Financial Counseling
A Strategic Approach

Second Edition

Charles J. Pulvino, Ph. D.

James L. Lee, Ph. D.

Carol A. Pulvino, Ph. D.

Instructional Enterprises

Madison, Wisconsin

Edition 2: First Printing

ISBN 0-9715491-0-9

Published by

Instructional Enterprises

P. O. Box 55064

Madison, WI 53705

Book Layout and Design: Carol A. Pulvino

Cover Design: Printing and Binding: EconoPrint, Inc. Madison, WI

Manufactured in the United States of America

Prologue

An Example of Poor Communication

Consider the following interaction between a client and a financial counselor. The client sought counseling because she had a number of financial concerns. She entered counseling in the hope that the counselor would be able to help her clarify her financial situation and arrive at a way to reduce her mounting debt. The counselor had little professional experience as a counselor but was sincerely interested in helping people.

Client: "I have a number of things to talk about. I don't really know where to begin."

Counselor: "How can I help you?"

Client: "I don't know. Maybe you can give me some ideas as to what I might do."

Counselor: "What you might do?" What do you mean?"

Client: "I've got a lot of bills. When I get done paying them I don't have enough money left to buy food for the month."

Counselor: "That does sound like a problem. What can I do for you?"

Client: "Help me pay my bills."

Counselor: "How can I do that?"

Client: "I don't know."

Counselor: " I'm not sure counseling will help you."

Client: "Why?"

Counselor: "I can't do anything for you if I don't more about your problem."

Client: "What do you need."

Counselor: "Whatever you can tell me."

Preface

We are aware of the need for facilitative communication skills. We see this need not only in our daily interactions but more importantly in our encounters with professional financial counselors. We previously applied interviewing skills to the financial counseling process and the financial planning process. In this edition of ***Financial Counseling: A Strategic Approach***, we focus our efforts on using specific skills and strategies for achieving effective financial counseling. We have expanded our earlier thoughts on interviewing, broadened our view of communication, integrated communication concepts that have emerged from solution oriented counseling, and expanded psychological elements that enhance the financial counseling process.

We believe that financial counselors can use this book as a map for effective counseling because it considers basic and advanced communication skills and strategies that foster client responsibility and independence. Skills and strategies are presented in ways that reflect the unique relationship that exists between financial counselors and their clients. We believe that effective communication skills, always beneficial in daily life, take on added significance when applied in situations that revolve around the management of personal resources.

It is our intention that the reader be given a chance to think about concepts, to see how they are applied, and to practice their use. With that end in mind, we discuss principles, share positive interactions, highlight practical examples, and provide opportunities for practicing the ideas presented. To the degree we were successful in our efforts, the reader will be a more informed communicator and ultimately a more efficient, effective financial counselor.

An Example of GOOD Communication

Now review the following interaction between a client and a financial counselor. The client sought counseling because she had a number of financial concerns. She entered counseling in the hope that the counselor would be able to help her clarify her financial situation and arrive at a way to reduce her mounting debt. The counselor had considerable professional experience as a counselor. The counselor believed the best way to help people was to help them become financially responsible.

Client: "I have a number of things to talk about. I don't really know where to begin."

Counselor: "We can deal with all your concerns but let's look a the most important first. What is the most pressing thing you would like to talk about?"

Client: "I feel like I'm in a financial quagmire. It's like I'm sinking in debt."

Counselor: "You have a feeling that your debt is about to overwhelm you."

Client: "Yes, exactly."

Counselor: "I think I can understand your feeling. Let's see what is contributing to your feeling."

Client: "Okay."

Counselor: "Your general feeling probably is a result of your total financial situation. Let's break that apart by focusing on specifics of your finances."

Client: "What specifics do you mean?"

Counselor: "I'd like us to look at both your income and where your money goes and then to examine ways that you can get to a point of financial stability." "I think that when you get to that point your feeling about being in a financial quagmire while disappear."

Client: " I sure hope so. How do we start?"

Counselor: "Actually, we have started. Your commitment to do something about your financial situation is the real beginning. I give you credit for coming to see me. Now, we can move forward by looking at the details of your financial world." "To begin, let's list all your sources of income…"

In the above situation, the counselor *heard* the client's plea and *blended* with what the client's *words* and *emotions*. The counselor *applauded* the client for taking an initial step toward resolution of the financial concern and offered the client *hope* that the financial quagmire could be overcome. Also, it is evident that the counselor was willing to work *cooperatively* with the client and to work *systematically* to help the client overcome his/her financial concern.

Each of the italicized words in the summary immediately above indicates a concept, strategy, or approach discussed in the body of the text.

Contents

SECTION 1

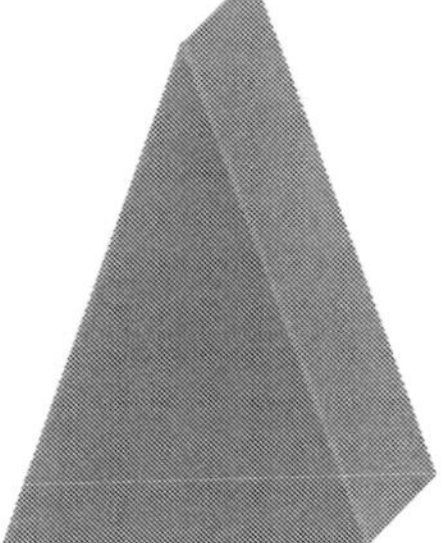

Foundations for Financial Counseling

1 AN INTRODUCTION

Every time people set themselves to learn, they need to labor as hard as they can, and the limits of their learning are determined by their own nature.

Therefore, there is no point in talking about knowledge. Fear of knowledge is natural; all of us experience it, and there is nothing we can do about it. But no matter how frightening learning is, it is more terrible to think of a person without knowledge.

from *The Teachings of Don Juan*
by Carlos Castaneda

A STRATEGIC APPROACH

This book addresses financial counseling strategies to help clients help themselves. The strategies are ones that employ facilitative communications skills, practical problem solving approaches, and decision- making techniques that have been found to be effective in personal and professional interactions. We have chosen to approach the task of financial counseling from a strategic perspective because it is our experience that counseling is a *complex* process. This process deals with client problems that have many dimensions, many levels of severity, and many different solution possibilities. A strategic perspective suggests that counselors approach the task of counseling in an orderly manner, a manner that provides the greatest hope for obtaining solutions in the shortest amount of time. This kind of approach takes planning. A haphazard approach, by contrast, has a minimal chance for success, is more likely to place the client in a precarious position, and fails to utilize what we know about human growth and development, learning styles, decision-making and change.

DEFINITIONS

There are a number of definitions of *strategy*. *Strategy* is " a) a careful plan or method: a careful stratagem b) the art of devising or employing plans or stratagems toward a goal" (Webster). Within definitions is the further notion of a *stratagem* which is defined as a "...cleverly contrived trick or scheme for gaining an end" (p.1150). A synonym of stratagem is *tactic* which is defined as "...a device for accomplishing an end" (p.1186). While these terms are often used to refer to military processes they also are applied to general problem solving. These definitions point to an orderly operation, one that uses thoughtful plans and devices to accomplish specific objectives.

It is interesting to note that within the word *tactic*, describing the central concept of a strategic approach, is another word that captures the essence of the process of applying tactics in counseling. That is the word *tact*. Tact is defined as, " a keen sense of what to do or say in order to maintain good relations with others or avoid offense" (Webster, p.1186). Strategic financial counseling relies on all three concepts of *stratagem, tactic, and tact* for its substance. We can define strategic financial counseling as a process of defining specific objectives (ends), developing workable plans (stratagems), and using appropriate skills (tactical devices) in a humanistic way (tact) to achieve the objectives.

The overall strategy entails knowing the client in as much detail as possible. First, knowing the client's current and long term situation, knowing the environmental contingencies facing the client, and knowing the resources that are available to the client are the basis for establishing appropriate objectives. Second, the financial counselor, with the client, develops specific plans (stratagems) that are thought to be the best to achieve the objectives. Third, the financial counselor utilizes various communication skills (tactical devices) to help the client through the process of establishing appropriate objectives and plans. Finally, strategic financial counseling occurs best when counselors use tact in their interactions. For counselors to use tact they must be able to spontaneously do the right thing at the right time in ways appropriate to the clients' circumstances. They must be able to relate to clients in a manner that is wholesome, honest, helpful, concerned, and real. Their interactions must encourage and facilitate clients in movement toward their goals and objectives. It is through the counselor's quality of tact that the counseling relationship gets its power, the power that is needed to move the client toward personal responsibility.

Tactics depend on the technical knowledge of knowing how to help clients to accomplish their goals and objectives. This knowledge becomes part of the counselor's arsenal that can be used to accomplish the goals of counseling. One of our primary purposes in this text is to increase your skills by sharing with you a number of tactics that are both appropriate and useful. Hopefully, as a result of reading the ensuing chapters, you will have a greater appreciation for a strategic approach to counseling, be more aware of specific tactics that can be used with particular clients, and gain a greater appreciation for the need for tact in counseling. While we can discuss technical skills, give you examples of their use, and suggest ways to practice them, you will only be able to spontaneously use the appropriate skills if you practice them until they become second nature.

PURPOSE OF THE BOOK

We hope to provide you with two ingredients for counseling, a *strategic* perspective that will enhance the counseling enterprise and specific *tactics* that can be used to facilitate clients in their development. While doing this, we will implicitly or explicitly encourage you to be *tactful* in your counseling. More specifically, we will discuss how to use strategy to identify, state, and accomplish appropriate counseling goals in a manner that will maximize client responsibility and increase positive counseling outcomes. To achieve this end, we will discuss tactics that facilitate problem identification, goal setting, specification of objectives, differentiation between outcomes and processes, individual and multiple communications, problem solving, and decision making.

OVERVIEW

Section I of the book provides a discussion of communication, listening, exploring techniques, systems for fostering client responsibility, and strategies for helping clients to solve problems and make appropriate decisions. The focus of Section II is on issues that influence counseling, examination of the counseling relationship, strategic perspectives foundational to specific forms of financial counseling, examination of how the physical environment influences the counseling process, discussion of evaluation and termination, and finally, a chapter on multiple counseling. Both sections contain theoretical and applied components. In general, however, Section I creates the foundation for applications stressed in Section II.

FORMS OF FINANCIAL COUNSELING

There is a natural tendency to think of financial counseling as being a remedial process, a process to help clients who have developed severe financial problems. However, the stratagems and skills useful in helping clients *after* they developed financial problems are also useful *before* problems begin. The occurrence of serious consequences for both the financial institution and the client can be *prevented*. There are three basic forms of financial counseling: remedial, preventive and productive. These forms are not necessarily mutually exclusive. There are times when a financial counselor might initiate remedial financial counseling with a client to solve an immediate financial crises and then move naturally, over time, into preventive counseling so that a similar problem won't occur again in the future. Finally, as the client's financial situation stabilizes the financial counselor might move into productive financial counseling to help the client establish long term financial goals and plans. The three forms are discussed separately below. Keep in mind that one might transform into another depending upon client needs.

Remedial Financial Counseling

Remedial financial counseling is used when clients have reached a state of financial, emotional and/or personal discomfort. This form of financial counseling attempts to help clients to understand their present financial state and to learn ways to resolve their situation. It is based on caring, understanding, planning, and follow through. Usually, remedial financial counseling will be effective if clients learn to accept responsibility for their actions and will fail when they don't. Consider the following example:

Jim and Betty are a young couple who have been married for three years. They have sought financial counseling because of conflicts over the use and misuse of money. As Jim and Betty enter the financial counseling relationship, they both discuss having more bills than they have money to pay for those bills.

Notice, the financial counselor has been presented with two problems. The first is that Jim and Betty are having conflicts. The financial counselor may choose to deal with this directly, refer the couple to a suitable professional source, ignore the conflict, or delay dealing with the conflict. The second problem presented is that the couple is spending more than they are earning. This problem is definitely within the financial counselor's professional domain.

To deal with the financial problem the financial counselor should:

1. Develop a relationship in which Jim and Betty will feel comfortable discussing all aspects of the problem.
2. Systematically clarify elements of the problem. Isolate elements that can be changed within financial counseling and identify those that cannot. Refer Jim and Betty to pertinent professional sources for those concerns that are not appropriate for financial counseling.
3. Specify the financial goals and objectives that Jim and Betty will work toward.

4. With Jim and Betty, generate solutions for overcoming the financial counseling problem.
5. Determine conditions under which Jim and Betty will employ the solutions determined. Encourage Jim and Betty to apply solutions to their problem.
6. Stay involved at a distance. Serve as a resource but let primary responsibility rest with Jim and Betty. Help Jim and Betty evaluate effectiveness of solutions they try.
7. Develop a program that Jim and Betty can follow which will help them avoid difficulties they have had in the past.

The model presented above is based on the idea that financial counselors will accept responsibility to work with clients on issues that are within their realm of professional expertise, but refer clients to other professionals for those issues outside their area of skill, training, and/or licensing. The model indicates distinct roles for the client and counselor. The role of clients is to accept responsibility for their behavior. The role of financial counselors is to provide a systematic means for helping clients overcome remedial concerns over the short and long term.

Productive Financial Counseling

Productive financial counseling is appropriate when clients are financially stable, but desirous of finding ways to use their resources more beneficially. Consider the following case as an example of productive financial counseling:

> Marti is a 55-year-old woman whose husband died recently. Marti has a part time job as a secretary with an income minimally sufficient to meet current fixed expenses. In addition to her income, Marti has $150,000 from her husband's life insurance policy and a house worth $95,000 with no mortgage payment. Marti's reason for entering financial counseling is not to overcome financial difficulties, but rather to discuss the most productive use of her resources.

As in all types of financial counseling, the counselor's first task is to develop an adequate relationship so that Marti will feel comfortable in discussing her needs. Once a relationship has been established, the financial counselor can help Marti to discuss her personal goals and to establish a process wherein they can be achieved.

The key components of the productive financial counseling process are:

1. Establish a trusting counseling relationship.
2. Accurately determine the client's short and long-term goals.
3. Discuss ways to achieve both types of goals.
4. Develop an action plan to achieve goals and objectives.
5. Develop a system of evaluation that can be used to assess whether goals and objectives have been achieved.
6. Initiate a process that will lead to achievement of goals and objectives.
7. Monitor the client's progress. This should be coupled with systematic, timely input about adjustments or changes that could facilitate achievement of the client's goals and objectives.

Preventive Financial Counseling

Preventive financial counseling has aspects of both remedial and productive financial counseling and is used when a client perceives a need for the productive use of resources to prevent the need for remediation.

> Katie and Ken, a 40-year-old couple, have two children in high school. Both of the children expect to go to college. Katie and Ken feel an obligation to contribute to their children's college education, but realize the financial difficulties they will have with both children in college at the same time. They enter financial counseling with the hope of finding ways of providing for their children's education without diminishing their present life style.

The financial counselor's task is to determine what Katie and Ken see as their current life style and to determine as accurately as possible the financial resources needed to maintain it. The financial counselor must be able to help Katie and Ken project financial costs that will accrue when both children are in college and to devise a plan that will allow Katie and Ken to retain a significant portion of their life style while helping their children through college.

To achieve this goal, the financial counselor must work with two components: the financial resources that Katie and Ken have now and will have while their children are in college, and the psychological aspects that Katie and Ken bring to the financial counselor. These two are interwoven. If Katie and Ken have adequate resources to maintain their life style while sending their children to college, then the psychological effect on Katie and Ken will be minimal. However, if Katie and Ken have to make drastic changes in order to finance their children's education, they will have to develop plans for the psychological adjustment that could be necessary because of reduced financial resources. In both cases, the financial counselor will be helping Katie and Ken prepare to face the situation. Preparation is preventive.

In summary, preventive financial counselors:

1. Establish a trusting counseling relationship.
2. Help clients to discuss and understand their goals and objectives.
3. Help clients to determine forces that could impinge upon achieving their goals and objectives.
4. Help clients to develop a system for achieving their goals and objectives in the most satisfying manner.
5. Help clients prepare for a number of courses of action before they are needed.
6. Allow clients time to adjust to changes in life style, attitudes, or behaviors.

Remedial, productive and preventive financial counseling use a similar process. All three use the financial counseling relationship to help clients to determine needs, set goals, establish objectives, and devise plans of action. The difference in the three strategies is the difference in counseling goals and, consequently, the specific plans of action that are used to help clients.

INTRODUCTORY EXAMPLES

One of our desires in writing this book was to provide examples to demonstrate the skills and techniques discussed. Following you will find two such examples. The first demonstrates a number of the communication skills useful in facilitating the financial counseling process. The second demonstrates a decision making technique that can be used with clients. Principles and relevant information that underlie both examples are provided in subsequent chapters.

EXAMPLE 1: USING A COMMUNICATIONS SKILLS STRATEGY

We can examine how focusing skills are utilized during a counseling session by reviewing a transcript of a counseling session. This is the second meeting for a counselor and client. During the first session the primary counseling concern of learning how to budget more wisely was identified. The general underlying client theme is a feeling of powerlessness or impotency to control impulsive buying.

Client: Well, you know, since the last time we talked, I've been giving my problems some more thought and there are some other things which we should take into consideration.

Counselor: Why don't you tell me about them.

Client: Yeah, well, it's not just me I guess. You know, there are all the pressures from society to buy, buy, buy and then I see all my friends buying the things I would like to have and I'm making good money so I think why shouldn't I have the things my friends have and so I buy them.

Counselor: So, you're telling me that your inability to budget ...which is what we identified as the primary thing you needed to learn ... is caused by advertising and the fact that you would like the things your friends have. It's like you have no control over them.

Client: Well ... it's not that I don't have any control over them ... it's just that our culture makes it hard to do what you know is best.

Counselor: You're saying almost the same thing we talked about last week. Because of the pressures you feel from society and because you would like to keep up with your friends you don't think about the possible consequences and just go out and buy.

Client: Yeah, I guess I am in a way ... but it sure doesn't make it any easier when you have things like that around you constantly.

Counselor: You have identified two of the things you have to be aware of as you are trying to overcome your impulsive buying. If you are aware of the feeling you have when you listen to advertising and when you see one of your friends getting something you would like, it will help you in saying no to yourself. What other kinds of issues ... or things should you be aware of?

Client: I ... uh ... don't know.

Counselor: Uh, hmm. (silence for a few seconds)

Client: Well, I guess if I just didn't feel like I was in competition with everyone all the time.

Counselor: You're always in competition with everyone.

Client: It's like I have to prove myself by the things I buy.

Counselor: It sounds like, "Nobody will like me unless I buy all these things and prove to them that I am successful."

Client: Yeah, that's it. I guess I figure if I have all these neat things that will prove I've made it and I'm an okay guy.

Counselor: You said a minute ago that you have to impress *everybody*.

Client: Well, it really isn't everybody.

Counselor: Who is it you really want to impress by spending all this money?

Client: I guess it's mostly women.

Counselor: Your impulsive buying is primarily to impress women. Is it women in general or any woman in particular?

Client: It's just women in general. I'm not going with anyone at the moment. I just want to have all the things women seem to like in a man.

Counselor: From what you have said before, that means you buy a lot of things because you hope it will make the right impression on women...you are afraid they really won't like you if you are just you... And in this whole process you have run up quite a few bills ... hoping to impress women.

Client: When you put it that way, it sounds kind of silly doesn't it?

Counselor: There seems to be several problems here ... You have gotten yourself into a financial bind ... not too serious...you spend your money impulsively until it's all gone; and then, you buy most of these things hoping you will make a good impression on women... I'm not sure we can deal with all of these at one time... The area that I can be of most help to you is the one which relates to how you budget and spend your money... Maybe in that process we can also relate that to how you feel about yourself and the kind of impression you want to make on women.

Client: That sounds okay to me.

Counselor: Now then, what specifically do you spend your money on?

Client: There are the usual things ... you know, rent, car payments, utilities ... insurance and all that kind of stuff is taken out of my paycheck before I get it so I don't have to worry.

Counselor: Do you know how to make out a budget?

Client: I'm not really sure.

Counselor: Would you like to learn a budgeting process? ... It will help both of us figure out just where your money is going and how you use it... Then, maybe we will have a better idea of what can be done about your problem... It might help us discover some of the things related to your impulsive buying.

Client: Sure.

The counseling session continued with the client and counselor discussing specifics of the client's financial situation. Throughout the discussion, the counselor also indirectly helped the client learn a simple budgeting procedure which could be used to generate ideas for how to control the client's impulsive buying habits and how to meet the present financial obligations. This particular financial counseling session demonstrates a number of counseling strategies.

The counselor
- Attended
- Listened
- Refocused
- Summarized
- Clarified ambiguities
- Responded to theme and content
- Reacted to client generalities

This approach would encourage the client to start taking more responsibility for himself and for defining the problem so that appropriate goals could be established. These skills, and many more, will be discussed in detail within the text.

Example 2: Using a decision-making strategy.

There are many different problem-solving and decision-making strategies available to counselors. A number of these are presented in Chapter Seven. The following example is intended to introduce you to how these strategies can be applied to financial counseling. The strategy chosen for this example is a relatively simple one, one that most readers will have used at one point in their lives. In reading this example, please note how the counselor uses the strategy to emphasize the client's responsibility for solving her own problem.

In this session, a client has approached the financial counselor to obtain help in making a decision about the purchase of a new residence. The counselor and client have established a relationship in previous professional encounters. The counselor is familiar with the client, her financial resources, and her decision-making style. The goal for the counselor is to help the client make a decision regarding her residence while helping her learn a decision-making strategy that she will be able to use in future situations.

Client: I hope you can help me solve a *big* problem.

Counselor: Tell me what you are concerned about.

Client: Well...as you might recall, I got transferred to a branch office on the other side of the city.

Counselor: Um hmm, I do.

Client: Well, the problem is, now I have to consider moving so that I'll be closer to my work.

Counselor: Closer? What specifically are you looking for in terms of distance?

Client: If I stay in my present location I am 20 minutes from the branch office. I used to be five minutes away. I'd prefer something only five minutes away.

Counselor: Okay, that helps me to understand what you're after. What have you done so far about solving your problem?

Client: I started to look... That's about all... That's when I decided to come to see you.

Counselor: What would you like me to help you with, specifically?

Client: I guess to help me look at my options...to come to some decision.

Counselor: Ok, that sounds reasonable...To do this, lets use a model that I've found helpful in working with other clients with similar concerns...okay?

Client: Sounds good to me...How do we begin?

Counselor: First, I'm going to ask you to be as specific as possible about *what the decision is*. Write down the decision you wish to make.

Client: What do you mean?

Counselor: Well, is the decision to move or not move... to move, but only if close to my new job... to move for sure, but to the location closest to my job... What specifically are you trying to decide?

Client: I see...The decision I want to make is *should I move*?

Counselor: Good... Now I would like you to *list* all the reasons you can think of *for* moving and then *list* all the reasons you can think of *against* moving.

Once the client has listed all of the reasons *for* and *against* moving, the counselor would help the client make sure that every possibility had been considered. Leads like, "Can you think of any other reason to move?" and "What do you think is particularly attractive about your present location?" can help the client examine all possibilities.

Once these have been discussed and listed, the counselor would ask the client to *assign point values to both sets of reasons*. This step is designed to evaluate which of the listed reasons is the most important. A higher value is assigned to a more important reason, no matter if it was for or against moving. Once the client had assigned points, the counselor could have the client inspect her ratings to make sure she assigned the points in the manner she most desired. Finally, the counselor would have the client total the point values and determine which was larger. Theoretically, the higher total of the *for* and *against* columns should indicate in which direction the decision should be made. The listing might look like the following:

For Moving		**Against Moving**	
closer to work	4	friends where I live	6
less travel time	3	familiar surroundings	4
I don't like driving	1	I like my house	7
I could get a bigger place	1	I enjoy my neighbors	3
Total Points	**9**	**Total Points**	**20**

Let's return to the client counselor interchange to see how this final tally could be used.

Counselor: Well, in your tally, the *against* moving came out considerably higher than the *for* moving. Does that surprise you?

Client: Yes, it does...I thought it would come out the other way.

Counselor: Where does all of this leave you?

Client: I have to give this more thought... I wasn't aware that I liked where I live so much... My present home would be hard for me to give up.

Counselor: Can I assist you any further?

Client: Not right now ... Maybe after I've given the whole thing more thought ... but ... in any event ... thanks!

The above interchange is not necessarily one a financial counselor would encounter, but it is one a financial counselor *could* encounter. In examining this case, one should be aware that the counselor's strategy was threefold.

- The counselor chose to reflect the client's statements which helped the client to add specificity to the original, more vague concern.
- The counselor taught the client a system that could be applied to similar problems in the future by using a specific decision making model.
- The counselor chose a strategy that placed primary responsibility for action on the client.

The client determined what decision was to be made, what reasons existed for and against the decision, what points were to be assigned, and the meaning of the total score. This strategy can lead clients to greater responsibility for their actions.

COUNSELING TENETS

Counseling can be viewed in many ways. Some counselors attempt to help clients to change their behavior. Other counselors help clients examine their self-talk while still others focus on helping clients to understand and/or reconstruct their past, to deal more appropriately with their emotional state, or to alter their cognitive processes. All of these approaches work with some clients some of the time. However, when one examines the underlying tenets of all of these approaches it becomes obvious that in most counseling approaches counselors expect clients to accept responsibility for their personal development and psychological growth.

Counseling, as presented in this text, is built on the following beliefs.

- Counseling can be accomplished in many ways.
- Needs of clients and the pre-dispositions of counselors influence the counseling process.

- Clients have a better chance of achieving psychological growth if they accept responsibility for themselves.

In the process of counseling, clients and counselors both have choices. Choices made by each influence the process of counseling and have a direct impact upon what is achieved.

All of life is about making choices. On a basic level we begin our days making choices, what will we wear, what will we eat for breakfast, or when we will leave for work. Of course, choices have consequences. The consequences can be satisfying or they can lead to disasters. All of us have made choices where, in hindsight, we wish we had chosen differently. Clients seek financial counseling because they made life choices that lead to financial problems. Most did not purposely make those choices. Most clients knew that if they spent more than they made, debt and financial difficulty would follow. We believe financial problems occur because people make choices to satisfy basic human needs. Sometimes choices work in favor of the client. Sometimes they do not. When choices do not work in the client's favor financial problems can occur.

The financial counseling process provides clients and financial counselors many opportunities to make creative choices. Typically, choices made by clients reflect their personal needs and reasons they sought counseling. By contrast, choices by counselors are professional, not personal and typically reflect the counselor's theoretical perspective and counseling approach.

In any counseling process, therefore, there are three components, the client's perspective, the counselor's perspective, and the counselor-client interaction.

Client Perspective

- Clients have more knowledge about their situation than anyone else. They know what they like, what they despise, who their friends are, what actions they have taken that have resulted in difficulties, what steps they have taken to solve previous problems, and why they have come to the counselor's office. Clients have motivation and ability to use that knowledge.

- Clients have an inherent desire to overcome their problems, to arrive at meaningful solution, and the wherewithal to act responsibly in their own behalf. It is the counselor's task to help clients generate solutions to their problems and to facilitate them as they develop responsible behavior. Both clients and counselors have resources that can be used to help clients achieve their counseling goals. These resources are as varied as the human condition, e.g., desire for change, willingness to work hard, motivation for a better life, or need to be a good person.

- Clients expect counselors to know how to counsel. They usually are not concerned about the theoretical rationale that will provide the basis for counseling. Clients focus on themselves, not on counseling process. When clients enter counseling they typically know a great deal about themselves and why they came to counseling. They also may be aware of what led up to their need for counseling and what they would like to gain from the process. Clients control the information used in counseling whereas counselors control how that information is ordered, evaluated, and acted upon.

Counselor Perspective

- Counselors control the counseling *process* while clients control *what* is discussed. Counselors are educated to provide theoretically based psychological assistance. Their training usually advocates a specific theoretical rationale, subsequent guidelines for interaction, and practice in controlling the flow of counseling with a given theoretical rationale. In essence, counselors are educated to control the *process* or *how* counseling will occur.

- Counselors can have a great effect on clients. Hugh Prather (1977, p.5) in *Notes on Love And Courage* states that "There are people whose feelings and well-being are within my influence. I will never escape that fact." This statement is true for all individuals but particularly true of counselors. When interpersonal influence is combined with the counselor's high status social position it can be understood why counselors are in a position of extreme influence. Counselors can and should use their influence to help clients achieve their financial goals.

- Counselors must have a thoughtful, purposeful rationale for their *professional* existence. The rationale should be based on tested theoretical perspectives but should reflect the uniqueness of the individual counselor. Counselors should counsel in a manner consistent with their rationale.

- Counselors should try to work themselves out of a job. Meier and Davis (1997, p.4) suggest that counselors should "explain counseling to the client." It is their contention that clients should know the process that will be used and what can be expected from participating in counseling. We agree with this but believe that counselors must go beyond merely explaining what will be done. Rather, counselors should actively teach clients techniques for solving their own problems. Counseling is considered to be successful when clients are able to deal effectively with the concerns they bring to counseling *and* when they have developed skill for effectively confronting future concerns.

- Counselors should be culturally aware. Cormier and Hackney put it well when they said that, "...counseling cannot occur outside of a culture. It may be the counselor's culture that is the medium, then, unless the client is of the same cultural background, the process of counseling will miss the target at best, or be irrelevant and useless at worst. There is no substitute for working in the client's cultural medium if counseling is to be effective (1993, p. 319)." For a financial counselors to be effective they must be able to understand another's world and be able to offer assistance that *will work within that world.* A primary way of doing this is through creation of many counseling choices, some which work in most client environments with most clients and some that are specifically tailored to specific needs of specific populations. The following list is not inclusive but it does provide a springboard for understanding many aspects of clients' worlds.

Race and Ethnicity: Understanding the influence of cultural backgrounds and the impact of backgrounds on communications, decision-making, and problem-solving.

Gender Issues: Attending to sex role stereotyping, changing roles, abuse, sex-fair counseling, gender devaluing, discrimination, and sexual harassment.

Sexuality: Being knowledgeable about sexually transmitted diseases including Acquired Immune Deficiency Syndrome (AIDS), sexual performance, and gay and lesbian concerns.

Older Adults: Dealing with adjustment to retirement, adjusting to diminished abilities and capacities, grieving lost friends and relatives, and facing one's own death.

People with Disabilities: Being conversant with adjustment to disabilities produced by genetics, by accidents, and by disease, e.g., multiple sclerosis and muscular dystrophy.

- Counselors may not be able to work effectively with all clients. Counselors sometimes work with clients who have needs that go beyond the counselor's ability to provide. When this occurs, counselors should refer. In school settings, when school counselors face this situation they may refer to school psychologists, psychiatrists, social workers, priests, rabbis, or ministers, governmental agencies, or other professional sources. Financial counselors might refer to professional communications experts, Credit Bureaus, government agencies, or family services. All counselors must be prepared to refer before they ever meet their first client.

Client-Counselor Interaction

- It is more helpful and productive to focus clients on *solutions to their problems* than on *causes for those problems*. This belief is based on two understandings. First, the mind focuses in one direction at a time. Said another way, two antagonistically opposed forces cannot exist simultaneously. For example, love and hate cannot co-exist. If one focuses on love, then hate disappears. If the focus is on hate, then love disappears. More directly, if one focuses on problems, energies will be spent on understanding those problems and efforts will be made to resolve those problems. Although this focus on problems could be productive, this concern with problems takes time, energy, and concentration away from determining solutions for the problem. However, if one concentrates on solutions, problems become less of a focus, individuals feel less vulnerable, hope is established, and potentially helpful choices can be entertained. In essence, problems lose their importance while solutions gain in importance.

- When focus is on creation of alternatives, or suggestion of problem-solving strategies early in a counseling encounter client resistance to suggestions is increased. Timing is important. Problem solving is most effective if it occurs after a relationship has been adequately established, the clients have had an opportunity to discuss how they have attempted to deal with counseling concerns in the past, and counseling goals have been established.

- Examination of the past can provide insight. However, the past cannot be changed. Change occurs in the present. That which is changed in the present has potential for impacting the future. There are elements of the past that can provide counselors and clients information about how to act in the present. These elements will be discussed later in the book under title *Personal History*. For now it is sufficient to say that the past is a reservoir of information for action in the present with an eye to the future. Solutions thus created move clients forward toward positive consequences.

- Counseling is a gentle, tender human interaction in which counselors use their professional knowledge and expertise to help clients deal with their financial concerns. In most cases listening, supporting, facilitating, and teaching are the most effective skills needed by counselors. However, there are times when the best thing a counselor can do is to confront clients with their ambivalence, distortions, or inconsistencies. Also, counselors can empathetically help clients become aware of their blind zone, that characteristic of an individual apparent to others but not apparent to one's self. By helping clients to understand how their observed behaviors are inconsistent with their stated preferences counselors can help clients make choices more consistent with their stated goals.

- The life of any person can be broken down into three distinct time periods, the past, the present and the future. Simply, a person's past encompasses all of his/her learned responses, memories, subconsciously stored information, and in general, personal history. The present is that moment in time of present conscious awareness and subconscious processing. The future is the vision of what will be. If there is relatively little external influence on individuals at any specific time they will be, and act, in accordance to what they know from the past, what they are aware of in the present, and what they envision for themselves in the future. Counselors can help clients to use the past to act more financially responsible in the present and to prepare them to do so in the future.

- Counselors, because of their influential position and inherent status, can stop their clients' normal routine. Carlos Castaneda (1972) in *Journey to Ixtalan*, said "The flow of life is continuous unless something or someone of significance influences it in a way to alter that flow." He coined the phrase "stopping one's world" to describe the process of altering one's normal flow. The significance of this is that once one's world is stopped then the past can be examined, the present changed, and the future opened to new or different possibilities. Counselors can stop their clients' normal routine or flow through many means including educating, advising, confronting, teaching, facilitating, and of course, counseling. Counselors can help clients to examine their beliefs and behaviors and to examine and try new possibilities. Counselors can "stop the world" of clients, change their normal flow, and consequently, open clients to alternate *choices* for the present and future.

In the *Financial Counseling: A Strategic Approach* model emphasis is placed on effects of behavior and choices. If the client does not like the effects produced, then counseling focus is placed on clarifying effects the client wants and how these might be produced.

Focus in this model is on the future and solutions, how to produce desired effects, rather than on solving or removing causes of problems.

In presenting this model, we discuss assumptions, natural processes that unfold as people grow and adjust to changes in their environments, and communication principles. *All are foundational to the counseling process*. Finally, therapeutic *frames* are discussed in detail. Frames provide a structure for focusing financial counselors' efforts. They provide a basis for creative counseling choices and a way to influence client behavior.

RESOURCES

Castanadas, C. (1972). *Journey to Ixtalan.*

Cormier, L.S. & Hackney, H. (1993). *The Professional Counselor: A Process Guide To Helping*. Boston: Allyn and Bacon.

Meier, S.T. & Davis, S.R. (1997). *Elements of counseling* (3rd. Ed.). Pacific Grove: Brooks Cole.

Prather, H. (1977). *Notes On Love And Courage.* Garden City: Doubleday.

Webster, M. (1983). *New Collegiate Dictionary*. Springfield: G. & C. Merriam Company Publishers

2 FOUNDATIONS OF COUNSELING

There are four ways, and only four ways, in which we have contact with the world. We are evaluated and classified by these four contacts: what we do, how we look, what we say, and how we say it.

Dale Carnegie

INTRODUCTION

The Chinese philosopher Lao-Tzo, once said, "The longest journey begins with but a single step." That important first step in professional communication is the development of an effective communicative relationship between yourself and your clients. Accomplishing this first step in a positive way begins with an understanding of the communicative process. Since communication revolves around the transmittal of information, in this chapter we will focus on how people process information internally and how information affects the way people behave. This will provide a foundation for strategies that can be used to help clients with financial concerns.

The principles to be covered in this chapter are as follows:

***Principle* 2.1:**	There is no best way to communicate.
***Principle* 2.2:**	People develop personal representations of experience.
***Principle* 2.3:**	People develop preferential ways of processing information.
***Principle* 2.4:**	Changing information in one processing mode changes information in other processing modes.
***Principle* 2.5:**	The number of choices people have at any point in time is directly related to the amount of detail in their representational maps.
***Principle* 2.6:**	People naturally generalize.
***Principle* 2.7:**	People process information differentially.
***Principle* 2.8:**	People seek informational harmony and closure.
***Principle* 2.9:**	People usually do what is best for themselves using stored information.

***Principle* 2.10:**	Communicative interactions are reciprocal.
***Principle* 2.11:**	The majority of stored information/learning is not conscious.
***Principle* 2.12:**	People are vulnerable to elements of persuasion.

Every professional relationship depends upon effective communication, whether it is a financial counseling session, an encounter between manager and employee, or a meeting between counselor and client. Our goal is to remind you of things you probably already know about effective communication, to add structure to the relationships you build in your professional life, and to show you how to develop effective helping relationships with clients.

THE ROLE OF INFORMATION PROCESSING

The success of your work as a financial counselor depends on how well you communicate. You communicate every day. It probably seems like a normal and natural process. Few of us consciously decide what to say when we communicate. The thoughts and words just flow. Yet, have you ever thought about how complicated the process is? How do people decide what to communicate? Where do their thoughts and words come from? How can two people experience the same event and respond with two entirely different reactions?

When you begin to examine the process, it becomes apparent that we do many things without consciously thinking about them. We act and react from experience or habit. There are a number of explanations for why we respond as we do. Most explanations involve concepts about how people gather, store, and process information. The following principles provide a partial explanation for the very complex process of communication and its inherent dependence on information.

◈ Principle 2.1: There is no best way to communicate.

In a book about developing effective counseling relationships it may seem odd to begin with a principle that says there is no best way to communicate. The underlying meaning of this principle might be better understood through an example:

Suppose you want to travel from Madison, Wisconsin, to Buffalo, New York. There are many ways to get there and numerous routes that can be used. You can get from Madison to Buffalo by train, plane, car, or bicycle. If you are raising money for a charitable organization, you might even walk. If you choose to fly to Buffalo, you can fly directly to Buffalo. You can fly through Chicago. You can even fly to San Francisco, then fly on around the world and back to Buffalo. It is only when you assign certain values and goals to the trip that one route or method becomes better than another. If efficiency is most important, you will probably choose the most direct flying route. If you are on vacation, and want to relax and experience the various forms of American culture in the process, you might drive and make a number of side trips. For example, you could go through Michigan and stop to see how cars are made in Detroit and then move on to Pennsylvania and see how chocolates are made in Hershey. Each new set of values and goals makes one form of transportation *better* than others.

The same is true of communication. The value system and the goals you have affect the choices you make. You can accomplish your communicative goals in a variety of ways. Some ways become better than others depending on your values or specific goals. Psychiatrist Milton H. Erickson is credited with an anecdote about several dentists who developed an effective way of dealing with children who were so afraid of dentists that they responded with crying, screaming fits when brought into their offices. The dentists wanted to have cooperative patients. They told the children as they arrived that they had nothing to fear. Then the dentists tied towels around the children's mouths and tied the children into their chairs. The dentists reported that the children were always very cooperative at their next appointments.

Anyone would be cooperative if they knew that they were going to get their mouths stuffed with towels and their hands tied to the chair if they didn't cooperate! So, in one sense, we can say that the dentists used effective communication because it produced their desired goal. It resulted in cooperative patients.

The dentists' system does not teach children how to deal with their fear of dentists. They merely learn a new fear on top of an underlying fear. So the same episode shows ineffective communication.

In this book we identify two underlying values to distinguish effective, professional communication from less effective communication.

Humanistic, Growth-Producing Treatment: By humanistic and growth-producing, we refer to communication that maximizes a person's potential while treating the person as being worthwhile. This is the *tact* in a strategic approach.

Efficiency And Parsimony: Effective communication attempts to achieve goals as quickly and effortlessly as possible. While one might accomplish a goal a number of different ways, we think that accomplishing the goal in the most efficient way is better. Efficient and parsimonious strategies not only save clients and financial counselors time, but will ultimately save individuals and financial institutions money.

◈ Principle 2.2: People develop personal representations of experience.

As people grow and develop, they store their life experiences and their reactions to those experiences. A person's experiences are gradually woven into a personal representation of the world. These finely woven representations have been called perceptions, tapes, personal rules, and maps. Each person's package of life experiences is analogous to a fine tapestry. New experiences are like new threads. They have an identity of their own. They become woven into the tapestry, and eventually they form a small design that becomes part of the greater design.

In this book we will refer to these finely woven personal representations as *maps*. We believe that people build unique maps of the world because no two people have identical experiences. On the other hand, it is true that there are many similarities among people and, therefore, among representational maps. For example, most people will have a similar map of the word *table*. When someone mentions a table, we probably form a picture of a four-legged piece of furniture. It may not be exactly the same representation as the person who said the word, but we probably would agree on basic characteristics, for example, a piece of furniture with four legs and a flat top.

As we use abstract words, we wouldn't have the same degree of mutual understanding. An abstract word like *fun* will have as many representations as there are people. Some people think that running two or three miles a day is *fun.* They enjoy using their body, working up a good sweat, and feeling better about their health. They might say, "Running is fun!" A second group of people might respond in a totally different manner. They might dislike the idea of exerting that much energy. They might think that sitting and reading a book is *fun,* and that running or jogging is agony.

Maps

It is important to realize that individuals' maps influence behaviors. People's maps govern how they behave and, to a large degree, how they think. People who think running is fun will arrange their schedules to engage in this activity. In like manner, people who would rather do something else will arrange their schedules to allow time for their personal *kind of fun.*

An understanding of representational maps provides a basis for understanding two common errors people make, errors that can have a very negative impact on effective communication.

- **People may assume that their representational maps are the same as reality**: Frequently, individuals fail to recognize that their experience is a combination of what their present sensory experience is telling them and what their representational maps allow them to perceive at any point in time.

- **People may assume that what is true for them must be true for others**. In essence, it is very easy for individuals to believe that what they perceive must be what is.

These two errors are the basis for miscommunication and misunderstanding. The beginning of an effective, professional counseling relationship is the recognition that the client's map of the world is potentially different from yours. An important first strategy in financial counseling is for you to understand the client's map of the world and how it is similar to and dissimilar from yours. Clients' maps affect how they make decisions; how they use money; how willing or capable they are to take risks; and how they view their personal, business, or financial goals. By understanding clients' maps, you have a better basis for communicating with them and for developing helping strategies.

◈ Principle 2.3: People develop preferential ways of processing information.

Over time, people build representational maps through accumulation of their life experiences. We use the five senses of seeing (visual), hearing (auditory), tasting (gustatory), smelling (olfactory), and feeling/action (kinesthetic) to acquire these experiences. Any one experience usually incorporates each of the five sensory elements. The same memory can be activated through any one of the five senses. While the smell of a bakery may activate images of home and childhood, a particular taste, sound, or visual image may activate the same memory. When we activate one sensory memory system, the others are automatically activated. Sensory-based representational maps provide the foundation for past, present, and future experiences and the basis for how we communicate about those experiences.

As people mature, they usually develop a preference for using one sensory system as a way of thinking about, or representing, the information they acquire. These preferences, often referred to as learning styles, include:

Auditory Learning

One person may prefer to learn and think about information he or she acquires through talking and listening.

Visual Learning

Another person may prefer to learn by watching others, seeing a film, or studying diagrams.

Kinesthetic Learning

A third person might prefer to learn through active participation. This type of learner usually uses trial and error or physical activity as a method of learning.

People very seldom develop only one learning style. Over time, and through formal education, individuals experience learning in all three ways. Usually, however, people develop preferences for one or more of the three styles. Counselors should be aware of all three learning styles. If a person learns best through experience, an auditory approach using lectures or discussions probably will be less effective than a method of communication that uses direct personal involvement. In this situation, some form of hands-on experience would facilitate communication. It may be sufficient to explain a new budgeting process to a client who has an auditory learning preference; but, with a client who prefers a more kinesthetic learning mode, it may be necessary to actually spend time with the client using and applying the budgeting process.

Effective communication begins with knowledge you have about yourself and your clients. As a financial counselor, you must be able to understand your client's representational map, and be able to understand how this map is activated through your client's learning style. There are two aspects to this understanding.

- First, you must assess your client's experiential, representational map as it relates to the purpose of your communication. In every financial counseling relationship there are important issues, goals, or concerns. It is important for you to understand how your client views each so that you know what your client wants to achieve. A divorce lawyer needs to know a client's feelings about separation, divorce, communal assets, custody, and related issues. Similarly, a financial counselor needs to determine elements of a client's representational map such as sources of income, present and anticipated debts, present budgeting processes, savings, and use of credit cards.

- Second, it is important to know how your client prefers to process and represent information. If you have an awareness of how your client prefers to communicate, you will be able to alter your counseling strategies and tactics to engage your clients in their preferred style. You will be able to enhance communication by speaking your client's language. This enables clients to accept you and your ideas and leads to more effective communication.

◈ Principle 2.4: Changing information in one processing mode changes information in other processing modes.

The three learning styles refer to specific ways of processing information: visual, auditory, and kinesthetic. As indicated in the discussion of Principle 2.3, most experiences incorporate elements of all senses. Therefore, when one sensory mode is activated, there is a tendency for each of the other sensory aspects of the experience to be activated.

For most adults in our culture, the strongest sensory and learning preferences are limited to auditory, visual, and kinesthetic processing. While we use our senses of taste and smell to respond to the world around us, we seldom use them to learn new things. Visual and auditory learning preferences are fairly straightforward. Kinesthetic learning, however, has two aspects. One form of kinesthetic processing refers to internal experiences: emotions, muscular, and glandular changes. The other form refers to external actions and activities. When we separate kinesthetic into internal and external experiences, we have an interactive system similar to Figure 2.1.

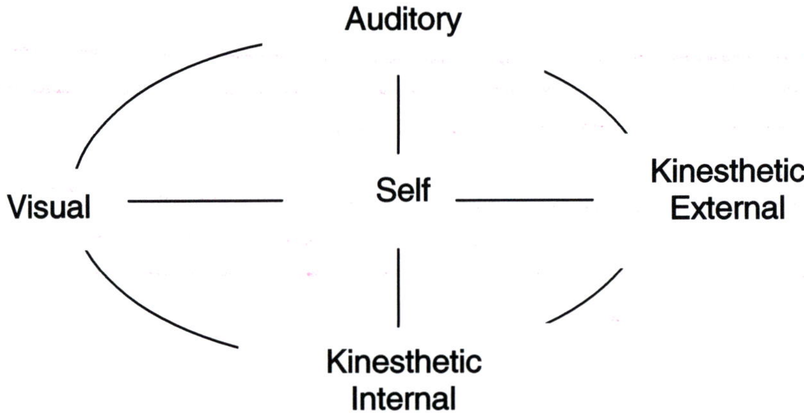

Figure 2.1

The lines in the figure indicate that the processing modes are connected.

Try This

Visualize a lemon.
Then visualize cutting the lemon into quarters.
Visualize yourself holding the lemon close to your nose.
Finally, visualize yourself biting into the juicy lemon.

If you clearly visualize all this, you probably will become aware of an increase in saliva in your mouth and may feel your neck glands respond. The process of holding the images (visual) in your mind has an effect upon another processing mode (kinesthetic internal). This principle has a number of practical applications.

Individuals can control their feelings, moods, and behavior by controlling what information they are processing. When individuals visualize a calm, relaxing place, they tend to have thoughts that are pleasant. As a result their bodies relax. This circle of experiences can become reinforcing. Feeling relaxed strengthens the visual images of relaxing places which, in turn, increases relaxing thoughts. This process is the basis for many stress reduction techniques.

If you wish to change the way you think about a situation, but you find it difficult to do so, you can purposefully act in a manner opposite to the way you feel. This can actually affect your thoughts and feelings. When someone asked Teddy Roosevelt how he could be so brave charging up San Juan Hill, Teddy responded, "I was really quite frightened, but if you act brave, then it can become true." Acting *as if* can lead to new thoughts and perceptions.

Clients can achieve goals or change behavior more easily when counselors invoke their processing modes to convey information. This is sometimes more effective than trying to *convince* clients through logical argument.

One of the authors, for instance, discovered that this principle could be used to control unnecessary spending. A client, who frequently used credit cards, was having difficulty with overspending. In an attempt to help the client to get in touch with his spending habits the author suggested that the client limit himself to cash purchases for a one-week period. The client began by withdrawing $100.00 from his savings account. He thought that amount of money should last for the week. After going shopping for new tennis shoes for one of the children and purchasing several small items at a drug store, the $100.00 was gone and the client had to draw additional cash from savings. This experience was repeated several times during the week. As a result the client realized how easy credit cards were to use, how little thought he gave to using them, and, from the opposite perspective, how much thought he gave to spending cash! This short-term *experience* succeeded where previous logical *discussions* had failed.

◈ **Principle 2.5: The number of choices people have at any point in time is directly related to the amount of detail in their representational maps.**

This principle is best understood by example. Suppose you want to travel between two major cities in the same state. When you look at an average map you might notice a description of major state and federal highways but little else. In this situation your choice would be limited by the map's restricted detail. However, if you were to obtain official county maps for all of the counties between the two cities, you would have enough detail to find every possible road between the two cities. With the additional maps and the additional detail, you would have a vastly increased array of choices. As detail on the map increases, the number of choices available increases. People's representational maps are similar. Freedom of choice increases with the amount of detailed information in a person's representational and experiential map.

In financial counseling, as you increase informational detail available to clients, you increase their freedom of choice. Many times clients need additional information in order to solve their financial problems or achieve their financial goals. Increasing freedom of choice increases likelihood that clients will find appropriate and satisfying solutions to their problems and, as a consequence, increases trust in the counseling process.

There is, however, a possible danger with this principle. Sometimes there can be too much detail. Choice can then become difficult or even impossible. People may have information overload. Consider this scenario witnessed by one of the authors.

A mother and father took their young son to a Baskin Robbins ice cream store. While they waited their turn to be served, the parents took turns picking the boy up and showing him all of the 31 flavors he could choose.

Two things became very obvious. First, this was the boy's first trip to a Baskin Robbins. Second, the boy had no idea that there were so many ice cream choices! As their number got closer, the parents put increased pressure on the boy to make his choice. The boy had never had so many choices. He had too *much* detail. When their number was called for service, the boy, when asked what flavor he wanted, said, "I guess I'll just take chocolate." The boy's parents then became irritated with the boy and said, "That's what you always have at home. Why do you think we brought you here?"

The boy, not unlike many people in similar situations, had so many choices he had become confused. Too many options *can be* troublesome. When people, like the boy at Baskin Robbins, get confused from too much detail, they usually fall back on what they know best. Counselors can help clients integrate new information by monitoring and adjusting the amount of detail that is being presented.

◈ Principle 2.6: People naturally generalize.

Each of us is continuously subjected to large quantities of information. To maintain sanity in a confusing environment, we learn to distinguish important messages from less important ones and, for efficiency, we learn to categorize sensory information into classes and subclasses. At a simple level, we soon learn that the burners on all stoves can be hot and that touching them can cause pain. We do not have to learn this lesson with each new stove that we encounter. We quickly form generalizations about stoves, burners, and physical pain.

When you talk with clients, you soon become aware of generalizations they have created. A counselor may note that a particular client is against all life insurance because the individual previously had an unfavorable experience with an insurance agent. In a similar manner, the counselor may notice that the client has an unusual degree of mistrust for the medical profession because of several bad experiences with one doctor. In both of these examples the client developed negative generalizations that can adversely affect the manner in which communication occurs with subsequent insurance representatives or physicians. An important task of financial counselors is to help clients be aware of their generalizations and how they impact financial decisions.

Financial counselors also form generalizations. As they encounter clients, counselors classify them into categories. They may apply adjectives like open, resistant, cordial, willing, or risk adverse to clients. In addition, they may classify clients by culture, gender, or economic standing. Effective counselors are aware of their generalizations about clients and how these generalizations influence counseling.

Counselors also form generalizations about the most appropriate ways of handling certain situations. As counselors gain experience their awareness of alternative actions increases. They form generalizations of concerns, problems, and possible solutions. To a large degree, generalizations help counselors to be more effective and helpful to clients. The danger that exists, however, is that counselors may assume that their generalizations are true and then take action as if they were. There is little danger if the counselor's generalization is an accurate representation of events. A real danger can occur, however, when a generalization is inaccurate or inappropriate.

Generalizations are hypotheses that we support from our experience. When we learn from experience that stove burners can be hot, we subsequently generalize and learn to be careful when testing stove burners. The generalization does not mean that all burners on all stoves are always hot, but it is a strong hypothesis. We learn to look carefully at burners, look to see if we can determine a recognizable color that would indicate heat, carefully place our hand over the burner to feel any possible heat, and, as a last resort, actually touch it. We are, in essence, testing our hypothesis. We must remember that our generalizations about people are only strong hypotheses. We must test them in a manner similar to testing hot burners. If we remember that they are only hypotheses, we will be one step closer to developing effective communicative relationships.

◈ Principle 2.7: People process information differentially.

Research has indicated that the human brain is composed of two primary components, the left and right hemispheres, which have overlapping yet distinct functions. For most right-handed people, the left hemisphere of the brain specializes in logical-analytical thought and verbalization. Reading, writing, language, inference generation, theory building, and mathematics represent left hemispheric processes. The right hemisphere, by contrast, is primarily in control of spatial perception, perceptual insight, tactile sensation, and visualization. Intuitive, metaphoric, and inventive capacities; divergent thought; and some components of music and art ability are said to be functions of the brain's right hemisphere.

In his book *The Social Brain,* M.S. Gazzaniga (1985) suggests that the brain has within it a number of *mental modules* The mental modules vary among individuals in number, location, and capacity. It is his belief that these modules express themselves through action (behavior) and not through verbal communication. Gazzaniga suggests that the brain's activities, the functions of both the left and right hemispheres and of the *mental modules,* are governed by a left hemispheric function he labels the *interpreter.*

In essence, the *interpreter* is responsible for integration of the individual's beliefs about the world *and* his or her actions in the world. Its task is to compare present action with previously held conscious and sub conscious belief systems. When a conflict occurs between belief and action, the *interpreter* attempts to reduce the conflict by one of two processes: changing the original belief or altering the conflicting behavior. For example, consider Bob, who for years has been telling everyone that when he can afford it, he is going to buy a particular make of automobile. Finally the time comes. Bob buys his desired car. Let's say, to Bob's chagrin, that the new automobile turns out to be a real lemon, a dud, a zero! When Bob is asked how he likes the car he probably will say, "Oh, it's the greatest car I've ever owned!" Privately, however, Bob will question his belief about this particular brand of automobile. He will be faced with the task of reducing the psychological gap created by his new knowledge and his previously held beliefs.

As people process information, they attempt to reduce "psychological gaps" through their left hemispheric *interpreter.* All humans operate, more or less, in a similar manner. Yet, each individual also is unique. Males are different than females, right-handed people respond differently than those who are left-handed, and adolescents respond differently than adults. As counselors, it is important to understand similarities and differences, to understand the importance of these differences in terms of communication, and to know how to assess differences.

◈ Principle 2.8: People seek informational harmony and closure.

As discussed in Principle 2.7, the interpreter module in the human brain seeks to organize behavior, beliefs, values, and needs in a consistent manner. The interpreter module does this by reducing psychological gaps. Whenever there is dissonance among any of our beliefs, values, or needs, there is motivation to reduce the dissonance and create *harmony*. This usually entails changing either values or beliefs so that they are consistent. For example, suppose a person has a basic need for security with financial resources. This *belief* would usually lead that person to choose very conservative investment instruments such as insured savings notes. At the same time, the person may place a high *value* on financial independence and learn from a financial counselor that conservative investments will barely keep up with the inflation rate.

As a result of the new learning the person may develop a new *belief* that minimal risks must be taken if financial independence is to be achieved. However, this attitude may be in direct conflict with the individual's need for security. A person in such conflict will be motivated to change the need, value, or belief. Such a person may decide that financial security may not be as important as financial independence. Conversely, the person may decide that financial independence is not as important as financial security, and despite the information provided by the financial counselor, stick to very secure, conservative investments. The latter decision could be reached even though the individual knows it may be contrary to "good" logic or "good" financial planning.

All of us have experienced times when we have an uneasiness or sense that something must be done. The feeling may be fear, nervousness, or frustration that results when we are forced to make choices relating to things that may be contrary to our beliefs, values, or needs. A third alternative always exists. We could avoid any action and do nothing, hoping that the situation will resolve itself. When we choose this alternative, we usually are left with the uneasy feeling of unresolved issues in our lives. When something in our lives activates beliefs, values, needs, or emotions associated with a previously unresolved issue, the issue itself can be triggered or be transformed into a new problem or issue. Suppose you had a bad day at work when everyone seemed to be very demanding. You did not have any time for your self or your own work. The feelings did not get resolved at work. You go home and when the children or your spouse ask an innocent question like, "Did you remember to return the video?" You fly off the handle and respond with anger and frustration. The unresolved issues from work get transformed and acted out on others.

This need for informational harmony and the accompanying need to reduce dissonance are central in most decision-making problems. Financial counselors should be aware of this and be patient. If clients are pressed when they are experiencing dissonance, expect resistance. The counselor's persuasive efforts may be viewed as high-pressure sales pitches. Dissonance cannot be resolved easily or quickly. It is best to allow the client time to resolve the dilemma and, when asked, provide information that can aid the client in the decision-making process.

The second aspect of Principle 2.8 is *closure.* Consider this scenario.

> You are driving down the highway with a friend and you hear a song on the car radio. Your friend asks, "What's the name of that song?" You recognize the song as one that is very familiar to you. You have heard it a hundred times but, for the life of you, you can't remember the title. You may say something like, "Just a minute. It's on the tip of my tongue." You think for several seconds and can't remember it and then forget about it as you continue talking about other things.
>
> Later that evening, while you are doing something else, the title of the song pops into your head! What happened? Evidently, the human brain does not like to be left with unfinished business!

Below our level of awareness, at the subconscious level, analysis of problems continues until answers are found. There are a number of popular television commercials that incorporate this principle. One of the Budweiser beer commercials several years ago used the jingle, "When you say Budweiser, you've said it all!" At the end of the commercial you would hear the jingle again, but it ended after the word Budweiser, "When you say

Budweiser..." Invariably, when people heard that phrase of the jingle, they would say to themselves, "you've said it all!". Even as you read the words now, there is the strong possibility that you have finished the jingle to yourself. This need to finish what has been started is the need for *closure*.

When people seek information and closure, the information they find is likely to stay with them. In the example above, if you had attempted to remember the name of a song, you would be likely to remember the title because of the work of your subconscious. In like manner, you would be more likely to remember Budweiser, when asked by a bartender for your choice of beer, if you had just heard the Budweiser jingle. It does not mean you will order a Budweiser, but it increases the likelihood that you will think of Budweiser when trying to decide which beer to order. The Budweiser corporation successfully uses this strategy to increase sales.

The principle of closure has direct application in financial counseling. One of the best times to apply this principle is when alternatives for action have been discussed but decisions for action have yet to be determined. A financial counselor might say to a client, "Now that we've discussed a number of possibilities it would be helpful if you gave some additional thought to the one that you'd like to try. Think about the possibilities. Next week when we get together you can tell me about your decision. You might be surprised by what you come up with!"

The last sentence of the counselor's statement probably would leave the client wondering what he or she might be surprised about. This is similar to the beer jingle in that the client would be left with a feeling of unfinished business. This approach allows the client an opportunity to digest consciously and subconsciously what has been discussed while allowing the natural process of closure to occur.

◈ Principle 2.9: People usually do what is best for themselves using stored information.

Each of us is dependent on information we have obtained and stored. We gain new information, form new insights, and experience new situations. As new events occur, we respond to them from the perspective of our experiential map. We cannot do otherwise.

"He's doing the best he can!" exemplifies this concept. An individual's actions will reflect stored information that, in some situations, may be incomplete or inaccurate.

This principle suggests two areas important in financial counseling. First, you must help clients to assess information they have, help them to become aware of additional information important to their decision making, and help them to correct information that may be misleading or inaccurate.

Second, you are obligated to continuously update your knowledge so that your professional interactions are based on the best possible information. Like your clients, you are limited by the information you have. The quality of professional suggestion, advice, or counsel is dependent on continuously updated and relevant information.

There are two additional implications of the principle. First, sometimes simply correcting or adding new information may be enough to bring about dramatic changes in people's behavior. In financial counseling one focus of the communicative interaction is on providing new information. New information can motivate people in desired directions while providing them a basis for problem-solving and decision-making.

Second, we may have the opinion that our clients are engaging in self-defeating behavior. It must be remembered, however, given the information they have, they may be doing *the best they can*. Granted, *the best they can* at any particular moment could be self-defeating. Additional information may be needed to affect their lives in a positive direction.

The most dramatic example of this principle is the person who attempts or commits suicide. For an outsider observing such behavior, it makes little sense that the individual chooses this act as an alternative to solve a problem. Yet, for the victim, with the information she or he has to work with, this may appear to be the best of bad choices. Remember people do the best that they can with stored information, even though from the outside the choice may appear to be totally inappropriate.

◈ Principle 2.10: Communicative interactions are reciprocal.

When two people communicate, they have direct impact on one another. What one person says has an effect on the other. When the second person responds, it has an effect on the first. Communication is not random but rather, ordered by the communication that has preceded it. There is mutual influence. When someone talks to you, you are affected in two ways.

Effect 1: The content of what is said usually limits the responses. If someone remarks on the weather, a typical listener response would be related to the weather in some way. By contrast, the following example demonstrates a conversation in which this basic rule is violated. It is obvious that this interaction is dysfunctional because what the patient said is *not* tied to what had been said by the psychiatrist.

> **Psychiatrist***:* Well, how are you today, Mr. Fitzgerald?
>
> **Patient***:* What do you mean always barging in here and attacking me!

Effect 2: There is an emotional undertone to what people say: Usually emotional undertones are expressed in tone of voice, volume of speech, and nonverbal behavior. If the tone of voice, volume, and nonverbal behavior are consistent, we usually respond to the content with a similar emotional undertone. When they are inconsistent, we are likely to become confused, and not know if we should react to the content or how the content was presented. It is possible that we would choose to respond to the speaker's emotional undertone rather than to the content of what was said. For example:

> **Client:** (very loudly, while clenching his fist): I am not angry!
>
> **Counselor:** (shouting back and looking very angry): "You are too, and don't yell at me like that!"

The client's words were not as relevant to the counselor as the client's emotional undertone which was communicated through the client's nonverbal behavior. The counselor's reaction was prompted by the client's verbal and nonverbal communication. The manner the counselor responded is an example of *reciprocal interaction.*

Principle 2.10 indicates that people will usually influence the kinds of responses they receive from others. As our examples indicate, the reciprocal nature of communication can lead to a spiral in which one negative output generates a negative response, which in turn generates another negative output. The same concept of reciprocity can produce positive communication spirals. Effective communication, of course, usually leads to positive spirals that are mutually beneficial.

A corollary concept is that we subconsciously form first impressions and expectations of how our communicative interaction will proceed. When the response we get from another person does not meet those expectations or fit our initial impressions, either we become confused or we respond to nonverbal messages that accompany the content. Verbal messages typically used by parents exemplify this. For example:

Parent: "Don't look at me in that tone of voice!"

or

Parent: "Wipe that silly grin off your face!"

These familiar phrases are the parent's response to the child's nonverbal behavior rather than to the child's words.

◈ Principle 2.11: The majority of stored information and learning is not conscious.

Humans seem to equate learning and knowledge with what they *know*. What individuals *know* is what they are *conscious* of. Yet, this conscious knowledge is a very small portion of total knowledge. The world we are aware of includes both the environment around us and the thoughts that are constantly active in our minds. Consider this typical activity.

> We are busily engaged at a computer. As we work, we are aware of the computer keyboard, the monitor, music playing in the background, and papers next to the computer. These are all in the *environment* outside. If attention is focused more broadly, we can become aware of the chair we are sitting on, and our feet on the floor. While typing, we may be aware of the various thoughts that come to mind as we look at the monitor. This is quite a bit to be aware of at one time.

> This is what we are *conscious* of while we are typing. We are not aware of, or do not have in our consciousness, all of the things that happened at work during the day. We are not aware of memories about last week or memories of things that happened last year or several years ago.

Stored information is below the level of consciousness and provides the basis for behavior. For example, one of the authors spent many months learning how to type. It was a frustrating experience and took a great deal of time and effort. The process of learning to type was a slow process of identifying a key, finding it on the keyboard, placing the correct finger over it, and pressing. Each letter had to be *consciously* found and *consciously* pressed. With each practice session, finding the keys became more automatic, or subconsciously controlled. With enough practice, the author didn't think about letters or keys any longer, just words, and his fingers seemed to respond "on their own" to produce words on the keyboard. In a real sense the process of typing became a subconscious process. Development of behaviors, feelings, values, and beliefs follow a similar pattern. Once learned, they function *automatically* or *subconsciously*.

A second concept is related to Principle 2.11. Usually, explanations for people's behavior represent only a portion of information that was used to generate the behavior. Previously, we discussed Gazzaniga's concept of the *interpreter*. He suggested that the interpreter attempts to explain our behavior in a congruent and socially acceptable manner. When it does, the person may be *conscious* of only a small portion of the information that formed the basis for the behavior. The socially acceptable explanation may represent only part of the information.

This does not mean that people deliberately lie to you or to themselves. It does mean that, very often, conscious information used to explain behavior is only part of a fuller explanation. It is this deeper and fuller understanding of the information people use to generate behavior that is the focus of most counseling or therapy processes. We are not implying that counselors must become therapists to become effective financial counselors. However, effective financial counselors are aware that there are fuller explanations for an individual's behavior than even the person understands.

◈ Principle 2.12: People are vulnerable to elements of persuasion.

People exist in an interpersonal environment, an environment in which they *learn* how to respond to others. In today's world, this environment is continuously becoming more complex with progressively more stimuli. According to authors such as Land and Jarman (1992), the amount of information available to individuals is increasing in geometric proportions. The consequence of both of these human conditions, interpersonal learning and increased exposure to stimuli, forces people to find the most expedient manner to arrive at meaningful decisions. The secondary result is that people increasingly become more vulnerable to persuasive appeals that promise *shortcuts* for making decisions, saving time, conserving energy, or retaining resources.

One way that individuals select shortcuts is to rely on *trigger features*. Trigger features are elements that individuals have found to be reliable, effective, or efficient in the past. For example, a parent concerned about her child's playmates might use her perception of the potential playmate's parents as her trigger feature. If she considers the parents to be honorable, she probably will let her child play with their offspring. For this parent, the trigger feature is the degree to which the child's parents were honorable.

Robert Cialdini (1988, 1993), a leading researcher in understanding the power of persuasion, suggests that people have automatic responses that develop from *rules* that were learned while growing up. As adults, people are unaware that they ascribe to these *rules*. Our learned responses (*rules*) direct our behavior and provide the basis for persuasion. From a professional perspective, it is important that financial counselors are aware of the mechanical process by which these responses can be activated and the inherent automatic influence that exists to those individuals who have chosen to exploit them. Five *universal rules* that have the potential to influence interpersonal interactions have been identified. A brief description of each follows:

Reciprocation: We are obligated to give back to others the kind of behavior that they have given us.

People have a natural desire to return to others that which they have received. If complimented by someone, you will have a natural tendency to respond with a compliment. If someone gives you a gift, you have a desire to reciprocate. When someone treats you kindly, you probably respond in a similar manner. These are positive examples. Think of how reciprocation can be, and often is exploited. Consider the following example.

> Jennifer is walking through Chicago's Midway Airport. A flower is pinned on her lapel by a member of a religious sect. Jennifer gave the individual money.

Jennifer's tendency was to abide by one of her *rules*, i.e., to *give something in return.* Jennifer didn't have a flower to give. She gave money instead. This scenario was probably repeated many times over the period of a day.

A corollary exists for the **rule of reciprocation**, i.e., *If I concede something, you will too.* Robert Cialdini provides two excellent examples of this corollary. In the first, he discusses how Boy Scouts were seeking $2.00 donations for their troop and met with little success. They consequently changed their strategy. Instead of asking for $2.00 donations they asked for $5.00 donations. Obviously, they were turned down at this higher level. However, upon being turned down, the Boy Scouts countered with a second request for a $2.00 donation. In most cases, they then received the $2.00 donation! In the first case, the Boy Scouts had given nothing, while in the latter, they created the *illusion* of having given up $3.00!

In a second example, people were asked to act as Big Brothers for youth from a Juvenile Detention Center. They were asked to spend one day with the selected youth. Of those individuals that were asked, seventeen per cent agreed. In an attempt to increase the percentage of positive response, the strategy of solicitation was changed. Individuals were asked to serve as Big Brothers for one year. In most cases this request was turned down. However, upon being turned down, the potential Big Brothers were asked, "Well, could you just spend one day a year as a Big Brother?" The positive response to this second request jumped to fifty per cent! By giving up the request to be a Big Brother for most of the year (an illusion), the solicitors increased their rate of positive response from 17% to 50%.

Consider the following interchange between a financial counselor and a client to see how this *rule* might be used:

> *Financial Counselor* (talking to a client who is hesitant about discussing his financial situation): "I am here to help you in any way that I can... I realize that it is difficult to talk about your financial situation with an outsider... You don't have to tell me anything you don't want to... You can discuss whatever you'd like."

In this simple statement, the financial counselor created an illusion that the counselor has given up control of what is talked about and used a persuasive strategy to encourage the client to accept responsibility for content of the session.

Scarcity: People try to seize those items or opportunities that are scarce or are becoming unavailable.

In particular, information that is exclusive, that not everyone can access, is more persuasive and has more impact than information that is available to everyone. This *rule* underlies why people will speculate on stocks, bonds, and other investments. on the basis of "inside tips." It is important for financial counselors to help clients be aware of this natural tendency and help them understand the potential financial consequences of responding to this *rule*.

Authority: People tend to follow suggestions of persons whom they see as having legitimate authority.

Clients can make financial decisions that can have negative consequences by blindly abiding by this *rule*. A client may view a particular financial counselor as being an authority on real estate investments and, on the basis of the counselor's recommendation, invest a significant percentage of his assets in one specific real estate venture. The client may be so influenced by the authority aspect of the financial counselor that the client does not consider the true merits/limitations of the investment. Obviously, this kind of financial decision making can have dire consequences.

Credibility: Authorities are more influential if they have credibility.

Individuals who are viewed as having knowledge and who are perceived as being trustworthy achieve credibility. Knowledge is demonstrated by the manner in which individuals manage information. Having ready access to information and being able to communicate it, through both oral and written formats, increases one's credibility. Trustworthiness is less direct. This is achieved by *how* and *what* one communicates. To be viewed as being credible one must provide consistently relevant information in a straightforward, direct manner. However, an interesting aspect of this *rule* is that trustworthiness is frequently gained through the earlier *rule* of **reciprocation**. For example, if I acknowledge my shortcomings (give up my perfection) I will be viewed as being more trust worthy than if I don't. Consider this concept in the following advertisements:

> AVIS, "We're number two, but we try harder!";
> and
> VOLKSWAGEN, "We're ugly, but..."

In both of these highly successful advertisements, the opening thought was self-defacing, an approach that builds credibility. In essence, what is communicated is, "If I can be this open about my shortcomings, I must *be honest*."

Comparability: When viewed in isolation, events are perceived differently than when viewed in comparison.

Comparability provides a powerful, useful *rule* of persuasion. Consider the following story .

> A manager of a small corporation was discussing with employees the financial condition of the organization. The manager's statement was, "Well, it has been an unusual year. We are expanding very quickly and we can't hire any more employees to meet the demands. Every one is going to have to work longer hours until we can catch up. I'm going to have to ask some of you to take a cut in pay; We may have to lay a few people off and I'm going to have to cut fringe benefits."

"Now, wait a second, it has been an unusual year, but we are not expanding too fast, no one will have to work longer hours, nobody will be asked to take a cut in pay, nobody will be laid off, and fringe benefits will not be cut,... But,... I *do* have to reduce the size of the New Year bonus."

When *compared* to all of the possible negative consequences, a cut in the New Year bonus seems trivial. Consequently, it would probably appear more palatable.

Financial counselors can use this *rule* to help clients see events more clearly. For example, consider the following:

Client: "I've got so many bills. It is real hard to save for a rainy day."

Financial Counselor: "I can see that you're having trouble seeing how you might save a few dollars. I was wondering, in a couple of years you'll have two kids in college and have all of the expenses you presently have. How do you plan to handle that situation?"

In conclusion, it is important that financial counselors have a working knowledge of all twelve communication principles. All will be applied to the financial counseling interaction in subsequent chapters.

RESOURCES

Cialdini, R.B. (1988). *Influence: Science and Practice* (2nd. Ed.) Glenview: Scott Foresman.

Cialdini, R.B. (1993). *Influence: The Science Of Persuasion* (2nd.Ed.). New York: W.W. Morrow Company.

Gazzaniga, M.S. (1985). *The Social Brain: Discovering The Networks Of The Mind.* New York: Harper.

Land. G. & Jarman, B. (1992). *Breakpoint And Beyond.* New York: Harper Business.

Rosen, S. (1982). *My Voice Will Go With You.* New York: W.W. Norton Company.

3 THE COMMUNICATION PROCESS

Our best evidence of people's true feelings and beliefs comes less from their words than their deeds. Observers trying to decide what people are like look closely at their actions. What the Chinese have discovered is that people themselves use this same evidence to decide what they are like.

Cialdini, R. B. (1988, p.75).

INTRODUCTION

Understanding basic communication provides the foundation for strategies in financial counseling. Everything a person does, communicates something. This includes even doing nothing. People communicate through words, nonverbal behavior, space, and variations in voice tonality, volume, and speed. There are important differences between the ways males and females communicate, differences that can have a major impact on counseling relationships. There are a number of influences on and obstacles to effective communication. This chapter presents eight principles which provide a basis for understanding the communication process.

***Principle* 3.1:** An individual cannot NOT communicate.
***Principle* 3.2:** People use words, actions, space, and tonality, rate, and volume to communicate.
***Principle* 3.3:** Males and females develop different communicative styles.
***Principle* 3.4:** Initial impressions affect communicative interactions.
***Principle* 3.5:** When a person's world is stopped, he or she pays full attention.
***Principle* 3.6:** Communication has five major components and two process elements.
***Principle* 3.7:** Communication is constantly being influenced.
***Principle* 3.8:** Communication always has its obstacles.

PRINCIPLES

◈ Principle 3.1: People cannot NOT communicate.

Everything an individual does communicates something. What is communicated may not be what was intended, but communication does occur nonetheless. Consider the following:

> George was interested in helping his youngest daughter obtain information about trade schools. George identified an educational consultant, one he knew on a casual basis. He called him, told him of his needs, and scheduled an appointment. To George's disbelief, his consultant "friend" said, "George, don't worry about that nonsense. Your daughter will do fine without your help!" George overcame his initial shock and again asked for an appointment.
>
> A date was set for late Friday afternoon the following week. George prepared himself for the meeting by carefully examining his information needs, collecting what he thought were relevant materials, and preparing himself mentally for the discussion. George entered the meeting with high hopes and a great deal of curiosity. To George's chagrin, the consultant was late for the meeting (in his own office!), came dressed in shorts and a T-shirt, didn't appear to be prepared for the meeting, lounged behind his desk, and, in general, acted in an unprofessional manner. George left the meeting confused and frustrated.

Let's look at all that the educational consultant conveyed to George. He probably conveyed some educational information but his dress, lack of preparation, and lateness for the meeting conveyed a lack of interest in George and in his problem. Should George try again to work with the educational consultant? Probably not. Will this experience have an effect on George's future interactions with other educational consultants or people in similar positions. It may.

Picture this scenario. Some individuals, when confronted with a new situation, become withdrawn and very silent. Are these individuals *not* communicating, or could they be communicating that they are shy, uneasy, and unsure? On another level, the withdrawn and silent behavior may be a means of communicating "please help me". You might think you really don't know what a person is thinking or feeling. This is probably true. Yet, you will, and do, form opinions about people. These opinions are formed from your observations of the person. Your subsequent thoughts and actions will be triggered by these opinions. In a true sense, *something* about the person's inner world has been communicated to you and this *something* has affected you.

Let's look again at our friend George and his encounter with the educational consultant. George's reaction to the encounter probably included

- the consultant did not care enough to prepare himself for his interview
- George was relatively unimportant,
- George's fears or worries were unfounded.

On what basis might George form these opinions? Principle 3.2 provides an answer.

◈ Principle 3.2: People use words, actions, space, tonality, rate, and volume to communicate.

Communication occurs in many ways. Some ways are more obvious than others. Edward T. Hall (1973) in a classic text, *The Silent Language,* documented a number of communication channels that people use. We will consider four of them.

Verbal Channel

The verbal channel is most familiar to us. The words we speak and the concepts we express through language are the primary focus of most of our communicative behavior. But, words do not have the same meaning for everyone. For example, *risk taking* to one person may mean making a five-dollar wager on a sporting event, while to another person it may mean borrowing a substantial amount of money to make an investment. We depend on the verbal channel for communication. Yet, we must keep in mind that the words people use is only the tip of the iceberg. Words provide us *some* information, but by no means *all* of what we must know to understand another's experiential map of the world.

George's words expressed a desire to provide for his daughter's well being. The consultant's words suggested that George shouldn't worry. In both cases the *words* provided a portion of the entire message, but not all that transpired between the two men.

Nonverbal Channel

The second channel is nonverbal. The old saying, "A picture is worth a thousand words" also is appropriate in communications. Some experts say that up to 90 per cent of all communication is nonverbal. Remember when, as a child, a look from one of your parents would freeze you with fear. Non-verbally, your parents communicated to you clearly. Most parents intuitively learn to use the power of nonverbal communication. Skilled communicators, like skilled parents, use this channel easily and purposefully. Financial counselors can become more powerful in their interactions and more skilled in communications by paying attention to their own nonverbal communication and to that of their clients.

Once more, let's review George and his interaction. It is clear that George cared about his meeting. He came prepared with questions. He was on time. He was seeking solutions to his concerns. On the other hand, the consultant was late for the meeting. He was dressed in sports attire, and he was casual in posture and actions. In this interaction the *nonverbal* communication has a greater impact than the *verbal*.

Space Channel

Space can be a powerful form of communication. An experience we have all had demonstrates the power of spatial communication. Consider friends or acquaintances that meet on the street and stop to say hello. Frequently, when they are about to part they say something like "Let's get together sometime for lunch." This statement is usually made as both people are backing away from each other. A typical "Yeah, let's do that sometime..." concludes the conversation. In this situation both parties are implying "Let's get together; it's fun to talk." However, the increasing space as they talk communicates distance and separateness. Usually, the space speaks more loudly and with more authority than the words. The individuals probably will not get together for lunch.

Other examples of how we have been conditioned to use personal space can be drawn from our daily lives. Hall (1973) refers to *dimensions* of space. His findings provide us an interesting description of how we use space to communicate. He suggests that people, as a result of cultural influences, abide by unwritten, yet clearly defined rules of space. Here is typical American practice:

- We normally keep people we don't know at least 36 inches away. This is considered to be *public* space.
- We allow individuals we know, but not well, a little closer, approximately 30-36 inches. This is called *social* space.
- Individuals whom we know and trust we will allow to get as close as 24 inches from us. This is called *personal* space.
- For us to allow individuals closer than 24 inches, we must be very comfortable with them and usually know them extremely well. This distance, 0-24 inches, is called *intimate* space.

All of these space distances are averages and are subject to gender, religious, and subculture variances. Nonetheless, they provide a basis for understanding communication and a means for influencing the communicative process. A simple pat on the back intended as a gesture of friendliness on the part of a financial counselor may make a client uncomfortable. If both the client and the financial counselor are men, the client may think the financial counselor is being too friendly. If the client is female and the financial counselor male, a pat on the back may be experienced as too intimate. Consider a financial counselor, wishing to emphasize a point: the counselor leans forward to talk intently to a client. As a result, the client may experience pressure to choose a particular solution. Effective communicators are aware of how their use of space affects others, and consequently it becomes part of their strategy to make others feel comfortable.

How was the concept of space used in George's situation? If you recall, George and the consultant were separated by the consultant's desk. This physical barrier can be a psychological barrier and can interfere with the communication process. As an effective communicator you should be aware of the power of space and use it as part of your strategy to enhance relationships and not to impede them. (For more on strategies for effective use of space, see Chapter 12.)

Tonality, Rate and Volume

We also communicate with our voice, with the limitless combinations of tonality, speech rate, and volume we can create. It is relatively easy to tell whether someone is angry or depressed by his or her tone of voice, speech volume, and speech rate. Angry people tend to talk loudly, have a sharp edge to their voices, and speak much faster than normal. Sad people tend to talk with very flat tones, speak with lower volume, and speak much slower than normal. While these two extremes are relatively easy to identify, there are many gradations between the two.

Paying attention to the subtle differences you detect can enhance communication. There are times when people are unaware of how they use tonality, rate, and volume to express aspects of their experience. It often happens between spouses. One spouse will say something in a loud, angry voice, such as, "Why didn't you enter the last two checks you wrote?" The other spouse might reply, "Don't yell at me!" to which the first spouse responds with a shout, "I'm not yelling!" In this familiar situation, the second spouse didn't respond to the words of the first spouse as much as to the tone and volume of what was said. The first spouse's response indicates that there was little or no awareness of the tone and volume of the initial communication.

This kind of situation raises an interesting question. In an interaction, is it more important to respond to *words* or the *tone, rate, and volume*? In general, effective communicators respond to both. They respond to the words in such a way that they communicate understanding and, also, recognize the second message communicated through tone, rate, and volume. Using our spouse example once again, an effective communicator might reply, "You sound angry at me for not recording the checks." Effective communicators learn to recognize all of the channels of communication and to respond to them appropriately.

There is another issue related to the differences that exists between words and tone, rate, and volume. There are situations in which a person's words communicate one meaning and tone, rate, and volume communicate something different. A person might say in a low, flat tone of voice and very slowly, "I'm so happy." When we hear such a statement, we intuitively know that something is wrong. Happy people usually don't speak in those tones.

The tone, rate, and volume are inconsistent with the words. Often, when people speak to us that way, they aren't aware of the inconsistency. What are we to respond to - the words or tone, rate, or volume? What usually occurs in such a situation is that people are happy at a conscious level and they are sad, depressed, or feeling low at a subconscious level. There is the tendency to automatically respond to the second message as if it were the more important. Effective communicators usually respond to both messages by labeling each half of the communication. A response could be "You say you're happy, but you sound sad," or "While you say you're happy, your voice sounds depressed." Effective communicators do not assume that one message is more important than the other.

Nonverbal behavior, space, tonality, rates, and volume provides subtle cues to another person's map of the world. It is important that we notice these cues so that we form meaningful hypotheses about what they might mean. In the Movie "10", the hero, played by Dudley Moore, is enthralled by the heroine, played by Bo Derek. He observes her from afar and creates, in his mind, a picture of who she is and how she would act. Yet, when he pursues a relationship with her, he finds her to be quite different than anticipated. In fact, she is so different that he is shocked!

Many of us like the hero of "10", observe individuals, form an impression, and only later realize that our impression was inaccurate. We respond to the many individual nuances of the person and compare our observations of this person with persons we have known in the past. If we see a high degree of similarity between the new acquaintance and others we have known, we assume that the new person is *like* the others we have known. At a subconscious level, we depend on our interpersonal observations and history with others to provide a basis for our interpersonal interactions.

◈ Principle 3.3: Males and females develop different communicative styles.

Carli (1991), Lurito (2000), Mills (1995), Pearson (1985), Rosener (1990), and Tannen (1990, 1994) provide insight into differences in male and female communicative styles. Carli, Lurito, Mills, Pearson, and Tannen focus on the communicative process whereas Rosener examines communication in leadership. We have chosen to highlight elements of their works that appear to be most important in counseling relationships.

Gender Difference in the *Listening* Channel

Differences in communication between the sexes can be found in all channels of communication. Lurito, a radiology professor at the Indiana School of Medicine indicates a gender difference in the listening channel. He completed a study in which he used functional magnetic resonance imaging of male and female brains to study brain functions. His initial conclusion is that men use less of their brains while listening than women do. His study of men and women brain scans indicated men, when listening, used the left sides of their brains, the region usually associated with language. Women used both sides of their brains. Women, it would seem, have more of their brain focused when listening than men. This may account for the observation that women are more adept at listening to simultaneous conversations, are more easily distracted by competing details, and are more adept at picking up emotional overtones. Males appear to be goal oriented and attend to incoming information that is consistent with their goals. They don't *hear* inconsistent or competing information.

Gender Differences in the *Verbal* Channel

In the verbal channel there are a number of differences between how males and females communicate. Pearson highlights some of these differences.

Formality of Language. Females tend to use formal words and phrases, whereas males are more likely to use informal ones. A female might say, "I understand what you are trying to tell me," while, by contrast, a male might say, "I get the picture."

Specificity and Hypercorrection. Females appear to prefer the *specificity* that language can provide. They tend to respond with precision to the meaning of words, while males appear to be content with the general meaning that is conveyed. Females respond to lack of specificity by *hypercorrecting*. A man may describe a shirt as "blue", but a women may typically correct that description and describe the same shirt as "teal". It seems to be more important for females to respond to the exact meaning of the spoken word and for males to react to the totality of the communication.

From a male perspective, males often feel they are explaining a concept and find that females responding to their statements, focus on the accuracy of the words being used rather than on the ideas being relayed. Males then may judge that the females do not understand or are being unnecessarily critical about the choice of words. For example, assume that a financial planner says the following:

> "When we consider real estate limited partnerships as a tax shelter, there is always the question of risk. We have to consider the risk relative to the potential losses. Suppose we consider taxes paid as a *loss.* If the limited partnership investment reduces your taxes 80% for the length of the partnership, and if it does fold, you have *lost* the amount you invested less the amount saved in your taxes.
>
> According to Pearson's work, a female might respond, "Hmmm. What do you mean *lost*? I don't consider the money I pay in taxes *lost.*

In the example, the female focussed on her specific interpretation of the word *lost*, while the counselor had a more general meaning of the word *lost* in mind. For females, hypercorrection may be a means of evaluating whether they have understood the speaker's message. Males, apparently, are content with understanding the overall message and are less concerned about how the message is given. In the above example, a male may find no difficulty with the word *lost* used in that context. If such misunderstandings occur during a financial counseling session, it is the counselor's responsibility to understand what is happening and to correct the situation.

Misunderstandings often occur when people use examples to illustrate a point. A male may think the example helps to clarify the concept, only to find the female taking exception with the example or the words used. The example can lead to confusion instead of clarification.

Guttural. Another major difference can be found in the *nature* of the words or phrases used. Males and females differ in their tendencies to use hostile words, profanity, or expletives. Males are considerably more likely to lace their conversation with words of this type than are females. In general, men tend to have a much more *earthy* quality to their language. Females, by contrast, use more precise descriptions and are less likely to reveal overt aggressiveness in their speech.

Intensifiers, Fillers and Qualifiers. According to Pearson, males are less likely to use intensifiers, fillers, qualifiers, or disclaimers than females. Let's look at each of these.

Intensifiers include words such as *"so"*, *"quite"*, and *"awfully"*. Females are more likely to say something like, "This is an *awfully* big challenge," or "That is a *great* deal more than I had hoped for." Males would probably say, "This is a challenge," or "That's more than I had hoped for." Females, in general, use intensifiers to express the strong feelings that are connected to what is being stated.

Both sexes use fillers, but females use them more frequently, especially as feedback. Fillers like "um hmm," "okay," and "right" are vocalized utterances that are used to assure the speaker that they are being attended to or understood. Males are more likely to provide such feedback to the speaker in a nonverbal manner, perhaps through direct eye contact or through nonverbal behavior such as a head nod.

Qualifiers like "maybe," "in my opinion," "perhaps," "somewhat," and "in general" are used not only to generalize specific statements, but also to soften the impact of what has been communicated. If you look back through this discussion, you will see a number of "qualifiers." These have been used to suggest that "in many cases but not exclusively" males and females respond differently. Females use this form of communication more frequently than males do.

Disclaimers are phrases such as: "I know I don't know much about this, but,..." or "I probably will get in your way, but,..." or "If you don't mind, could you...?" They weaken the speaker's request or statement. Disclaimers are found in females' speech more often than in males' speech.

One way isn't better than the other. However, they are different. The difference can lead to misunderstanding and conflict. When financial counselors work with couples, it is beneficial to be aware of male and female communication. Counselors should adjust their speech so that both parties are accommodated.

Interactive Quality of Communication

In two controlled studies, Carli examined the communication patterns and verbal interaction of males and females. She found that females used *disclaimer* questions such as, "I don't know, but..." three times as frequently as males. Second, Carli found that females used *tag* questions like, "More people drive big cars, don't they?" two and half times more frequently than males and finally that females used *hedges* such as *"sort of"*, *"perhaps"*, and *"maybe"*, one and one-half times more frequently than males.

A second aspect of Carli's study was to determine how females and males were viewed by others when they exhibited use of these linguistic forms in their speech. She addressed competence and influence. Carli found that when females used disclaimers, tag questions, or hedges, both females and males viewed them as being less competent and less knowledgeable than females who did not use them. By contrast, perception of males' competence and knowledge was *not* effected by use of these linguistic forms. When influence was evaluated, Carli found that females using these forms of communication were viewed by males as being *more* influential than females who did not use them. They were viewed as *less* influential by other females. Assertive females, ones who did not use disclaimers, tag questions, or hedges, were viewed by males as being *less* influential. Finally, both sexes rated males to have equal influence whether or not they used disclaimers, tag questions, or hedges.

Carli's findings are important because they stress the interactive quality of communications. What is clear in Carli's work is that interaction between the sender and the receiver determines the *meaning* of the transmission. What is less clear is *why* males and females respond differently to identical messages and why males and females are viewed differently when they speak. It is not our purpose here to argue that one form is better than another nor to raise issues about gender bias in judgements. Rather, a financial counselor needs to understand that these basic differences exist and that these differences do affect the transmission of meaning.

Tannen (1990), in *You Just Don't Understand*, adds a slightly different perspective to our understanding of differences between male and female communicative styles. Her emphasis is placed on the fundamental goals or purposes one has for communicating. In general, she suggests that *most* male communication is aimed at achieving independence, whereas a *significant* portion of female communication is geared toward relationship development or maintenance. Differences between the sexes can be noted in the categorical ways of communicating listed below:

MALES	**FEMALES**
Value independence	Value intimacy
Emphasize report talk	Emphasize rapport talk
Talk more than women	Talk less than men
Talk for information	Talk for interaction
Overestimate word power	Underestimate word power
Argue categorically	Argue personally
Argue from external data	Argue from internal data
Focus on external events	Focus on personal data
Focus on large picture	Focus on personal details
Lecture	Listen
Seek respect	Seek to be liked
Offer information	Seek understanding
Focus on content	Focus on emotions
Listen silently	Give feedback as they listen

The perspectives advanced above are apparent in an article by Rosener (1990) entitled, *Ways Women Lead*. The major points of the article are that women managers emphasize interactions, encourage participation, share power and information, work at enhancing the self worth of others, and tend to energize co-workers. Male managers, by contrast, encourage independent action, retain power and information, and focus on the task at hand more than on the individuals attempting to achieve the task.

All three of the authors discussed above emphasize that males and females communicate *differently*, but that one way of communicating is not necessarily *better*. To exemplify this point, consider the interchange that follows between a male financial counselor and a female client:

> **Client:** I just received an inheritance of $10,000.
>
> **Financial Counselor***:* What would you like to do with it?
>
> **Client***:* I haven't had a chance to talk with my husband yet, so I don't know.
>
> **Financial Counselor***:* Well, haven't you considered some things yourself?
>
> **Client***:* No, I want to talk with my husband first.
>
> **Financial Counselor***:* Why don't we spend a few minutes and discuss some possibilities.
>
> **Client:** Not until I talk with my husband!

Obviously, the above interchange was designed to be stereotypical. However, this interchange demonstrates one of the key differences between males and females. Males have been socially conditioned to value independent action, females to value relationships. Whereas the client in the above interchange wants to make a financial decision that will be determined in *conjunction* with her husband, the financial counselor seems to be pressing her to make a decision *independent* of her husband. Both male and female financial counselors should be aware of how they have been conditioned. This conditioning can have a subtle, yet powerful, impact on their counseling.

◈ Principle 3.4: Initial impressions affect communicative interactions.

In a book titled *Contact,* Zunin and Zunin (1975) state that the first four minutes of an interpersonal interaction are "the key to establishing social relationships, family harmony, business success, and sexual pleasure." This first four minutes is the average time span in which people assess each other and arrive at decisions of whether to pursue or to terminate the relationship. Given the significance of these first minutes, one might ask, "What, specifically, are people responding to?" The following elements appear to be most important.

Trustworthiness: An individual will trust another initially if certain criteria are met. The first reaction is visually based. When you meet people for the first time, you subconsciously assess what they are wearing, how they stand or sit, how they posture themselves, how they move, and how they use nonverbal gestures in communication. You pay particular attention to eye contact, the manner in which they say or form words, the sound of the voice, and the speed of their speech. You use each of these bits of data to arrive at your overall assessment, usually at a subconscious level.

At a more conscious level, you also attend to what is said. If you determine that the person does understand the important issues under discussion, then you probably will be more favorably disposed toward him or her. Your overall rating of trustworthiness is dependent upon your reactions to all of these variables.

Societal Expectations: We have all met people we immediately like. By contrast, we have met people who turn us off! What is the difference? Probably some combination of the factors outlined above.

For example, imagine yourself going to a meeting in which you are introduced to a 40-year-old man. He is clean-shaven and is wearing a well-tailored, navy blue pinstriped suit. He carries himself in an athletic manner, has a ready smile, and appears to be interested in what you have to say. He looks at you when you talk. He nods his head in understanding. Overall, he demonstrates good listening skills. Most people would immediately like such a person. The person described fits a number of normal societal expectations. In general, the more we fit societal and subgroup expectations of success, the more likely we will be accepted by others. In this regard, being viewed as different is a disadvantage. To avoid being viewed as different, we must become aware of what is expected and learn to act accordingly.

Dynamic Quality: A person who demonstrates a sense of excitement for living, a forceful presence, an enthusiasm for interpersonal involvement, and a willingness to entertain new ideas or behaviors usually will be viewed in a positive manner by others. People who demonstrate these characteristics in initial encounters will attract others to them.

Basic Value Similarity: In initial interactions, people attempt to determine the basic values of others. The degree to which another is open minded, the degree to which an individual is impartial or unbiased, and the degree to which another expresses views similar to one's own all are determined very early in a relationship. If you determine that another is similar to you, then a basic sense of trust and liking probably will follow.

Status: In addition to the above, there are status determinants of trust and liking. In this regard, people of higher status command, and receive, communicative responses that reflect their status position. For example, the manager of a financial institution, by the nature of position, will be given greater credibility than an employee of the financial institution by those people who are aware of the status of both persons. As unfair as it may seem, position or status carries power or influence. The higher the status, the greater the power.

◈ Principle 3.5: When a person's world is stopped, he or she pays full attention.

This principle is founded on the work of Carlos Castaneda (1972) in his book *Journey to Ixtlan*. It may seem abstract. Yet, an understanding of this principle can facilitate communication. The *orienting reflex* underlies this principle. The orienting reflex is a mental process that allows us to shut off our internal dialogue at potentially crucial times. For instance, when something different happens in the environment we pay attention long enough to decide whether it is dangerous or, said another way, when an environmental stimulus differs from normal expectations we stop *self-talk* to focus our full attention on the external event. We pay limited attention to stimuli that bombard us. Normally we habituate, or adjust, to any stimuli that aren't included in our immediate focus of attention or that do not pose a threat to us.

Consider this example. While you are watching television you gradually pay less and less attention to the normal noise of the children playing in the house. You habituate to the playing noises and pay attention to the television. However, when one of the children screams, you suddenly pay attention. You focus on the scream to see if it indicates that it is just part of normal play or whether it means someone is hurt. If you decide it is part of normal play, you focus your attention back on the television. If you decide it may mean someone is hurt, you will rush to see what happened. When the orienting reflex is activated, you give your full attention for a moment. By full attention we mean that all of your senses are focused on the stimulus until you decide, consciously or subconsciously, how you need to respond.

We are aware that unusual occurrences cause us to stop and reassess our world. The teenager who has a close friend die in a car accident, the man who has his youngest child leave home, the woman who loses a job, those who observe a televised space shuttle explosion, or watch a terrorist attack on the World Trade Center exemplify this point. In all of these situations, individuals are forced to reconsider what they believe to be important in life.

Even though the nature of most intervening events may not be as dramatic as those presented above, financial counselors can use this human capacity for attending to important circumstances to help clients. A financial counselor working in a small town in New York had a client who was interested in purchasing a recreational cottage. As a result of a number of conversations, she learned that the client frequently sought out such property, but never purchased. In the course of discussing mortgage rates, the counselor said, "I'm aware that you have looked at property in the past and that you look but don't buy. Could it be that you are afraid to take the risk?" This question caught the client off guard and led to an in-depth discussion that focused on all the positives and negatives of owning a recreational residence. The counselor, in this situation, had gone beyond the words of the client and had addressed an apparently deeper concern. To get at this concern, the counselor had to confront the client with his own behavior. The counselor's statement stopped the client's usual means of operating, and that led to greater understanding for both.

A second way to look at this principle is to consider the concept of psychological patterns. Patterns are generalizations that make it easier to function in a stimulus-loaded environment. For instance, we have learned that when we see a police officer we should behave lawfully. When we see a school bus we should drive cautiously. When we are at public events and the National Anthem is played we should stand and place our hands over our hearts. Each of these situations represents a learned pattern that no longer requires conscious thought. Each helps us to function in society. There are patterns, however, that interfere with our functioning. In the example presented above, the financial counselor became aware of her client's pattern and by making an unexpected comment helped the client examine how that pattern influenced his decisions. By helping a person recognize a pattern, a financial counselor can help clients *stop their world* and gain control over an otherwise subconscious occurrence.

◈ Principle 3.6: Communication has five major components and two process elements.

Communication is a complex act in which two or more people attempt to share internal thoughts and feelings. In the process of this sharing, a number of variables affect the nature and content of communication. The major components of this process are the *sender,* the *message,* the *channel,* the *receiver,* and the *environment.* The process elements inherent in this act are *feedback* and *noise.*

Sender

The *sender is* the originator of the message. In communicative interactions, the sender is the person who wishes to convey a thought or feeling. A financial counselor who expresses an opinion about a specific investment to a client is a sender. A client who mentions to a financial counselor that he wants to shelter more income is a sender. A financial counselor who explains the use of options to a client is a sender. Obviously, at different times both the client and the counselor will be the sender.

Message

The *message is* the idea or feeling that is conveyed by the sender. The message for the financial counselor mentioned above might be that the investment under discussion can meet the client's specific needs. For the client working with the financial counselor the message might be "I want help." For the financial counselor, the message might be "These are the implications of options that I would like you to understand." In each case, the message serves as the content being transmitted.

Channels

Communicative messages are sent through *channels.* In the human system the five senses of sight, sound, touch, taste, and smell are the channels through which messages are exchanged. Of these, sight and sound are the most important. Hamilton, Parker, and Smith (1982) suggest that language, paralanguage, and nonverbal language are the three primary channels of communication. They suggest that the spoken word accounts for 7% of communication, 38% of communication is through paralanguage (voice intonation, rhythm, inflection, etc.), and nonverbal language (gestures, use of space, body movements, etc.) is responsible for the remaining 55% of what is communicated. It is noteworthy that they ascribe 100% of communication to channels involving sight and sound and totally disregard taste or smell as channels of communication. They do, however, consider touch as an important variable in nonverbal language. (They are talking about the process of channeling communication. People do store information with elements of *all* the senses.) Finally, sight and sound are emphasized because of cultural expectations. Generally, in the United States, sight and sound are the primary channels. In other cultures or subcultures, smell and taste may be very important communication channels.

The three channels of sight, sound, and touch are primarily responsible for the degree to which an intended message is communicated. For example, if a client said to a counselor, "I'm very happy to be working with you," while he looked and acted disinterested, a dual message could be communicated. On the one hand, the client might be stating, "I'm happy to be working with you." On the other hand, the client, through paralanguage and nonverbal language, appears to be saying, "I'm not happy to be working with you." For accurate communication, it is important that the individual sending the message, the *sender,* be consistent across channels. That is, it is important that the same message be sent across all of the channels of communication. This will assure that the message is transmitted with the greatest clarity. It is the sender's responsibility to assure that the message that is intended is communicated in a consistent manner.

Receiver

The *receiver* is recipient of the message, the person, to whom the message is directed, and as such has an obvious influence on whether communication will occur. In this capacity the *receiver* must demonstrate openness to the incoming message and capability for responding.

Feedback

Receivers use *feedback,* the first of the process elements, to carry out their responsibility. Feedback is the response or reaction the receiver provides the sender about the message and how it was communicated. As a result of the receiver's feedback, the client would have an opportunity to correct or alter his or her message. The counselor in the example above might provide feedback to the client by saying, "I'm confused. You say that you are happy to be working with me, but you don't seem happy." This allows the client to clarify which message is most important, the verbal or the nonverbal.

Environment

The *environment is* the context in which communication takes place. Obviously, it is difficult to hold another's attention in a hot, humid, or poorly ventilated room. The receiver's ability to attend is directly related to the degree of his or her physical comfort. Therefore, it is very important for financial counselors to provide a physical environment that is conducive to attentiveness and understanding. Chapter 12 will provide strategies that can be used in this regard.

The second environmental variable that must be considered is psychological in nature. Environments, by their very nature, will be comfortable or uncomfortable. For example, a student in a principal's office will be less comfortable than the principal. A loan officer in her office will be more comfortable than a client seeking a loan. From a practical, applied point of view, a financial counselor must consider the psychological environment and do whatever is necessary to ensure that the receiver (the client) is psychologically comfortable. In some circumstances, this may mean holding conferences in the client's environment or in a neutral arena.

Noise

Noise can be either internal or external in nature. Internal noise occurs in communication when either participant has a physical or psychological malady; if either party is preoccupied with other thoughts; or, in general, when one or both of the people involved have difficulty focusing on the message. External noise is usually easier to detect and, frequently, easier to remedy. External noise consists of variables such as heat, sounds, humidity, odors, or ventilation. Each of these can influence the attentiveness of the receiver and the communicative impact of the sender. It is the financial counselor's responsibility to be aware of the influence of environment on communications and to create a physical environment that is conducive to attentiveness and understanding.

◈ Principle 3.7: Communication is constantly being influenced.

There are many influences on the communicative process.

Motivation

Motivation is a key influence in interaction that refers to the internal state of both the sender and receiver. If either party is not motivated to communicate, then the degree to which both parties understand the primary meaning of messages will be decreased. For instance, if an accountant is attempting to help her client to understand the necessities of obtaining tax-sheltered investments, while the client is thinking about an upcoming golf outing, then meaningful message transfer probably is not taking place. What could cause such a situation? Many things! The client could be overworked, the room might be too hot, or the financial need, at the moment, may not be sufficiently pressing to the client. The important point is that for true communication to occur, both parties have to be motivated. In counseling relationships, it is the financial counselor's responsibility to promote motivated interaction and to be aware when this is not occurring. One of the purposes of this book is to indicate strategies to accomplish this end. Subsequent chapters will present skills and strategies designed for making communication more effective.

Source credibility

Source credibility is a second issue to be considered. If we believe someone is important, we are more likely to listen to him or her. If we accept this basic assumption, then it becomes crucial for us to be viewed by our clients as being important. A financial counselor obtains credibility in many ways: by demonstrating excellence with past clients; by behaving in a professionally competent manner with current clients; and by establishing a reputation for excellence in the professional field. Source credibility is important, yet fragile. It is difficult to achieve and relatively easy to lose. A credible financial counselor must continuously work to stay abreast of current developments in the field and must demonstrate credibility in interactions with clients. In essence, credibility occurs when professionals have a substantial knowledge base, stay current with their field, and demonstrate their knowledge through a caring interaction.

Information difficulty

Information difficulty is an important variable to consider. We may assume that the financial counselor is motivated and able to motivate the client. Further, we may assume that the counselor has a high degree of credibility. Given these two assumptions, we might then assume that clients would be willing to expend effort to learn what is necessary for making meaningful changes in their lives. This assumption probably would hold if the information clients are asked to learn or deal with is not overly difficult. For many clients, the difficulty level of communicated information determines whether they pay attention to the counselor's message. Information that is too difficult will not be attended to or will not be accepted in a manner that is beneficial. This is true for both written and verbal communication.

Organization

Organization has a significant impact on the degree to which information is learned. Two basic principles can be applied to organization.

> **Principle 1: The Principle Of Primacy.** The principle of *primacy,* suggests that information that occurs early in an interchange is likely to be remembered longer and in greater detail than material that occurs in the middle of the interchange.
>
> **Principle 2: The Principle Of Recency.** The second principle, the principle of *recency,* suggests that the last information presented will be remembered with clarity.

Although it is not entirely clear which of these two principles is dominant, it is clear that information occurring early (primacy) and information occurring late (recency) are more likely to be remembered than materials presented in the middle of an interchange.

A counselor can utilize these principles by organizing materials in such a way that the most important elements of a message occur early and/or late in the interaction. For example, a doctor, in consultation with a patient, could use these principles by saying the following: "It is important that you consume more fluids than normal. One of the problems that you are presently experiencing is related to your diet, the amount of exercise that you are getting, and the way that your body is processing what you have been ingesting. This problem is quite common and not very serious, but I would suggest that you consume more fluids than you normally do." Notice that the doctor's primary message about increasing fluids is given both early and late in his statement.

Communicative Style

Communicative style is the final influence on communication to be discussed here. Although style can be viewed from many perspectives, we will be concentrating on one that emphasizes interaction. *Style* refers to how you, as a counselor, represent yourself to the client. We will present three possibilities, even though, by forming combinations of the three, many others exist.

- ***Possibility 1:*** As a financial counselor you can approach the client from an authority/expert perspective. From this stance, communication focuses on what you *know* and how the client can benefit from your knowledge. Information is emphasized. Decisions are reached from logical analysis of known data. Although you can be cordial in the interchange, the communicative atmosphere is structured. You determine what will be discussed and how decisions should be reached. A brief example of this approach might look like the following:

Financial Counselor: The best investment possibility open to you is a limited partnership. This will provide you all of the tax sheltering you need and give a fair cash flow advantage.

Client: Why is this the best for me?

Financial Counselor*:* Your tax bracket makes it imperative that you shelter some of your income. Also, this vehicle has the best combination of shelter and income. You will benefit more from this investment than from any of the others I've described to you.

▶ ***Possibility 2:*** A financial counselor could also adopt a communicative style that would emphasize facilitation. In this approach, you provide relevant information but emphasize the *client's understanding* and use of the information. You can use communicative skills to help the client to arrive at personally relevant decisions. In contrast to the authority or expert approach, this approach places greater responsibility on the client. An interchange using this approach might flow like the following:

Counselor*:* We've examined a number of savings possibilities. Which one looks best to you?

Client*:* From what we've discussed I'm leaning toward a certificate of deposit.

Counselor*:* What is it about certificates of deposit that you find attractive?

▶ ***Possibility 3:*** Finally, a financial counselor could adopt a communicative style that is *low key* or laissez faire in nature. In this approach you place almost all of the responsibility on the client and provide information specifically sought by the client. This approach is reactive instead of proactive. Again, an example might clarify this style:

Counselor*:* What are your needs?

Client*:* I'd like to examine some savings possibilities.

Counselor*:* Which ones have you considered?

Client*:* Well, I've looked at a number of them.

Counselor*:* Have you settled on any in particular?

Client*:* Certificates of deposit look quite good. What can you tell me about them?

It should be obvious that the examples presented above are stereotypical. Yet, they do reflect a variety of communicative styles open to professionals. The choice of any one style, or combination of styles, is dependent on client needs, your counseling competency, personality variables of the financial counselor and his or her clients, the context in which the communication is occurring, and the nature of the counseling endeavor. In summary, the choice depends upon what you want to accomplish and the strategies available to accomplish those ends.

◈ Principle 3.8: Communication always has its obstacles.

Communication, by its very nature, is less than perfect. The message transmitted from sender to receiver will always be less than 100%. As a financial counselor, your goal should be to maximize the receiver's understanding of the message. To do this, awareness of a number of obstacles can help you communicate more effectively.

Inadequate Preparation

Inadequate preparation is one of the potential obstacles. A loan officer who does not know current mortgage rates, a doctor who does not know current practices, a financial counselor who does not know current financial institution loan rates, or an insurance salesperson who does not know insurance benefits will communicate, but not what they might want to communicate. Effective communication is based on credibility. As discussed earlier, credibility results when knowledge is demonstrated. Inadequate preparation prevents you from displaying this knowledge and destroys credibility. The end result can be the client's lack of faith in you, a subsequent lack of motivation in the communicative process, and eventually, a severing of the counseling relationship. Without this relationship, there is no communication!

Vague Instructions

Vague instructions can interfere with the communicative process. Clients frequently are unaware of the subtle aspects of professional discussions. Consequently, vague statements, unclear instructions, inexact definitions, or obscure procedures can lead to client confusion. It is important for you to be clear and succinct so that interference to communication is prevented.

Rules: Failure to follow rules is a general category. There are a number of rules, which, when neglected, prevent facilitative communication.

- ***Rule One:*** You should attempt to provide an overall perspective about the topic under discussion. Communication is enhanced when clients know how specific pieces of data fit into the overall picture.
- ***Rule Two:*** You should use the simplest words possible to get your message across. A minimum of simple, succinct words is far superior to many confusing terms.
- ***Rule Three*:** Be specific. A client should know what, exactly, is being discussed. You should try to avoid generalities and to be specific in the messages you communicate.
- ***Rule Four*:** Use repetition in your communication. Clients are more likely to *hear* messages that are repeated a number of times. This rule becomes especially important when it is coupled with the principles of *primacy* and *recency.*

Culture

Cultural nuances add to the difficulty of communication. Different cultures employ different conventions for listening or responding to others, for sequencing their thoughts in a linear, spiral or circular manner, and for determining when in a relationship important issues should be discussed. They also use different conventions for evoking stylistic differences such as animated, personally confrontational approaches as contrasted with low key, impersonal, non-challenging communication, and finally, for using candor, specificity, and assertiveness. Additional difficulties occur from voice accents and professional uses of communication media such as telephones. Each culture has its own rules. Consequently, it is imperative that financial counselors become aware of culturally different client nuances and use this awareness to communicate more effectively. Counselors can gain further insight into cultural nuances by reading Judith A. Starkey's (1996) book, *Multicultural Communication Strategies.*

RESOURCES

Carli, L.L. (1989). *Gender differences in interaction style and influence*. Journal of Personality and Social Psychology. Vol. 57(6), p.964.

Cialdini, R.B. (1988). *Influence: Science And Practice* (2nd.ed). New York: Harper Collins Publisher.

Hall, E. T. (1973). *The Silent Language*. New York: Anchor Books.

Hamilton, C, Parker, C., & Smith, D.D. (1982). *Communicating For Results.* Belmont: Wadsworth Publishing Company.

Lurito, J. T. (2000). *Did you hear me*? Presentation made at Radiological Society of North America's annual meeting, Chicago, Illinois.

Mills, S. (Ed.). (1995). *Language & Gender*. New York: Longman.

Pearson, J.C. (1985). *Gender And Communication*. Dubuque: W.C. Brown.

Rosener, J.B. (1990). *Ways Women Lead*. Harvard Business Review. November-December, pp. 119-125.

Starkey, J.A. (1996). *Multicultural Communication Strategies*. Chicago: JAMS Publishing Company.

Tannen, D. (1994).*Talking From 9 To 5*. New York: Avon Books.

Tannen, D. (1990). *You Just Don't Understand.* New York: William Morrow and Company.

Zunin, L. & Zunin, N. (1975). Contact: *The First Four Minutes.* New York: Ballantine Books.

4 THE LISTENING PROCESS

Our perceptions about the world are coded in the brain. Thoughts using pictures, sounds, and feelings determine our communication process. The words we select for communication reflect our favorite sensory system: visual, auditory, or kinesthetic. By translating our thoughts into familiar words of another person's favorite representation system, we can increase rapport and understanding.

Laborde, G.Z. (1984, p.73).

Listening skills and processes are used to establish and maintain effective working relationships, relationships that are characterized by openness, honesty and trust. We will discuss the important dimensions of listening, examine specific rules for the process, investigate a number of issues that influence how people listen, and indicate potential effects these concepts have on an overall financial counseling strategy.

DIMENSIONS OF LISTENING

Consider the following dialogue between Fred, a financial counselor, and Mary a member transferring funds from a money market account into a certificate of deposit.

> ***Fred:*** Mary, the certificate I've been talking about is the best kind of immediate investment you can make. It is insured by a federal agency and is as secure as the Rock of Gibraltar. There is no way you can lose with the interest our CD's are paying right now. Why, if I had the money, I'd put into this kind of savings vehicle in a minute.

> ***Client:*** Well, I don't know if I'm interested in tying up my savings for that length of time.

Keep in mind, as we discussed in the previous chapter, that the *words* in the interchange are only the surface of the communication that took place. Integral parts of the communication process also include the *thoughts* that provide a basis for the words. With this example as a backdrop, we can discuss a number of the primary dimensions of listening.

Attending

Attending refers to the process of paying attention to internal or external stimuli. We live in a world full of stimuli, some of which are important to us, while others are relatively unimportant. We learn to selectively screen what is important from that which is *not* important. This process allows us to function in a manner that is consistent with our personal needs, values, and goals. It allows us to use stimuli that will be helpful to us in our quest for personal satisfaction.

From a negative perspective, selective attention can prevent us from experiencing elements that are important. We frequently hear the words but, unfortunately, do not pay attention to the message. In interactions, selective attention can impede meaningful communication

In our example, Fred could be so intent on convincing Mary about the value of investing in the Certificate of Deposit that he would selectively attend to Mary's response *only* if it agreed with what he wanted. He could miss any response that was inconsistent with his point of view. Thus, he might selectively attend only to the words, "I don't know if I'm interested," which might mean that there is still hope, thus providing some encouragement for him to continue. Mary also could attend selectively. She might believe that financial counselors are only interested in selling other services at the financial institution. Her tentative reply seems to imply that she thinks Fred is using a hard-sell approach. Once she placed Fred in this category, Mary would attend to Fred's style and would not attend to his message. The result probably would be Mary's rejection of Fred and his suggestions.

Assigning Meaning

Once stimuli are attended to, meaning is assigned. Let's assume Mary attended to Fred's style and determined that Fred was untrustworthy. To arrive at this conclusion, Mary probably compared Fred to other people she has known and to how she has viewed these people. This process of comparison to stored experiences, a portion of her representational map, is the primary method for assigning meaning.

Mary's response to Fred was based on her previous interactions. In a way, Fred was the victim of Mary's history. Fred, however, is also a victim of his own history. He probably learned that a *selling* approach would be the best method to help clients. In general, he might be correct, but in this interaction, it appears that he was wrong.

Categorizing

For meaning to occur, previous experiences have to be accessible to the individual. Although it is not clear how data are stored by the human system, it is clear that certain events will evoke categorical responses. Mary's behavior exemplified this. She responded to Fred in a manner that is similar to how she would or did respond to salespeople who behaved like Fred. Her thoughts and feelings in her encounter with Fred were immediate and spontaneous. Mary did not have to create a response; rather, her response was automatic and specific to the situation. Stimuli that are attended to are assigned meaning and categorized according to specifics of the situation similar to stored experiences.

Remembering

Remembering, whether conscious or subconscious, is the process of recalling thoughts or feelings about previous occurrences. Without this final dimension, categorization could not occur and meaning would have no reference point.

At times the remembering process is conscious, while at other times it is subconscious. For example, you may consciously try to recall the name of a high school teacher, the title of a favorite movie, or the call letters of a stock on the stock exchange. In most cases, that which you are able to recall will depend on how well you attended to specifics of the original data and on the degree to which you assigned meaning to that data.

The subconscious process of remembering is less predictable but of equal importance. Two key components of subconscious remembering are important.

> **Component 1:** The subconscious process can be set in motion consciously. By using our inherent tendency to finish what is set in motion, we can *program* subconscious memory. For example, a financial counselor trying to help a client might make the following suggestion,
>
> > "We've talked about a number of things that you could do to solve your dilemma. Yet, none of the ideas seems quite right. Instead of continuing to spin our wheels on this, between now and next Thursday when we will get together,

why don't you think of some other possibilities that don't have the limitations we've discussed."

In this example, the counselor has given the client a conscious message to continue the search for an appropriate solution *and* has provided the client's subconscious a strong suggestion to find an appropriate solution for the problem. The counselor also has set a time limit for the subconscious activity!

Component 2: A second feature of subconscious processing relates to the use of information stored in our representational maps as a basis for behavior. Our representational maps are a distillation of our previous experiences. These representational maps become the basis for our responses in new situations. This process is most often subconscious and can be exemplified by our emotional responses. Emotions exist in both conscious and subconscious awareness, but the impact from subconscious remembering frequently is more dramatic. There are many examples in our daily lives. Consider a mother who, upon seeing a college student hug his mother, starts to cry because she misses her son. Consider the serviceman who gets tears in his eyes when he hears the Marine Hymn. Consider the moviegoer who alternates between tears and laughter while watching a particularly good movie. In all of these, events trigger memories both consciously and subconsciously.

We have discussed the four dimensions of listening: *attending*, *assigning meaning*, *categorizing*, and *remembering*. You either attend or do not attend. In circumstances where you attend, you assign meaning to what is perceived; you classify specifics of the situation; and you remember, consciously and subconsciously, previous experiences that relate to that which you did attend. By contrast, what is not attended to will be lost and be unrecoverable. Listening, composed of its four dimensions, is the basic stratagem for effective communication.

RULES FOR LISTENING

There are a number of rules which increase the effectiveness of listening and facilitate communication.

Respond To The Main Idea

In listening to someone, always attempt to determine the person's main message. It is not uncommon for someone to express, through words and actions, a number of messages at one time. As listener, you may have to practice attentiveness and patience to get at the primary message. Consider the following interchange between a client and a financial counselor.

Client: I have to do something about a situation I find myself in.

Counselor: What seems to be the problem?

Client: I would like to purchase a new house that I've been wanting for a long time. The problem is that I'm not sure if my job is stable or not. On top of that, my oldest child is about to enter college. The house is perfect. I don't know what to do.

Counselor: So, the big problem is that you want this house and you are not sure you can have it.

Client: I don't think that's it.

Counselor: I see. Could it be that you are just frustrated that everything is happening at the same time...and you can't seem to control it?

Client: I hadn't thought about that, but I think you could be right.

In this interchange, the counselor was presented with five ideas: I want a new house; my job is not stable; my oldest child is about to enter college; I don't know what to do; and I'm frustrated by the entire situation. The counselor's first response to the client seemed to miss the mark. The counselor then adjusted his response. The client's final statement confirmed that the counselor made an appropriate adjustment. This example demonstrates the importance of attending as a dimension of listening. The counselor attended to the client. Consequently, he was able to determine the client's main message*: "I am frustrated by my inability to control the situation."* The goal for listening should be to understand the sender's message as soon as one can, but, more importantly, to make sure that the main message is understood. In the example, this was accomplished.

Respond To Emotional Messages

People simultaneously communicate at thinking and emotional levels. In financial counseling it is usually most appropriate to respond to clients' thoughts. However, since emotions can block rational decision making, financial counselors should listen for indicators of emotions. Consequently, financial counselors must be able to communicate with their clients in a manner that recognizes how emotions affect clients' goals. An example of this might be when a client states, "I'm afraid of being audited this year." If the client exhibits nervous characteristics that would lead the counselor to believe that the client is worried, then it would be appropriate for the counselor specifically to address the client's fears. Failure to address these fears probably would result in ineffective communication and could result in client dissatisfaction and in frustration for the client and the counselor.

Remember Significant Details

A good memory is a significant asset in listening and in communication. Clients invariably share a wealth of information relevant to their needs, goals, and circumstances. Effective financial counselors pay attention to almost everything that is shared, refer to appropriate details in their interactions with clients, and seek clarification of elements that are not clear. The major benefits of this attention to detail are threefold.

- Clients will learn to value themselves. Clients will develop the attitude that "My counselor is paying so much attention to me that she can tell me what I've said, so she must value me." This may seem far-fetched; yet, we probably would agree that if we are not interested in another person we don't pay close attention. Clients operate from the same frame of reference. They say to themselves, "If you pay attention to what I say, I must be important or at least worth listening to."

- The second significant value in paying attention to detail is that you obtain additional information to help clients achieve their goals. Detail adds flexibility, as we discussed in Chapter 2.

- By paying attention to and remembering details, you actively encourage clients to share what is important and relevant to them. In this regard, active listening encourages active client participation.

Make Justifiable Inferences

Effective financial counselors attempt to *make sense* of the data presented to them by clients and share their interpretations with their clients. To do this, you have to be willing to venture educated guesses from the data. For instance, a client, in talking with a loan officer, states, "I'd like a new car, one that will have a lot of room for the family; one that will get excellent gas mileage." The loan officer might infer that the client needs a vehicle with significant carrying capacity, but can't afford a large luxury wagon or van. If this is the loan officer's inference, he might say, "Can I assume that you need room in the car you buy, but that you are planning on borrowing just a moderate amount?" This statement provides the client with what the loan officer understands of the situation and allows the client an opportunity to make adjustments in what has been communicated.

At this point, the client could respond in a number of ways: "Yes, that about captures my situation", or "Oh no, I really would like a large automobile", or "I guess I haven't really thought about it." In any case, the loan officer will have stimulated the client, in a non-threatening manner, to consider what has been communicated. Sharing inferences provides you with a means for helping clients understand what has been communicated.

The rules are straightforward. Effective listening depends on responding to the speaker's main ideas; responding to the speaker's emotional message; remembering significant details of the interaction; and making inferences that are justified by understanding of the client's situation.

LISTENING ISSUES

Listening is a process that inherently makes the financial counselor responsible. When someone shares ideas or feelings with you, you are responsible. For financial counselors, responsibility comes with the territory. The issues highlighted in this section are included to help you understand subtle areas of responsibility in communications and to alert you to obvious areas where responsibility in listening can be anticipated.

Candor

How honest should a counselor be in a financial counseling interaction? The answer that immediately comes to mind is, *"I should be totally honest!"* Yet, when we examine this, it becomes apparent that we can't be totally open or honest in all situations. Total honesty is not always tactful! Remember, part of our strategic approach in financial counseling is to use stratagems and tactics in a tactful way. When thinking about honesty, we must consider *balance*.

Balance refers to the need for maintaining harmony between what you hear, what you feel or believe, and what you say. For instance, a client may say to his financial counselor, "All car salespeople are crooks!" If the financial counselor says to the client, "Yeah, I think you are right," the counselor may be stating something that, in fact the counselor does not believe to be true. If, on the other hand, the financial counselor says, "No, I think you are wrong when you say that," the counselor runs the risk of alienating the client and of destroying harmony or balance in the relationship. In most situations of this type, your best tack is to try to understand the client's emotional message and to *say nothing* or deal with the emotion directly. The financial counselor could respond, "You sound angry at car salespeople. Did you have a bad experience with one?" This is far more tactful. The financial counselor can then explore the client's perception and experience.

A candid response to a client's question is appropriate when a client specifically asks for your opinion, when your response can shed new light on the topic being discussed, or when there is a legal, ethical, or professional rationale for your input. A candid response may be inappropriate, however, in those situations in which the client is expressing a personal opinion, value, need, or goal. The client who stated, "All car salespeople are crooks!" was *not* asking a question; rather, the client was stating a value, and this does not require verification from the financial counselor.

Both candor and harmony are important. Yet, maintaining a balance between the two may be difficult. When in doubt, you should consider the appropriateness of any response. Consider as a first option not responding at all. As a second option, you may want to deal with the emotional content in your response.

Deception

The word "deception" automatically has negative connotations. Because of this, you might say to yourself, "I would never use deception in my counseling interactions." This may be true for you, but most people say or do things that could be classified as deceptive. Have you ever felt or believed one thing, but said another? Have you ever tried to hide how you felt about a particular issue? Have you ever told a "little white lie"? Have you ever communicated by omission? If your answer to any of these questions is yes, you have used deception.

How does deception relate to listening and financial counseling? In communication, there are many occasions for you, as a financial counselor, to listen to your clients. Certainly there are times in these interchanges in which you find your client's comments to be interesting or stimulating. There may be other times, however, in which you find it difficult to pay attention to what your client is saying. What do you do when you find it hard to pay attention? On some occasions, you fight your natural tendency to let your mind wander and force yourself to focus on your client. There probably are those occasions, however, when you succumb to your desire and, for a while, you lose contact with your client. You may pretend to be in contact, but in reality you are not paying attention. This *pretended attention* is a subtle form of deception. It is normal, and if not extreme, of little influence in the relationship. You should be cautioned, however, that if this form of deception becomes too prevalent, an effective counseling relationship will deteriorate and may cease to exist.

A second, more serious issue is related to listening and deception. If you listen to clients selectively, you will be practicing deception. Said another way, if you listen for what you want to hear, and selectively fail to hear what you don't want to hear, you will be acting deceptively. An example may clarify this point.

Bill, a financial counselor, had a conversation with Lennie, a client, about the value of a payroll deductions savings program. The conversation went like this:

> **Bill**: This payroll deduction program can provide you and your family all you'll need in the way of savings for years to come.
>
> **Lennie**: I appreciate what you have to offer, but I'm a little concerned about making sure I keep ahead of inflation.
>
> **Bill**: I'm glad to see that you value regular savings and what they can do for you.
>
> **Lennie**: Oh, I do value them, and I think that it is important that I save on a regular basis. I just want to make sure that my savings don't lose money.
>
> **Bill**: Good! Our program provides a good rate of interest and it is secure. You can't go wrong with this program.

And so on.

This second form of deception uses listening as a process for determining client needs and wants, and then uses deception to avoid issues that may be important. In the above example, the client wants to stay ahead of inflation whereas the counselor appears to be more concerned with enrolling the client in a regular savings program regardless of the rate of return. Deception of this type is unethical and can destroy a counseling relationship.

One final aspect of deception should be noted. Clients may interpret your behavior as being deceptive if they observe significant discrepancies between your words and your actions. When someone says one thing but behaves in a contradictory manner, observers frequently conclude that they are being deceived. To avoid the possibility of such an interpretation, counselors should be consistent in verbal and nonverbal communication.

Shared Information

Financial counselors, through the process of listening, are exposed to a wealth of information about clients. Some of what financial counselors learn is through direct client interactions. Some of their knowledge is a result of working with others in the clients' behalf. Still other information, usually of a more subtle nature, is gained from observations of clients. All information, no matter how it is gained, is private information. Because of the nature of professional relationships, financial counselors are obligated to maintain client confidentiality and to shield information shared within the professional relationship. Several issues related to shared information are discussed below.

Clients Must Maintain Confidences

Clients frequently share their opinions with financial counselors. It is important that they have an opportunity to do so. It is equally important that financial counselors treat all information in a confidential, protective manner. This is important for at least two reasons. First, information is shared under the assumption (by the client) that it will be confidential. A release or sharing of information, without the client's consent, will break the client's implicit trust in the relationship. Second, in most professional relationships, it is illegal or, at the very least, unethical to share client information without the client's release. When counselors choose to release information without client consent, they are risking severance of the relationship and, in some cases, may be breaking the law.

Counselors Must Learn Ways of Handling Client Secrets

As trust develops within counseling relationships, clients increasingly share significant aspects of their lives. At times, they share information that is personal, private, or confidential. In most cases, the information is pertinent to the purpose of the professional interaction. At other times, however, information provided may go beyond professional needs.

Access to client secrets is a natural occurrence, one that should be anticipated by financial counselors. Prepare yourself by devising guidelines for dealing with a number of common situations and how they should be handled. These guidelines should incorporate the fact that all materials shared within your professional relationships should be held in confidence, unless the material clearly indicates potential harm to the client or to society.

Most information that is shared will not indicate potential danger to the client or to others. Rather, the information probably will provide you an indication of the client's values. For instance, consider a financial counselor whose client brags about underpaying his income taxes. The financial counselor may not have any evidence that an impropriety has been committed, other than her client's statement. Yet, the financial counselor will have an insight into her client's value system, one that may cause the financial counselor some concern.

When we listen to others we find out about them. As professionals, we must be prepared to handle information we obtain, know how to respond in a manner that will be helpful to our clients, and maintain our professional integrity.

Privacy Is Important In Professional Relationships.

Clients have a right to privacy. Professionals also have a right to privacy. We already have discussed aspects of client confidentially, client sharing, and access to client secrets. These, although related to privacy, do not comprise privacy.

Privacy is the inherent right all clients have to reveal about themselves information that they "choose" to reveal. Clients have the "right" to tell counselors what they choose to tell them. What is shared may be insufficient for meaningful action, but, despite this, clients do have this choice. In most professional situations, clients maintain a "private" stance until they develop trust in the professional and in the professional relationship. By using listening in a caring way, you, as a financial counselor, can help foster a trusting relationship in which pertinent information will be shared from the client's private world.

By the nature of your professional relationships, you can be viewed as a model of action. Your clients observe how you function in the relationship and then use these observations as a point of reference for their own behavior. If you readily share your personal ideas or feelings, you will model self-disclosure. Your clients will thus learn that this style of interaction is acceptable and, consequently, will soon adopt a similar approach in the relationship.

If, by contrast, you are not comfortable in sharing your ideas and feelings, and hesitate to do so, you will model a non-sharing perspective. Clients will observe this and act accordingly. You should not feel obligated to act or behave in a manner that is uncomfortable for you, but you must be aware of the influence of your actions.

Privacy is important for both parties in professional relationships. Listening, and all the aspects of this process, encourages sharing of ideas and feelings. It is important that counselors work to keep these thoughts and feeling private. You are entrusted with using your skills to build trusting relationships so that shared materials, and the consequent reduction of privacy, are in the best interests of you and your clients.

ACTIVE LISTENING

Active listening is a process in which the listener actively engages the speaker. The goal of active listening is to facilitate communication between the client and counselor.

Pacing, the matching or mirroring of another person's behavior, is a technique of active listening. Pacing occurs at several levels. Nonverbal pacing is a process through which financial counselors can communicate with clients by mirroring their nonverbal behavior, e.g., posture, hand gestures, and use of space. Closely linked to nonverbal behavior is pacing relating to client voice tonality, rate of speech, and volume. Verbal pacing involves a number of communicative elements important in effective financial relationships: client content, emotional theme, specificity of language, and congruence. The verbal tactics of restatement, paraphrasing, and summarization are defined, explained, and illustrated in this chapter. Finally, advanced pacing skills dealing with learning styles and language levels are considered.

Pacing

Both nonverbal and verbal pacing tactics can be used to communicate acceptance, warmth, and understanding, and to build the trust necessary for effective relationships. In a study on the effects of nonverbal and verbal pacing, R.J. Storms (1982) made tapes of the same client and counselor under four different counseling situations. In the first situation, the counselor did not pace verbally or non-verbally. In the second situation, the counselor paced non-verbally (mirrored the client's behavior - sitting in the same posture as the client, using similar hand and other gestures) but not verbally. In the third situation, the counselor paced verbally (restated, paraphrased, or summarized client statements) but did not pace non-verbally. In the fourth, the counselor paced both verbally and non-verbally. Storms then showed the tapes to experienced counselors, to people with minimal counseling training, and to people with no training in counseling. None of these people had any training in pacing. All individuals were asked to rate the various situations in terms of the counselor's helpfulness, empathy or understanding, and effectiveness. As one might expect, in the situation in which the counselor paced on both the verbal and nonverbal levels, the counselor was rated as significantly more helpful, effective, and empathetic than the situation in which no pacing occurred.

The interesting finding in this research was that when the counselor paced non-verbally but not verbally, the counselor was rated as being as effective as in the situation where she paced both verbally and non-verbally. Nonverbal pacing used alone was also found to be more effective than verbal pacing alone.

Nonverbal Pacing

When one person deliberately paces, the second person usually reports feeling listened to, understood, and accepted. Nonverbal pacing requires that the counselor *model* or *copy* the nonverbal behavior of the client. In simple terms, if you fold your arms when your client folds his, you are pacing that behavior, arm folding. Because nonverbal pacing is a powerful and effective communication element, counselors should use it in developing open, honest interaction.

Nonverbal pacing is a normal, natural part of most communication. In studies done in England, films taken of people engaged in conversation were studied frame by frame. In these studies, nonverbal behavior between pairs of individuals matched better than 80% of the time. These studies support our intuitive observations about people and how they naturally pace each other. For example, we all know couples who have lived together for a few years and who seem to talk alike, walk alike, and, in general, exhibit many of the same mannerisms. They pace each other. How we talk with young children is a second example, we pace them. We get down to their physical level when we talk. We bend over or get down on one knee. This is a form of nonverbal pacing. (In addition, we often use language consistent with their level of understanding. We use simple language, even "baby talk" to verbally pace them.)

How should you non-verbally pace clients? You might sit the way they sit or use the same gestures they use. On a very gross level, this kind of mirroring may be distracting to you and to the client. If you are *caught* doing everything they do, clients may think you are making fun of them. The most effective nonverbal pacing takes place at more subtle levels. You might breathe at the same rate as the client. You can blink your eyes at a rate similar to the client's. You might assume the same general posture the client does, either sitting or standing. If the client leans forward, you may lean forward. All of these acts exemplify nonverbal pacing.

Since most communication takes place on the nonverbal level, nonverbal pacing communicates very powerfully, usually below clients' level of awareness. This form of communication indicates that you are interested in everything they have to say; that you accept them; and that you want to develop a facilitative working relationship. This acceptance and closeness form the basis for developing the trust and understanding necessary for effective long-term relationships. A second major benefit of nonverbal pacing is that it is the first step in understanding the client's perspective. Through your nonverbal mirroring, you can get a sense for what it feels like to be inside the client's world. This can facilitate your understanding of the client and the client's needs and goals.

Following are two experiments designed to help you understand and develop the skill of nonverbal pacing:

Experiment 1

Engage a colleague in a discussion and attempt to mirror all of his or her nonverbal behavior. After four or five minutes, ask your colleague for a reaction to you and discuss the preceding communication. Were you perceived as being interested? Did your colleague feel understood? Did he or she feel you were developing a relationship that encouraged discussion? Did your actions foster trust in your colleague? Did your colleague rate your interchange as being open and honest? When you have discussed these and similar questions, share with your colleague what you were doing. Ask if he or she noticed. In most cases, the paced person will not be aware that you mirrored her or his behavior and yet will feel understood and accepted.

Experiment 2

Practice nonverbal pacing each day. Instead of mirroring exactly what another person does, practice subtle levels of breathing, eye blinks, general body orientation, and voice intonation. To begin, you can practice without even engaging in conversation. For example, practice nonverbal pacing while waiting at an airport, shopping mall, or other well-populated place. Simply pick someone near you and practice the subtle art of pacing. This form of practice is most effective when done in situations where you can focus your entire attention on nonverbal behavior without having to engage in conversation. To be skilled at this valuable tactic, practice nonverbal pacing at very subtle levels until it becomes second nature to you.

Verbal Pacing

Verbal pacing also can be powerful. Verbal pacing tactics should be used throughout all stages of your relationship with clients, but they are especially effective during the initial stage.

Most humans can understand at a rate eight to ten times faster than someone else can talk. We can go to a lecture, speech, or sermon, listen to what is being said, and still think about other things. We can take mental side trips. For example, we might think about what we are going to have for dinner that night, imagine what we are going to do after work, or even think about what we need to get done at home. Despite these mental side trips, we can follow and understand the speaker's main thoughts. This listening speed differential allows us to be aware of our mental thoughts and listen to what someone else is talking about at the same time.

Despite this ability, the process can create problems. It is possible that during a counseling session a mental side trip may become more interesting than what the client is saying. When this happens, you pay greater attention to yourself than to your clients. It stands to reason that if you take mental side trips about a previous client, a person you are meeting for lunch, or a client scheduled later in the day, you will allow yourself to get pulled away from your present client. The message is clear. In financial counseling you must put your listening speed differential to work for you by focusing all of your extra attention on the client. You can begin by pacing non-verbally. The nonverbal pacing process forces you to attend to the client.

Try This Experiment

Talk to someone for a few minutes and establish good eye contact. You will find that while you are maintaining good eye contact you will have difficulty thinking about anything other than what the person is saying.

With clients, put your listening speed differential to good use by attending to four elements of communication. While all four are defined here, only the first two are important in verbal pacing. The final two are discussed in the next chapter as exploring tactics.

Content: The specific words, story line, or stated intent of the client.

Emotional theme: The client's feelings about what the client is saying. Usually this can be observed by attending to the client's voice tone, speech rate, and volume.

Specificity: Client words, primarily nouns and verbs, which refer to specific things or actions or which are vague and ambiguous.

Congruence: The logical consistency between what a client says and how the client says it. Usually, this refers to the consistency between verbal and nonverbal behavior.

It may seem overwhelming to listen to four elements of communication simultaneously. Keep in mind, however, that you can comprehend at a rate eight to ten times faster than someone can speak. If you focus all of your attention on the client, you will find that you can, indeed, listen for all four elements at the same time. Also, you already attend to them at an intuitive level. When people communicate in an emotional voice, with very low volume, and at a slow rate of speech, you probably would ask them, "What's wrong?" You do this without thought. At one level of awareness you know that they sound sad or upset. Your response reflects this awareness. Consider the following client statement expressed to a financial counselor.

> **Client** (in a slightly frustrated tone of voice): I've come to see you because I need to set money aside for retirement, but I'd rather save up for a vacation. I want both but can't see how to get them. What should I do?

The *content* or story line in this client statement is, I need to set money aside for retirement; I'd rather build up a vacation fund. I want both. I can't see how to get both, and tell me what to do.

The *emotional theme* underlying the client statement is understood when we take into account how the client presents the story. By attending to his tone of voice and watching his nonverbal behavior the theme could be determined. In this case the theme might be: "I'm frustrated" or "I'm agitated!"

Additional forms of verbal pacing revolve around tonality, rate, and volume. We naturally attend to these elements. When individuals raise their voices, it is common for listeners to respond in a similar manner. Or, when people whisper, listeners tend to lower their voices and whisper. While we do these things almost automatically, one advanced technique is to purposely match (pace) the client's level of communication. This process is useful in establishing rapport and a relationship with clients. We can use this natural process in another way. When a client is agitated or angry and we use a calm, slow speech rate in a low tone, the client will generally slow down to meet our level of communication. In other words, the client, because of his natural tendency to pace our speech pattern will start speaking in a slower, calmer manner.

Tactics

Several specific skills can help you pace your clients verbally:

Restating

Restating is a process in which counselors repeat what the client has stated. Emphasis is placed on specifics of content. For example, consider the ways you might restate the client's statement about his vacation and retirement needs.

> **Client** (in a slightly frustrated tone of voice): I've come to see you because I need to set money aside for retirement, but I'd rather save up for a vacation. I want both but can't see how to get them. What should I do?
>
> Here's how you might respond:
>
> > *Restating of content*: You've come to see me because you need to set money aside for retirement ... and you'd rather save for a vacation ... but you can't see how to do both ... and finally, you'd like me to tell you what to do.
> >
> > *Restating of theme*: You're feeling frustrated about how to use your money for two different purposes at the same time.
> >
> > *Restating of content and theme*: You need to save for retirement and would like a vacation fund ... and you're frustrated about it.

In restating the content there is no need to sound like a parrot or a tape recorder. You can change sentence order in such a way that restating does not sound like an echo. For example:

Client: I'm caught between making a real secure investment and taking a few more risks.

Financial Counselor: You're wondering if you should take a few more risks or stay with a real secure investment.

(or)

Financial Counselor: You're wondering if you should make a real secure investment or take a few more risks.

In this example there are two equivalent forms of restating content. The first reverses the order of the client's communication. The second maintains the order. By simply reversing the order you can add variety to restatements. Restating attempts to communicate back to clients the essence of what they have said. It thereby provides feedback to clients through which they can judge whether they are communicating what they desire. One of the primary purposes of restating is to assess accuracy of the information exchanged. Restating is analogous to holding up a mirror to the client. Whereas a mirror provides us with visual feedback, a restating response provides a verbal mirror so that you and the client can determine whether you are accomplishing what you want in the communicative process.

Restating is a way to communicate several qualities considered earlier. Through restating, you can communicate empathy or understanding, acceptance of the client and the problem or issue under discussion, warmth and willingness to engage the client in a personal relationship, and encouragement for further discussion of the problem.

When clients are encouraged to talk about problems, issues, or goals, they usually add detail. Addition of detail helps you in all aspects of working with clients.

Paraphrasing

A second way in which financial counselors can verbally pace is through paraphrasing. Paraphrasing, unlike restating, is the process of taking the essential content of the client's communication and restating it in your own words. Examples of paraphrasing are given below.

Client: I think I'm about ready to get involved in a riskier investment.

Financial Counselor: You feel like it's time to take a few financial chances.

Client: Do you think that I should be considering tax shelters?

Financial Counselor: You'd like to know if I think you're ready to shelter some of your capital.

Client: I've been thinking about mutual funds as a primary source of investment.

Financial Counselor: You think that mutual funds can best serve your financial needs.

In each of these examples, the counselor has attempted to repeat for the client the essential message the client wishes to communicate. The counselor does this in his or her own words. It is important to note that, like restating, each counselor paraphrase is essentially equivalent to the client statement and does not add any additional information.

Both restating and paraphrasing provide you a means of sharing your understanding of the client's message. Neither adds new information. Yet both communicate understanding, and consequently they open the interview to further and deeper discussion. A result of the effective use of restating and paraphrasing is development of mutual trust between you and your clients, trust that can lead to more accurate goal definition, better problem resolution, appropriate decision making, and eventually a more effective financial plan. Restating and paraphrasing cannot provide total communication in financial counseling. Rather, they serve as a form of verbal pacing. Along with summarizing, restating and paraphrasing establish a feedback link between you and your clients. This link is essential to effective professional relationships.

Summarizing

Summarizing serves a purpose similar to restating and paraphrasing. It is very useful when the client has talked for an extended period. Unlike restatement and paraphrasing summarizing can be done by either the counselor or client.

For example, consider the following counselor summary:

> **Client***:* As you know I'm just getting into this financial planning business ... I've got a lot of questions ... I mean ... I want to use my money wisely ... I've got a lot of plans for the future....
>
> **Financial Counselor***:* You're new at this way of planning your financial future and you want to make sure you make wise choices.

In this example, summarizing is used to tie a number of the client's ideas together. This provides clients with an opportunity to hear what they have said and an opportunity to correct any miscommunication between themselves and the counselor. A second use of summarizing is to bring closure to a portion of the client - counselor communication and to provide structure for further discussions. As a result of the above interchange the counselor could focus discussion on: (1) the client's newness to financial planning, (2) the client's need to make wise choices, or (3) the client's plans for her future, or on a combination of these points.

By contrast, consider the following interchange:

> **Client***:* As you know I'm just getting into this financial planning business ... I've got a lot of questions ... I mean ... I want to use my money wisely ... I've got a lot of plans for the future....
>
> **Financial Counselor***:* We've talked about a number of issues. It would be very helpful if you could summarize the points you think are most important.

In this use of a summary the counselor, by soliciting a summary from the client, can determine what the client regards as most important.

Summarizing also is an important technique to use in bringing a counseling session to a close. At the end of the session, it is important to know what has transpired and what, if anything, needs to be accomplished in the near future. For example, consider the situation in which the client expresses readiness to make a financial commitment to a real estate purchase but additional information about its liquidity is needed. If you were the financial counselor, you might summarize the financial planning session like this:

> **Financial Counselor***:* We've talked about a number of financial investment possibilities. In looking at a number of possibilities you've settled on real estate. But before you make a final decision you'd like me to check out the liquidity factor of this one particular offering.

After obtaining client agreement on the summarized material, you might conclude by saying, "By our next meeting I'll have the information you requested."

Finally, summarizing is a useful process to use in a counseling session with a client who has been seen before. Summarizing at the start of a session will provide a review of what has previously transpired and set the stage for the present meeting. As an example, consider the following:

> **Financial Counselor***:* The last time we met we talked about a number of financial possibilities. You settled on real estate, but you asked if I would check out the liquidity factor on one particular offering. I did. Here is the information you requested.

This summary included material from the earlier closing summary. This approach is one way of tying two sessions together, keeping the focus on the client, and avoiding undue repetition. A second session can begin where the first ended.

Restating, paraphrasing, and summarizing are used by counselors to build a sound relationship. These responses do not add to what a client says, but provide a feedback link between the professional and client. This allows the professional to check accuracy of communication and encourages participation.

The verbal pacing tactics of restating, paraphrasing, and summarizing are effective skills to help you begin understanding the client's experiential map. You can increase your understanding and communicative power if you also attend to several other elements as the client communicates with you.

Pacing Learning Styles

Earlier we discussed how people develop their personal experiential maps through use of their senses and how sensory experiences become part of the stored information in our experiential maps. As adults we use three primary information processing modes: visual (images), auditory (sounds), and kinesthetic (feeling or action).

Visual: The *visual* learning style usually refers to pictorial representations of events and is characterized by words that embody vision, for example, seeing, picturing, reflecting, and mirroring.

Auditory: The *auditory* learning style refers to hearing, word characterizations, abstract thinking, and verbal analysis. This learning style is typified by words such as thinking, knowing, analyzing, assessing, evaluating, and appraising.

Kinesthetic: The *kinesthetic* learning style encompasses feelings and actions and is represented by words like sensing, feeling, and exciting and words like forcing, being, doing, and acting.

As discussed previously, people usually develop a preferential way of acquiring, processing, storing, and communicating information. We referred to these preferences as learning styles. In financial counseling it is important to approach clients from their preferred learning styles to build and maintain rapport. The importance of pacing the basic learning style of clients can be understood if we examine common human experiences. For instance, have you ever had an argument or heated discussion with someone, only to find out later that you were both saying the same thing? This can happen if one person discusses the topic from one preferred learning style and the second person from another preferred learning style. While both may be sharing the same perspective, it may sound like they have quite different opinions. Frequently, the realization comes later that both were saying essentially the same thing. These kinds of interactions can be avoided in financial counseling if counselors verbally pace their clients' learning style preferences.

While there are formal ways to measure preferred learning styles and preferred information processing modes, there usually is neither the time nor the opportunity in financial counseling to do so. The easiest way to gather this information is to listen carefully to the client's use of language. When people speak, you can get a deeper understanding of their experiential map if you listen carefully to their verbs, adjectives, and adverbs. By pacing these kinds of words, you can restate, paraphrase, or summarize while matching the learning styles of your clients. Consider the following client statement:

> **Client***:* Well, I guess the issue is to *see* my financial *picture clearly* so that I can *look* toward the future. If I can *focus* on what is necessary for the kids' education, I might be able to *see* what I need to do.

When you examine the verbs, adverbs, and adjectives (the italicized words) in the client statement, you will notice that they are mostly visual. When people talk, the verbs, adverbs, and adjectives they use will give you an indication of their preferred sensory operation mode or learning style. Verbal pacing, using the tactics of restating, paraphrasing, and summarizing, would suggest that the professional attempt to match the type of verbs, adverbs, and adjectives used by the client.

For example, in response to the client statement above, you could verbally pace by saying, "You want to *focus* on what you *see* as necessary to prepare for your children's education." On the other hand, you could verbally pace the content of the client's statement without pacing the learning style level of the client's perceptual map by saying, "You want to analyze what will be necessary for your children's education." While the second example accurately reflects content, it does not pace the client's verbs, adverbs, or adjectives, and consequently does not match the client's experiential map. Verbal pacing that includes a matching of client verbs, adverbs, and adjectives deepens the client's feelings of acceptance and understanding. This leads to trust that is essential for effective financial counseling and action.

Other examples of statements that reveal visual representational maps:

I don't *see* how ...
I try to *watch* out for things that ...
I'm not *clear* right now. If only I could focus on ...

A client could say the same thing as our previous client, but from an auditory learning style:

> **Client***:* Well, I guess the issue is to *analyze* my situation enough to *know* what the future might be. If I can *analyze* what is necessary for the kids' education, I might be able to *talk* myself into doing what I need to do.

When you examine this client statement, you will notice that although it says essentially the same thing as the first client statement, the verbs, adverbs, and adjectives all relate to hearing or analyzing. If you respond with visual verbs, adverbs, and adjectives, you might be accurate about the content but would not match the client's preferred way of processing information.

Other examples of how auditory representational maps are reflected:

I keep *analyzing* the situation but can't find a solution.
I keep *telling* myself to plan better.
I give myself these pep *talks* all the time about ...

Again, we can go back to our original client statement to determine what it might sound like if the client's preferred learning style were kinesthetic.

Client: Well, I guess the issue is to *get* myself *straightened out* enough to *plan* for the future. If I can *get a handle on* what is necessary for the kids' education, I might be able to *force* myself into doing what I need to do.

Notice that the client's verbs, adverbs, and adjectives almost all deal with feelings and actions, kinesthetic responses. You can deepen your level of expressed understanding by matching the verbs, adverbs, and adjectives of the client when you verbally pace through restatement, paraphrasing, or summarizing.

Kinesthetic examples from an *emotional* perspective include the following:

It's so *depressing* to think about buying life insurance.
It's *really exciting* to think about all these possibilities.
You know, it's *really hard* to keep all the possibilities in mind.

Or from an *action* perspective:

Well, it's time I *really got going* with my finances.
It's *really hard to keep pushing* myself like this and having inflation *eat* things away.
I don't know where *to go* for ...

Or, finally, from a *sensory* perspective:

> It's a *bitter* pill *to swallow.*
> I just *keep getting* this deep *sense* that something may *go* wrong.
> I smell something *fishy* in this deal.

When people talk, their verbs, adverbs, and adjectives paint a picture that provides an understanding of how they experience their worlds. The verbs, adverbs, and adjectives also provide information about how they are processing and storing information in their representational maps. When we verbally pace clients, we communicate to them that we are listening to their general ideas and listening to how they are processing those ideas. When people feel *stuck* in decision making, they may be simultaneously having experiences in two different representational systems, or having two incompatible experiences. While they may *know* what they need to do, they may not be able to *see* how it will turn out or *feel* comfortable with the ensuing decision. The internal conflict precludes any decision.

Consider these statements, for example:

> I would really like to *get out* of this investment but I can't ever *see* my way *clear.*
> or
> I have *no idea* what the reason is and I can't ever *see* myself *doing it.*

Two important keys appear in these client statements. First, there are essentially two sentences held together by the words *but* or *and.* Second, when you examine the two sentences in the first example, you will notice that the verbs, adverbs, and adjectives in the two sentence segments are at different sensory levels. For example, *get out* (kinesthetic) and *see/clear* (visual). Sentences such as this convey the client's confusion about an issue. The confusion stems from having two different experiences at the same time, a feeling on the one side and seeing on the other.

It is possible to experience two different or conflicting things at the same time if there is a difference between the senses used for each experience: visual and auditory, or visual and kinesthetic, for example. It is very hard to have two opposing experiences at the same time through the same sensory system. That is, it is difficult to visually represent two contradictory objects at the same time or simultaneously experience two opposing feelings.

For example, it is highly unlikely that you would be both happy and sad at the same time or that you simultaneously could imagine both a peaceful situation and a chaotic one.

When a client has two distinct experiences, through two sensory levels, visual and kinesthetic, for example, you can use verbal pacing skills to help the client transpose both experiences into one or the other of the systems. This will help the client separate the experiences. The client will experience first one, then the other, but not both at the same time. To do this, you merely employ a listening response that uses similar verbs, adverbs, and adjectives in both halves of your response rather than using two different sensory systems as the client does.

Consider the following example of this idea.

> **Client**: *I* would really like to *get out* of this investment but I can't ever *see* my way *clear.*
>
> **Financial Counselor**: You would like to *see* yourself out of this investment but you can't *see* your way *clear.*

In this example the counselor has transformed the first kinesthetic verb into the visual mode to be consistent with the second half of the sentence. This sorting out process will help the client to relieve the confusion and sense of being stuck. A second alternative is to transform the client verbs, adverbs, or adjectives to the third sensory system, away from the two expressed by the client. For example:

> **Financial Counselor**: *You tell* yourself you ought to get rid of that investment but you also *tell* yourself you can't.

In this response the counselor has transformed the client's kinesthetic and visual verbs and adverbs into the third mode, auditory. This helps clients to separate their experiences, allowing them to deal with distinct or opposing issues one at a time.

As the previous discussion indicates, effective counselors identify how people experience their worlds by listening intently to their verbs, adverbs, and adjectives and respond to clients in a manner that mirrors how clients express themselves. Below are additional examples of how people might express themselves.

Visual Examples*:* Each of the examples below expresses something visual. When you read them or listen to someone talking this way, you can usually form a mental picture yourself. In the examples, it is clear the person speaking is processing information through some form of mental picture.

I don't see what you mean.
I can't see my way clear to do that right now.
I wish I could get a clear picture of what to do.
From my view ...
Everything is so black right now.
Everything is just so fuzzy.
I keep looking for the right answers.
I have this vision of what I want.
I need something to brighten up my life.

Auditory Examples*:* In each of the following examples the verbs, adjectives, or adverbs all refer to listening or talking. Words of this type are all associated with an auditory learning style.

I listen to all of this advice ...
I keep telling myself what I ought to do.
I can talk myself into just about anything.
I just keep hearing the same advice over and over.
I wish I had the right words to motivate myself.
I have trouble hearing what he is trying to say.
She never listens to me.
Just tell me what to do.

The kinesthetic examples which follow are broken into three subcategories; kinesthetic action, kinesthetic emotion, and kinesthetic sensory.

Kinesthetic Action Examples:

I've got to get going with my plans.
I keep trying but don't seem to get anywhere.

I want to find something that is meaningful.
I keep running around for advice.
That was an uplifting experience.
It's like I'll never get there.
No matter how I try ...
He drives himself until he drops.

Kinesthetic Emotion Examples:

I'm so depressed about ...
I'm about as happy with ______ as I've ever been.
I get so darn mad when ...
You feel so taken advantage of.
It's just such a sickening feeling.
I guess I can't be happy about _______ all the time.
Do you ever just feel blah about _______?

Kinesthetic Sensory Examples:

Things just smell fishy about that deal.
That deal smells!
I just get this bad taste in my mouth about it.
I'll just grit my teeth and choose something.
It's such a bitter pill to swallow.
That deal is so sweet!
She is so sickeningly sweet all the time.

The verbs, adjectives, and adverbs in the kinesthetic examples all indicate someone who is experiencing a world of action, feeling, taste or smell. Such people usually experience the world at a concrete sensory level. They may find it difficult to deal at a more *abstract* or *theorizing* level. This type of person frequently asks, "So, what does that mean in practical terms?" Effective financial counselors, despite their own natural tendencies or learning styles, must learn to assess the learning styles of clients and respond to clients in the client's style.

There is a final category called the "Metaphorical-Visual" category. In this category a client's verbs, adjectives, and adverbs may be difficult to classify, and yet, when you listen closely to content, it is fairly obvious that the client is trying to paint a verbal, but metaphorical, picture of personal experience.

Metaphorical-Visual Examples:

It's like being caught in a never-ending circle.
It's like being in a fun house and trying to find the way out.
I wish I could just find the right path up the mountain.
I feel like I'm caught on a Ferris wheel and can't get off.
Life is just one big garbage dump right now.
I guess I've got three strikes against me.
It's like a knife through hot butter.

In these examples some of the verbs, adjectives, and adverbs refer to kinesthetic, auditory, or visual experiences. However, the overall effect of the statements is to create a mental picture or metaphor to explain an experience. Such metaphorical language is very rich because it usually contains or activates elements of all three learning styles. You may have noticed that effective speakers usually use metaphorical language as a way of reaching each person in the audience. The same approach works for one-to-one communication.

Pacing Language Levels

Clients may not have the knowledge or the extensive vocabulary we have about our field. This is one of the reasons they come to see us. However, the difference in knowledge and vocabulary can become a source of problems. J*argon* financial counselors develop may be useful among counselors. Jargon is a shorthand way of expressing numerous and varied complicated and detailed concepts. However, when we use jargon with clients, we often forget that they might not know what we are talking about. Simple concepts like *open- end loan, debit,* and *cash value* may be foreign to the lay person.

When you begin building a counseling relationship, you should spend as much time as possible assessing the client's level of understanding and vocabulary. This should be done slowly and purposefully. Once you have a sense of the client's sophistication, you can choose vocabulary and concepts that pace the client's present level of knowledge or understanding. A quick way to destroy rapport and trust is to discuss important concepts with vocabulary the client has difficulty comprehending. Following are four examples that examine this attitude. The first two demonstrate non-pacing, the second two, pacing.

Don't Do This

Client: I don't want to take any risks with my money.

Financial Counselor: You believe that it is inappropriate to invest your resources in something that has low credibility and high expectation of forfeiture.

Client: *I* need some financial advice.

Financial Counselor: You'd like relevant information pertaining to acceptable investment opportunities.

In both of these examples, the professional has moved beyond the client and has used words that, although accurate, do not *pace* the client. The degree of sophistication in your response should match the sophistication level of the client's question or statement. Consider the next examples.

Do This

Client: I believe I'd like to expand my financial base.

Financial Counselor: You think it's time to enlarge your financial holdings.

Client: I can see that I need a clearer picture of investment opportunities.

Financial Counselor: I can help you look at some financial possibilities.

In these examples the counselor has paced the client on two levels. First, the counselor paced the content through a content paraphrase. Second, the client's verbs were paced. The word *believe* (auditory) was paced with the word *think* (auditory) and the word *expand* (kinesthetic) was paced with the word *enlarge* (kinesthetic). In a similar manner, the counselor paced *see* and *clearer picture* (both visual) with *look at* (visual).

In summary, effective communication is fostered when counselors use words similar (in level of sophistication) to the client's and when counselors pace the client's primary sensory system by attending to his or her verbs, adverbs, and adjectives.

RESOURCES

Griffith, J. L. & Griffith, M.E. (1994). *The Body Speaks*. New York: Basic Books.

Laborde, G.Z. (1984). *Influencing With Integrity*. Palo Alto: Syntony Press.

Palmer, W. (1994). *The Intuitive Body*. Berkeley: North Atlantic Books.

Walton, D. (1989). *Are You Communicating?* New York: McGraw-Hill.

Westra, M. (1996). *Active Communication*. Pacific Grove: Brooks Cole.

Young, M.E. (1998). *Learning The Art Of Helping*. Columbus: Merrill.

5 EXPLORING STRATEGIES

Nature has given us one tongue, but two ears, that we may hear from others twice as much as we speak.

Epictetus

INTRODUCTION

In Chapter 4 we discussed basic communication tactics and skills that flow from the concept of pacing. We now focus on tactics that can be used to gather information and explore details of the client's representational map. The normal and useful way of gathering information or exploring is through the use of questions. However, if you continuously use questions, the communicative interaction can take on characteristics of an interrogation. Additional tactics are needed to gather information and to explore.

One method of exploring was considered in the discussion of verbal pacing. If you recall, verbal pacing skills are used to help get in touch with the client's representational, which in turn helps to establish open, trusting relationships based on understanding. A second level of exploration is needed to generate quantitative and qualitative informational details relevant to client problems, goals, and resources. Without specific details, counselors are hampered in their efforts to make pertinent recommendations. Four basic tactics can be used to gather information and to explore with clients: *Selective Pacing*, *Imperative Statements*, *Declarative Leads*, and *Questions*.

Finally, advanced exploration techniques are needed to help clients clarify the meaning of their statements and to help them become aware of verbal and nonverbal discrepancies that are indicated through their implied ambivalence, stated or implied logical inconsistencies, unrealistic goals, areas of implied causation, and generalizations.

SELECTIVE PACING

Verbal pacing tactics of restating, paraphrasing, and summarizing can be used to gather information and explore. In Chapter 4 we discussed restatement as a way of building a relationship and providing communicative feedback. We also suggested that restatement could be used to check the accuracy of the communicative interaction. In addition, restatement of a selected portion of the client's statements can be used as a way of exploring one specific aspect of the client communication without having to ask a question.

Consider the following interaction:

> **Client**: Well, my last kid just graduated from college. I'm not getting any younger . I guess I'm ready to put a little more into my savings account . What do you think?
>
> **Financial Counselor** (using selective restatement): Let's see, you think you're ready to invest a little more in savings.
>
> **Client:** Well, yeah. Savings are nice and safe, and the money I was using for my kid's education I can now put to work. It seems like a good chance to build up a retirement nest egg.

This example indicates that you can explore and gather information without having to resort to questions. In the example, the financial counselor elicited additional information from the client by using selective restatement. This form of response allows you to respond to that portion of the client's statement that seems most appropriate. Once aspects of that segment of the client's statement are thoroughly discussed, you can continue the conversation by selectively restating another portion of the client's original statement. As an example, using the illustration above; "You say this is a good chance to build a nest egg". Or you can introduce an entirely different line of inquiry. For example, "What other forms of investment have you considered?" The advantage of a selective restatement is that you can use the client's statements to provide the basis for obtaining additional information. This approach adds variety to the interchange, helps you understand the client's representational map, and communicates caring and understanding to the client.

IMPERATIVE STATEMENTS

The simple imperative sentence can be used to clarify meaning, encourage client participation, and obtain additional information. For example:

Client: I think I'd like to start preparing for my retirement.

Financial Counselor: Tell me about your retirement plans.

The statement "Tell me ..." encourages the client to add information. Other imperative statements include "Expand on that ...," "Elaborate on that ...," "Explore that further ...," or "Give me more detail." Each of these leads places responsibility on the client to provide more detailed information about the topic under discussion. By using selective restatements (verbal pacing) and imperative statements, you can explore and gather a wealth of information without asking questions.

DECLARATIVE LEADS

The financial counselor can encourage clients to elaborate by stating or *declaring* what they are thinking. For instance, a financial counselor might say to a client, “I was wondering which of the suggestions I’ve made sounds best to you.” This counselor statement, when followed with silence, would prompt the client to share his thoughts about the counselor’s suggestions. This could lead to a fuller discussion of specific suggestions and open communication. Consider the following:

Client: I have a lot on my mind. At times I don’t know if I’ll ever get out of debt or ahead of my bills.

Financial Counselor: I can understand your concern. *I am curious* about what you think you should do.

Client: I’ve thought a lot about it. I think the first thing to do is to make sure I list everything I owe.

Financial Counselor: *I am interested* in knowing if you have started this process.

Client: Not formally, but informally. I’ve started thinking about it.

Financial Counselor: *I'm wondering* why you haven't been more assertive about putting all the information together.

Client: I could have but I knew I would be seeing you and I wanted to talk with you first to see if this was a good place to start.

Declarative leads effectively use inference to foster communication. When a financial counselor says to a client, "I'd like to know more about that" and then silently attends to the client, the client will know, by inference, that it is his or her turn to share more fully. Financial counselors can stimulate client exploration through leads like those used above or through others such as, "It would help me if…," "I am impressed with your …", or "I am confused by what you just said." All leads of this type, when followed with attentive silence, encourage clients to elaborate on their thoughts.

QUESTIONS

There are times when questions are appropriate for obtaining specific information. Six basic types of questions, along with their strengths and weaknesses, are discussed below.

Yes And No Questions

Questions of this type usually are asked in such a way that the client can respond with a simple *yes* or *no*. For example, "Did you bring the information I asked for?" This question can be answered *yes* or *no*. It does not encourage the client to offer additional information. Because the client is being asked to respond to the question, she may comply exactly, despite the fact that you may really want her to elaborate on the issue being discussed. If a positive relationship has been established with the client, you are more likely to receive additional information even if you ask a yes/no question. Otherwise, you may be forced to ask another question to keep the interchange going. If the client continues to respond with one-word answers, you should check to see if you are using too many yes/no questions.

Yes/no questions, although appearing in a question format, may be used to express a statement or belief. For example, "Don't you think the President's foreign policy is a good one?" is a disguised statement that says in effect, "I think the President's foreign policy is a good one." When we use this kind of yes/no question/statement, we strongly imply the desired answer. In this example, the speaker wants a *yes* response from the listener. If the listener does not give the expected *yes* a disagreement often results. You should be careful in using yes/no question/statements. It is much better to state ideas directly than to imply them through yes/no questions. Yes/no questions/statements frequently make people feel manipulated, which in turn affects trust in the relationship. When people feel manipulated they often become argumentative or resistant. Yes/no questions can be an effective tool if you use them purposefully. They can be used to control the type of information and the amount of client talk.

For example:

Client*:* I think that I'm ready for an ongoing investment program.

Financial Counselor: Are you willing to commit money to this program on a regular basis?

Client*:* Yes.

Financial Counselor*:* Are you willing to invest $100 every month?

Client*:* Yes.

In this situation the financial counselor used two yes/no questions to move the client from generalized thought about entering a regular investment program to a definite $100 per month commitment for such an investment.

Yes/no questions can be used to establish a *yes set.* This use of the yes/no question can be used to influence clients by establishing a pattern in which you ask a series of yes/no questions that imply a *yes* answer. This develops a *yes set* in the client. You can then make your final point, which is intended to influence the client in a particular direction. For example:

Financial Counselor: You've said you'd like to prepare for retirement. Is that right?

> **Client**: Yes.
>
> **Financial Counselor:** In our last discussion about this, you indicated that to retire at 55 you'd have to supplement your company pension plan, correct?
>
> **Client**: Yes.
>
> **Financial Counselor**: Well, since you're 43 now, don't you think that you'd better put money aside on a monthly basis to meet your goal?
>
> **Client**: Yes.

This use of the yes/no question has several dangers. The first, of course, is that the client may feel manipulated and then may resist all efforts at influence. While this *yes* set use of the yes/no question may be very powerful, it can sound like a typical sales pitch, which in turn may turn the client away. If used judicially, the *yes set* pattern of yes/no questions can be a powerful tactic in your arsenal of communicative skills.

Multiple-Choice Questions

This form of question usually provides the client with a number of alternative choices. For example:

> **Financial Counselor**: What sort of investment are you interested in? Certificates of Deposit? Shares? Money Market Account?

The usual motivation in asking a multiple-choice question is to help the client talk more about the topic at hand. Whereas multiple-choice questions can lead to open exploration by the client they present dangers similar to those found in yes/no questions, i.e., the client is forced to choose one of the alternatives presented. There may be times when you want to limit the client's response to a choice of one of a number of possibilities. However, if you want open exploration on the client's part, multiple choice questions may produce the opposite effect.

There are situations in which speakers use multiple-choice questions to make a statement. This usually is an attempt to convince someone to take a specific action. You can lay out a number of alternatives with a multiple-choice question and imply which one the client is to choose. This can be done in two ways. You can imply the *correct* response by making several of the alternatives ridiculous or by emphasizing one with your voice. For example:

> **Financial Counselor**: Well, what do you want to do, just leave your money in a regular savings account and let inflation take care of most of it, or invest in something that will really beat inflation?
>
> **Client**: Well, of course I want to stay ahead of inflation.

The danger with this approach is that the client may feel belittled or manipulated. Although there might be rare occasions when this may be appropriate, remember that an effective financial counseling relationship demonstrates openness, respect, and honesty. If you honestly believe the client should do what you have in mind, it is better to state it directly, and not imply the answer through multiple choice questions.

Dilemma Questions

A dilemma question provides limited choice or, in some cases, the illusion of choice. It is asked in such a way that no matter how clients respond they may be wrong, or neither alternative is what clients really want. The comic's question, for example, "Have you stopped kicking your dog?" cannot be answered without self-incrimination. If the person answers, "yes" it means he has been kicking his dog. If he says, "no" it means he still is kicking his dog. A dilemma question such as this usually is inappropriate in counseling relationships. Dilemma questions, like multiple choice questions, can have the effect of making clients feel manipulated and belittled.

A second form of the dilemma question, one giving the client a choice between two unwanted alternatives, is frequently used. At the doctor's office the nurse may ask, "Do you want your shot in the arm or in the fanny?" The nurse has assumed that you would prefer to get your medicine by means of injection rather than in oral form. The dilemma question precludes you from selecting alternative choices. A financial example of this form of the dilemma question might be, "Would you like to make your monthly mortgage payments through a savings account draft or by mailing them in directly?"

While there are dangers to the dilemma question in that the client may feel manipulated or belittled, there are times when you might use the second form of the dilemma question to help clients move toward needed decisions. This second form of the *dilemma* question can be used effectively to reduce resistance and will be discussed further in Chapter 6.

Level I Probes

Level I probes are used to gather factual information that is verifiable. Demographic data such as name, address, telephone number, and place of work are examples of level I probes. Level I probes usually follow normal interrogatives of *who, what, when, where, how,* and *why*. Demographic data usually is gathered easily and efficiently by using client information forms before sessions begin. However, some information necessary for counseling can be gathered during interviews.

Consider the following:

Financial Counselor*:* How long have you been with your present employer?

Client*:* Four years.

Financial Counselor*:* Hmm , what type of retirement plan is provided by your company?

Client*:* A complete package. I mean I can retire at 62 or with 30 years of service, whichever comes first, at 66 percent of my final base salary.

Financial Counselor*:* I see. That sounds quite good. When do you think you'll retire?

Client*:* I haven't figured out the exact year, but I know I'll be 62!

Financial Counselor*:* You sound very certain about how old you'll be. What would you like to have built up in investments by then?

Probes of the type used in this example are most effective when used in combination with the Level II probes discussed below.

Level II Probes

Level II probes are very similar in form to Level I probes; that is, they usually use interrogatives *who, what, how, when, where,* and *why*. The difference lies in the kind of information being acquired. While Level I probes get at factual information, Level II probes attempt to get to the client's deeper feelings about the information being discussed.

For example:

> **Level I Probe***:* What kind of account would you like to open?
>
> **Level II Probe:** What is there about that type of account that makes you think it will meet your needs?

The Level II probe attempts to get at information concerning the client's underlying feelings about a specific type of account. While the Level I probe provides necessary information for the beginning of planning, the Level II probe provides information that is necessary to develop potential action plans with the client. Level II probe questions solicit details about the client's representational map which form the basis for choosing one alternative over others. There may be a number of equally good action plans for the client. The counselor may need to understand deeper aspects of the client's map to help the client make decisions or to choose among various alternatives.

The Faulty Question

Faulty questions follow the normal Level I or Level II probe/question format, but if you analyze them, you will find them to be logically inappropriate. For example, a young lad comes home in the winter without his mittens and Dad asks, "Where did you lose them?" On the surface this sounds like a normal question. However, when examined, the question appears to be inappropriate. If the lad knew where he lost the mittens, he would have found them and brought them home. The usual answer from the boy is, "I don't know." At this point Dad might follow with another faulty question, "Why don't you know?" This second question asks the boy to make some statement about how he knows and remembers. If the boy knew the answer to this question, he wouldn't have lost his mittens in the first place. At this time, an appropriate response might be, "You see, Dad, as a human I have short-term memory and long-term memory. Where I set my mittens down must have gone into short-term memory, and since it has been longer than five minutes, I no longer remember." You can imagine what kind of response that would elicit from Dad! However, keep in mind that the potential negative interaction between the lad and his father was precipitated by Dad's faulty question.

In financial counseling there also are examples of faulty questions. "Why didn't you sell that investment when you saw that it was dropping so fast?" There are only two possible answers: "I thought it would go back up," and "If I had known it would drop that far, I would have sold it." The major point to be made is that if you ask questions, make sure they help clients explore further or add pertinent information.

ADVANCED EXPLORATION TECHNIQUES

When people talk, they assume that other people understand exactly what they are saying. That is, they assume that other people mean the same thing that they do with any word or phrase. As discussed earlier, the words we use are an attempt to express some part of our experiential map. The same word or phrase will not mean the same thing to each individual. What makes this even more difficult is that some words are more expressive than others (expressive in the sense of being open to many possible interpretations), while other words or phrases would be accepted unilaterally.

Clarifying Words and Concepts

The kinds of words we use to describe our experiences vary on a continuum from concrete to abstract. Concrete words have few possible interpretations, while abstract words have many possible interpretations. When you hear the word *dog* you intuitively know that the word does not refer to any particular dog or, sometimes, that the word may not even refer to an animal. While it may refer to a mutt, a Collie, or a Great Dane, it also may refer to an object, a bad show, or a slow car. The word *dog* lacks a *referential index.* Without a specific contextual reference point, the word *dog* does not refer to anything specifically. You may have experienced the lack of referential index in listening to others. An individual could talk for a long time, sound wonderful, but say very little. A financial example may illustrate this concept.

> **Client***:* Well, you know how it is. It's awfully hard to keep track of where my money goes!

While it appears that the client statement is understandable, it is filled with abstract words and has very little referential index.

In the above note the following:

> *You*, the pronoun may refer to the client, it may refer to a generalized group of people as with the word everyone, or it may refer to the financial counselor.
>
> *It/It's* refers to something, but what specifically is unclear.
>
> *To keep track.* Does this mean to know, to count, to be aware of, to watch, to follow, or something else? Each verb phrase, when substituted for the original in the client statement, changes the meaning slightly but importantly.
>
> *Money.* What money is being referred to is unclear at this point. Is the client referring to savings accounts, an IRA, bonds, direct participation programs, or a weekly/monthly pay check? Again, when investments are defined specifically, the client statement takes on a different meaning.

Although the client statement appears to have meaning, when the words are examined it becomes clear that there is much more that needs to be known before we can understand fully what the client is trying to express. On an emotional level, it is quite evident that the client is frustrated. Intuitively, the counselor might respond to the client's rate of speech, tonality, speech volume, and nonverbal clues. All of these clues, plus the context in which clients make statements, provide a basis for knowing what the client is saying, despite the use of abstract words and lack of referential index.

Another example may further clarify this concept. Suppose a parent hears a child say, "Mary hurt Johnny!" Immediately this announcement makes sense. An immediate intuitive reaction might be, "Is he hurt badly?" The usual secondary reaction is, "How did she hurt him?" Our intuition tells us that we really don't know how *hurt* is being used. Mary could have hurt Johnny by hitting him, pushing him, hugging him, or some other act, and *hurt* could mean physical or even emotional hurt. We intuitively know to ask for more specific information so that we can respond appropriately.

There are times in financial counseling when seeking specific information is very important. For instance, if a client stated, "I think that what I am paying for loan interest is way out of line, and further, it's just costing too much," you probably would respond intuitively to a number of elements in the client's statement. First, you might wonder what loan? A car loan? A second mortgage? Home equity loan? All of these? Second, you might question the phrase "way out of line." You might be curious about the client's reference point, "way out of line" as compared to what? Compared to another financial institution's finance company's or bank's loan rates? Compared to a friend's loan rates? The reference point needs to be defined to know what the client means. Third, the statement, "It's just costing too much" probably would lead you to wonder how much it actually costs; what "just costing too much" is being compared to. Finally, you may wonder whether the statement "just costing too much" is appropriate at the present moment but not in the past, or possibly, in the future. All of these intuitive responses are natural and appropriate. Answers to them would help you to understand your client's representational map and help in the counseling relationship.

You can foster the counseling process if you:

- become attuned to the words clients use, words such as debts, savings, investments, stock, money, expenditures, assets, and liabilities

- use your awareness to clarify words that are vague or unclear.

Examine the following client statements as examples that illustrate these points.

> I think my investments are quite sound, my cash reserves are good, and my income is steady.

My stocks are not doing very well in today's market and I'm starting to worry about what I should do.

I've got my money tied up in a certificate of deposit.

My expenditures are just too high.

I can use my assets as collateral.

My liabilities are out of proportion.

Selective restatement of vague words or phrases like those in the six client statements above usually will elicit further discussion, elaboration, and clarification. Imperative statements can be used to help clients be more specific about their needs and wants. Finally, questions about what the client specifically means can be used. The following interchange exemplifies how counselors can clarify client words or concepts.

Client: I think my investments are quite sound, my cash reserves are good, and my income is steady.

Financial Counselor (using a selective restatement): You say your *investments* are quite sound.

Use Silence

The counselor can use silence to motivate clients to elaborate. In reference to the above interchange, the counselor should restate the client's statement while placing emphasis on the word *investments*. Then, the counselor should wait silently for the client to discuss more fully specific investments. Word emphasis plus silence is the key in this tactic.

Client: My stocks are not doing very well in today's market and I'm starting to worry about what I should do.

Financial Counselor (using a selective restatement): You say your *stocks* are not *doing very well.*

What To Emphasize

Voice emphasis on the word *stocks* and possibly on the words *doing very well* coupled with appropriate silence can foster client exploration.

Client: I've got my money tied up in a certificate of deposit.

Financial Counselor (Using an imperative statement): Tell me specifically which money you've got tied up.

Client: My expenditures are just too high.

Financial Counselor (using an imperative statement): You say that your expenditures are too high. Tell me which expenditures you are referring to.

Imperative Response

In the client statements above, the words *money* and *expenditures,* respectively, were vague and lacked specificity. Imperative leads would help clients to state exactly what he/she had in mind.

Client: I can use my assets as collateral.

Financial Counselor (Using a questioning response): Which assets are you referring to?

Client: My liabilities are out of proportion.

Financial Counselor (Using a questioning response): You say that your liabilities are out of proportion. Which liabilities specifically are you thinking about?

or

Financial Counselor: You say that your liabilities are out of proportion. I'm curious, out of proportion as compared to what?

In summary, it is important that you utilize a variety of responses. It is through this variety that you can control the financial counseling process and help clients explore their experiential maps more deeply.

Failure to use a variety of tactics can result in a less powerful and productive interchange between you and clients. A variety of tactics will keep clients somewhat off guard, make you less predictable, provide stimulation for client thought, and generate specificity needed for helpful professional counseling.

VERBAL AND NONVERBAL DISCREPANCIES

Once information has been gathered financial counselors must help clients explore discrepancies in statements and behaviors. Discrepancies that exist are not intentional but can cause clients difficulty in decision making. Discrepancies usually occur when clients have two opposing feelings, when they are unable to openly accept opposing feelings or responsibilities appropriate to a situation, or when they want to achieve conflicting goals.

Expressed Or Implied Ambivalence

There are times when clients express conflicting emotions or thoughts about a situation. This can be done directly or be implied through nonverbal behavior that is inconsistent with words the client uses.

Expressed Ambivalence

Client*:* I'd like to save more, but life is so short I want to enjoy it now.

Financial Counselor*:* On the one hand you'd like to build up your savings account, but on the other hand you want to enjoy life now. It's confusing to want two things at the same time.

Implied Ambivalence

Client (said defensively): I'm going to spend my extra money for a vacation.

Financial Counselor: You say that you're going to spend the money on a vacation, but somehow you don't sound sure that's what you want to do.

Stated Or Implied Logical Inconsistencies

At times clients talk about their situation, their problems, or possible solutions without realizing that their statements are inconsistent.

Stated Inconsistency

Client*:* We do budget every month but, at the end of the month we just don't know where our money went.

Financial Counselor*:* You say that you budget and yet you don't know where your money goes.

Implied Inconsistency

Client: I guess playing the stock market is okay. We have to make our money work somehow.

Financial Counselor: It sounds as though you're not sure that the stock market is a sound way to invest your money.

Unrealistic Goals

At times a client's goals, when perceived by another, seem unrealistic. However, *in the client's mind*, the problem is in the situation, not in the perception of the situation.

Client: I'd like for us to invest $500 a month. I know that may seem like a lot, but, if we just cut down on eating out and a little recreation, I know we can do it.

Financial Counselor: I wonder how realistic it is to think that you'll be able to give up such a sizeable portion of your entertainment and budget yourself so tightly.

Implied Causation

In this form of discrepancy, clients imply that they have little or no control over an event or situation. This form of discrepancy is characterized by the word *but.* By implication, content that follows the word *but* explains what was said in the first part of the sentence. For example:

Client: I would like to save more, *but* I'm buying a new condo.

In this statement the second part of the sentence is used to explain the first part. The client is saying, in effect, that buying a condo is preventing him from saving more, and by implication, that there is no plausible alternative. Clients will frequently discuss issues in this manner. They may not realize that the implied causation does not prevent them from doing what they state they want, but that the decision they make does. Financial counselors can help clients overcome this situation by helping them clarify and understand exactly what they have said.

Consider the following responses to the client's statement above:

Question Response

Financial Counselor: How does buying a new condo prevent you from saving money?

Imperative Response

Financial Counselor: Tell me how buying a new condo prevents you from saving money.

Restatement

Financial Counselor: You'd *like to* save more, *but* buying a new condo is preventing you.

(Emphasis, by the financial professional, is on the words *like to* and *but.)*

You must listen closely to the client's response to any of your statements. The clients' explanations may indeed indicate a true causative relationship that prevents them from accomplishing a stated goal. On other occasions, you may determine that the major obstacle to client success is the client's financial attitude.

For example:

Client: I would like to save more money *but* something always comes up.

Financial Counselor:: Something always comes up to prevent you from saving.

Client: Yeah!. Well, you know how it is, I just keep seeing things that I'd really like and I have to buy them. I end up not saving.

Financial Counselor: Why do you say that you *have* to buy them?

Client: Well, I guess I don't *have* to.

Financial Counselor: I see. Tell me more about what you believe to be your long-term savings goals.

In the sequence presented above, the financial counselor's primary purpose was to help the client clarify what he wanted or desired. To do this, the counselor focused on the client's statements and through the tactics of restatement, questioning, and imperative leads helped the client see more clearly how statements were consistent or inconsistent with stated savings goals.

Generalizations

The natural way of dealing with the world is to put elements we experience into categories or to generalize. We generalize our experiences so that we can make predictions about future events or possibilities. For example, the generalization *"hot stoves burn"* is a useful way of categorizing our experience to prevent burning ourselves in the future. While this process is useful, it can cause problems. Generalizations can be limiting. Racial or prejudicial statements about social subgroups are limiting. The generalization *"women are terrible drivers"* leads one to believe that all women are bad drivers and fails to allow for the possibility that any woman can be a good driver. Generalizations lack detail that can help individuals respond differentially to unique situations. Thus, the individual who believes that all women are bad drivers is limited to experiencing only women who are bad drivers or making such judgments despite contrary experiences. When meeting a good woman driver, he will ignore her or use her as the exception that proves the rule.

Generalizations lack detail and thus limit the freedom of choice clients have relative to their concerns or goals. You can help clients explore their generalizations, thereby helping them add detail to their experiential maps. In this way you can help your clients increase the number of options available.

Let us examine how generalizations limit freedom of choice. Suppose that the first chair a little boy climbs into happens to be a broken rocking chair. When he climbs into the chair, it tips over, and he falls and hurts his head. In this situation the child can learn that chairs are dangerous; they will tip over; and he will hurt himself. As a result of this generalization, the child limits his potential freedom. He may hesitate to sit in any chair, thus limiting his options to sitting on sofas or the floor. However, the child might learn a different generalization; rocking chairs are dangerous. In this generalization the child has more freedom. He can now choose to sit on sofas, the floor, and on four-legged, non-rocking chairs. The child also could learn that broken rocking chairs are dangerous. With this generalization the child is left with even more options. He can sit on sofas, on the floor, on four-legged chairs, and on rocking chairs that do not have broken rockers.

As can be seen, generalizations have a limiting or freeing effect upon choice and eventual behavior. Many times, clients will talk about themselves and their concerns in generalizations that are extremely limiting. It is important in financial situations to help clients recognize how their generalizations limit their freedom of choice.

Generalizations are easily recognizable. They usually contain some word that indicates a universal element, such as *everyone, nobody, people, the guys, the gals, society, everybody,* or *all.* There also are a number of adverbs that indicate generalizations: *always, never,* or *sometimes*.

There are three basic ways you can help clients to explore generalizations: restating the content while emphasizing the generalization; asking the client for an exception to the generalization; and providing the client with an example that would be an exception to the generalization. These approaches are examined through the following examples.

Restatement With Emphasis

Client: I can't think of any situation in which a certificate of deposit would be helpful.

Financial Counselor: You can't think of *any* situation in which a certificate of deposit would be a useful way to save.

Asking For An Exception

Client: I'd never tie my money up for five years.

Financial Counselor: Can you think of any situation in which such a way of saving would benefit you?

Providing An Exception

Client*:* Loan insurance is always a bad idea.

Financial Counselor: I can understand your concern, yet loan insurance protects your family if something happens to you.

Responding to generalizations is important. By responding, you help clients to add detail to their personal mapping structure, which in turn increases their freedom of choice. One of the counseling tasks is to organize the amount of detail and information available to clients. This increases clients' options and can help them to achieve their financial goals.

BROADENING TACTICS

The following tactics of communication can help clients to broaden their perspective. Some of the tactics are *indirect* whereas others are *direct*. All are potentially useful for counselors. By incorporating a variety of techniques counselors can maintain control of the counseling process, maximize their counseling leverage, and focus counseling. A closer examination of these tactics follows:

Cooperation

Two individuals who work together potentially are more powerful than either working alone. To use this knowledge, counselors must refrain from doing everything for the client or from expecting the client to accomplish their goals on their own. Rather, counselors should cooperate with clients, share responsibility for movement toward clients' goals, and work together toward finding solutions to clients' concerns.

The following example demonstrates this concept:

> **Client:** "I can't seem to figure out how to get everyone off my back!"
>
> **Financial Counselor:** "You seem to be frustrated and starting to wonder if you can get your creditors to ease up a little."
>
> **Client:** "Yes, I'm very anxious about my finances and about dealing with everyone I owe."

Financial Counselor: "Let's see how we can work together to deal with your anxiety and how you might put a plan together for communicating with your creditors."

Client: "Thanks, I would like that."

Scaling

Scaling is the process of moving thoughts and actions form a binary scale to one with a larger scope. This process is one that provides a simple rating scale that clients can use to represent their needs, indicate their goals, or suggest levels of motivation.

Consider the following example:

Financial Counselor: "On a scale from one to ten in which one is low and ten is high, how would you rate this choice for yourself at this time?"

Client: "Oh, about a four."

Financial Counselor: "What would have to happen for you to move your rating up to nine or ten?"

Reframing

Reframing is the process of putting a new or different frame around one or more of life events to produce a different picture. When we put a new frame around an event we look at it from a new perspective. For reframing to be effective it must be closely related to the client's own experience and be an equally plausible explanation for that experience. Reframing accepts the client's feelings, fears, or anxieties as part of normal experience and does not attempt to change them or take them away. Reframing is the process of showing clients how the meaning they have ascribed life event(s) can be judged to have a different meaning.

Reframing can be accomplished in three ways. First, counselors can "provide the flip side of the coin", e.g., point out the counter-balancing desires or positive feelings to those expressed by the client. Second, the counselor can amplify or exaggerate the client's feelings, fears, or anxieties. Finally, the counselor can use the underlying experiential data in a negative frame and jump to a new positive frame. Reframing can be surprising, positive, sometimes humorous, and have a powerful affect on clients.

Consider the following examples.

Example 1: Flip Side

For most thoughts or feelings there is a "flip side." For instance, stubbornness is the flip side of tenacity. One is viewed negatively, the other positively. Yet, they are basically the same characteristic. Also, thoughts and feelings can have counter poles, those thoughts or feelings at the opposite end of the continuum from the stated thought of feeling. Listed below are a number of common thoughts or feelings and their corresponding counter-balancing thought or feeling.

Thoughts or Feelings	**Counter-Balancing Thought or Feeling**
Fear of failure	Desire to succeed
Hate	Love
Fear of death	Desire for life
Misunderstood	Accepted

Client: "I am really afraid of speaking to my friends about this.
Financial Counselor: "You have a very strong desire to be accepted and respected by your friends."

Example 2: Amplifying or Exaggerating

Amplifying and exaggerating are ways of focusing attention on clients' thoughts or feelings. When clients' statements are reframed in this way clients' understanding of what they have said increases.

Client: "I feel so guilty when I go on a buying spree."

Financial Counselor: "You obviously don't feel guilty enough to keep yourself from doing it."

Client: "I guess you are right. Maybe I need to feel more guilty."

Example 3: Frame Jumping

Frame jumping is based on an assumption that a thought or feeling stated negatively, at times, can be reframed in a positive manner. The thought of feeling can be moved from a *negative frame* to a *positive frame*. This concept is demonstrated in an event that occurred in the Korea conflict in 1950. The United States Fifth and Seventh Marine Corps were surrounded and cut off from the rest of their division. The press talked about their need to retreat. When asked about the impending retreat Major General O.P. Smith, the Marine Division commander statement was, "No, not a retreat. It will be an attack in another direction." Smith's comment is an excellent example of reframing. Consider another example.

Client: " My boss thinks I'm a know it all. He says I am rebellious."

Financial Counselor: "It sounds like you are someone who knows his own mind. You aren't afraid to tell people what you think and you'll stick up for your point of view. I wonder if the difficulty you are having is knowing when to act that way."

SOLICITING EXCEPTIONS

This approach focuses attention on when the problem is not occurring. The technique is built on an assumption that problems do not occur *all* of the time and that by examining when they are not occurring counselors can learn ways for assisting clients. Focusing on exceptions allows counselors to reframe the counseling process from solving problems to looking for solutions. Looking for solutions focuses counseling on the future. This process is a positive approach for mobilizing appropriate energies toward achieving counseling goals.

Consider the following example.

Client: "I can never do anything correct when keeping my budget."

Financial Counselor: "That is interesting. Can you think of any time when this isn't true?"

Client: "Well, one time maybe."

Financial Counselor: "Tell me about that time."

Client: "When I decided to buy a new car and had to save money I kept a close budget."

Financial Counselor: "I'm curious. What made that time different from other times?"

Counseling Statements Applying The Concept of Exceptions

When doesn't the problem occur?

Tell me about times when the problem doesn't occur.

I'd be interested in knowing about times that the problem isn't there.

When are you already doing what you want to do?

When are you already on track toward your goals?

Tell me about times when you are accomplishing some of your goals.

I'm wondering if there are times when you are already doing what you want to.

What is different about times when your problem doesn't occur?

What do you do differently during those times when the problem doesn't occur?

During those times when you are not experiencing the problem how would others see you?

GOAL SETTING

Goal statements provide counselors a basis for focusing the counseling process. They provide the client and counselor a means for determining the direction of counseling and material for the counselor's intervention. Clear goal statements provide a basis for intervention in the present, a working agenda for clients' action, and a vision of the future. Effective goals abide by several general principles.

Principle 1: The goals *are ones that are under the client's control.*

"I will pay my monthly bills on time."
"I will invest money toward my retirement."

Principle 2: The goals *emphasize what the client will do or how they will behave.*

"I will be patient in communicating with my spouse about our finances."
"I will call my creditors about the amount I am in debt to them."

Principle 3: The goals *specify what the client will be doing when on track toward achieving goals.*

"I will be spending less for nonessential items during the month."
"I will be saving a portion of every paycheck."

Principle 4: The goals *may specify the conditions under which behavior can be observed.*
"As soon as I receive my paycheck I will deposit part of it in my savings account."
"The next time my spouse and I talk about finances I will be open to her ideas."

Principle 5: The goals *may specify actions, in percentages, degrees, or numbers, that will be acceptable during a specific time period.*

"I will put 10% of every paycheck into savings."
"For the next three months I will pay creditors double monthly payments."

Principle 6: The goals *are stated in positive terms.*

"I will make regular monthly payments."
"I will consistently budget for the month."

Principle 7: The goals *are stated in the client's language.*

"I'll save on a regular basis."
"I'll keep track of my spending for the next two months."

Counselor statements that can result in goal statements include the following:

What do you want to get out of working together?
What do you want to do differently when counseling is done?
What is your goal from counseling?
I'm wondering what will be different for you once counseling is complete.
What could I expect to see differently about you after completing financial counseling?

The following example illustrates goal setting.

Client: " I wish I could get my finances straightened out."

Financial Counselor: "I am glad you are motivated to do that. How, specifically, would be a good way to get you started?"

Client: "Well, I could contact my major creditors and talk with them."

Financial Counselor: "Great. Tell me how you will arrange this."

Client: "I'll talk to them today to see what they might suggest."

FUTURE PACING

Future Pacing is a tactic for helping clients to impact their present situations by stimulating them to see themselves in the future. This process can be accomplished in a variety of ways. Exploring the future can be done through use of focused exploring skills, role playing, and visualization. All of these approaches help clients to address concerns before they occur.

Focused Exploring Skills

Use of questions, imperative leads, and declarative leads discussed earlier in this chapter can be used to stimulate clients' future pacing. Following are some examples of the process.

Questions:

What will you do differently in the future to keep the solution going?

When you see yourself in the future what will be different in your life?

Imperative Leads:

Tell me how you plan to apply what we've discussed in the next week or so.

Share with me, what you will be doing when you are past your current concern.

Declarative Leads:

I am curious how you are going to apply what we've discussed.

I am wondering what it will be like for you in five years if you don't get your concern under control.

Role Playing

Counselors can use role playing to have clients experience solutions to their concerns. This can be done in the safety of the counseling relationship. For example, clients may feel uncomfortable discussing their financial situation with their creditors. Counselors could role play representative situations in which clients communicate with creditors. This would provide clients practice in advance of their actual discussions with creditors and would allow counselors an opportunity to prepare clients for the interchange.

Visualization

A way to *future pace* is to ask clients to imagine a situation in the future, one using a solution behavior. As with role playing, the focus of visualization is on the future and practicing the use of solution actions or on possible negative consequences if solutions are not carried out. In visualization, the medium for practice is the client's imagination. For example, a counselor might say the following, "Let's imagine it is five years from now and your problem has been completely resolved. Visualize how you would be acting." Based on knowledge of the client's situation, the counselor can help the client to focus on specifics of the created image. As a follow-up to this process, counselors can help clients to set goals that will result in obtaining the desired future. The following example illustrates this concept.

Client: "I'm stuck on what I should do next."

Financial Counselor: "If you look into the future, what would you like the situation to be?"

Client: "I would like to have some money set aside for retirement and also have money for my daughter's education."

Financial Counselor: "Okay. Let's look at what you have to do in the short term to achieve those long term goals."

USE OF QUOTATIONS

People tend to resist direct suggestions. When suggestions are made indirectly, however, the person has the opportunity to accept or reject them without having to feel defensive. One way of making indirect suggestions is to imbed them in quotations. Quotations can be part of the ongoing dialogue or might be a quote from someone else. Consider this example between a counselor and client.

> When I was a counselor in training my supervisor once told me (looking directly into the client's eyes), "No wonder you have problems. You keep trying to control how people feel about you." That was really hard for me to hear because I wanted my supervisor to like me.

In this example, the counselor used a quote from the supervisor to make a suggestion to the client about the client's characteristic of trying to control people's feelings. If the suggestion has meaning to the client it will be used. If it does not have meaning, it will be passed off as part of the story the counselor was telling.

METAPHORS

A metaphor is a figure of speech in which one thing is spoken as if it were another, e.g., *All the world is a stage*. Metaphorical language has the quality of painting a verbal picture. It tends to activate the senses and transmit information in a representative manner. Examples of metaphorical language include the following:

I'm up the creek without a paddle.

I've got myself behind the eight ball.

I feel like I'm at the bottom of a pit and I can't get out.

Counselors can blend with clients and help them to elaborate on their thoughts by responding to clients' metaphors directly. This can be accomplished by entering the clients' metaphors as in the following example:

Client: "Taking on this expense is like entering a deep, dark tunnel."

Financial Counselor: "It's like you are getting into something blind…like you don't know what to expect."

Client: "Yeah, that's it. It is scary."

Financial Counselor: "What would make this experience less frightening?"

Client: "Well, maybe if I knew more about what it is going to be like."

In addition to responding to client metaphors, counselors can create metaphors that represent their knowledge of the client's world and use metaphors to focus on specific concerns. By doing so counselors can help reduce client reluctance to discuss sensitive issues. Consider the following interchange in which a client and counselor are talking about a client's spending habits:

Client: "I hate this time of year. I can't seem to control myself."

Financial Counselor: " As you describe your situation, I get a picture of a kid in a candy store. Everything looks good to the kid. He spends his entire allowance on sweets. Then, not only is his allowance gone but he doesn't feel so well either."

Client: "Yes, that is true. I blow the money and then feel guilty later.

Financial Counselor: " I wonder what advice we might give the kid before he enters the candy store."

Client: " Well, we could tell him to leave his allowance at home!"

Financial Counselor: "That is a great idea. Would that also work for you?"

Client: " I don't think so."

Financial Counselor: " Okay, other than the obvious differences of age, what do you see as being the differences between your situation and the kid's?"

CHEERLEADING

Clients frequently feel frustrated and have difficulty in seeing the bright side of their financial situation. Their negative perspective may inhibit them from taking the steps necessary to alter their current situation. Counselors, on the other hand, should not only be aware of negative elements of the situation but must keep positive possibilities in mind. By maintaining a positive stance, counselors can help clients overcome their negative, self-defeating, tendencies and encourage them to take the steps necessary to achieve success. Consider the following:

Client: "I've been working at getting a jump on holiday expenses before they get too big."

Financial Counselor: "That is fantastic. I am really happy to see you so motivated to stay in good financial shape."

Client: " I must admit that with all that is happening, sometimes I feel it isn't worth it and I feel like giving up."

Financial Counselor: "I can understand that. It is hard to keep restricting yourself, especially when you are working so hard. I give you a lot of credit for persisting."

Client: "I am feeling good about it."

USE OF IMPLICATION

Implication is one form of communication that contains two messages. The first message is carried in the words and the non-verbal communication. When one reads *between the lines* a second *indirect* message is implied. Consider the following counselor statement:

"Among some of the things you can learn is to trust your intuition."

In this statement the counselor tells the client *directly* that the client can learn to trust his/her intuitions. There is a second *indirect* message that is implied through the opening phrase, "*Among some of the things*". The implication is that trusting the client's intuition is only one of the things that the client might learn.

Statements Demonstrating The Use of Implication

"Tell me the first important thing that comes to mind about your concern."

"There probably are a number of things we should discuss about your concern."

" You've probably had a number of experiences in your life that might be useful in finding a solution."

"It goes without saying…"

"I don't have to tell you…"

"I assume you already know…"

"Someone with all of your experience already knows…"

SPECIALIZED QUESTIONS

Miracle Questions

Miracle Questions are questions that conceptually remove obstacles that hinder or prevent clients from taking action. This form of question is a way to construct a bridge between counselor and client built around a future occurrence. It is particularly helpful in helping clients to get beyond being stuck by their perceived problem. Miracle questions do this by separating clients' problems from possible solutions. They free clients to think about solutions in the *absence of problems*. The following exemplifies this approach:

Client: "I am at a loss of what I should do."

Financial Counselor: "If you went to sleep tonight and a miracle happened to remove the immediate concern how would you act differently?"

(or)

Financial Counselor: "If a miracle happened and the problem went away, what would you do?"

(or)

Financial Counselor: "If, while you were sleeping a miracle occurred to do away with your concern, what would then be most important to you?"

Hypothetical Questions

Like miracle questions, hypothetical questions can help clients to think beyond their immediate concern. By presupposing a certain condition, counselors' verbal leads like "What if…?" and "Suppose…" can be productive. These leads will help clients refocus their concentration on problems to exploration of possibilities for solution.

Statements Demonstrating Hypothetical Questions

"What if you were out of debt? How would your life than be different?"

"Suppose you didn't have the current problem. What impact would that have on your life?"

"Let's say your current financial situation changed for the better. What would that mean to you?"

"Let's suppose you were able to solve the immediate problem, then, what would you do differently?"

"Assume that you start making payments on a regular basis. How might that change the way your creditors are reacting to you?"

Presumptive Questions

Presumptive questions presume a particular state of being. These, like *miracle* and *hypothetical* questions, can move clients beyond conceptual barriers. Consider the following:

> "When you are on track to achieving your goal what will you be doing?"
>
> "When you are acting in a way that moves you toward your goals what will be different?"

Both questions presume the client will be on track and moving toward specified goals. Also, both focus the client on a time, in the future, when movement toward resolution of the current problem has begun. Presumptive questions, like these, can stimulate clients to consider, in advance, what they will do when the future time arrives.

CONCLUSION

Thirteen communication techniques have been presented in this section. It should be noted that some are *direct* forms of communication, ones that openly enlist client involvement. Cooperation, Scaling, Soliciting Exceptions, Goal Setting, Future Pacing, and Cheerleading fit this category. Other techniques that have been presented are *indirect* forms of communication. They use nuances of language to help clients to overcome natural resistance to change. Reframing, Quotations, Metaphors, Implication, Miracle Questions, Hypothetical Questions, and Presumptive Questions are included in the *indirect* category.

A Counseling Example

This example demonstrates a number of the skills that have been discussed in this chapter. The counselor uses a number of *direct* and *indirect* techniques to help the client to explore concerns and to arrive at a plan of action. Review the interview and try to determine which techniques were used.

Client: Talking in a low, soft voice, "I came into today to see if I could get some help."

Financial Counselor: Talking in a quiet, reserved manner, "What is it you would like help with?"

Client: "For a long time I thought I was doing fine but recently I started to realize that I wasn't."

Financial Counselor: "When you say you thought you were doing fine, I assume you mean in regard to your finances."

Client: "Yes, that is correct. Lately I have become aware that I never pay off my charge cards, and that I have opened more credit cards than I really need."

Financial Counselor: "I'd like to understand how intense you feel about this. On a scale from one to ten in which one is not very important to ten which is very important how would you rate your concern?"

Client: "That's interesting. At times it feels like a three but at other times more like a nine or ten."

Financial Counselor: "What rating would you give it today?"

Client: "Ten."

Financial Counselor: "Okay. Tell me about those times when you would rate your feeling a three."

Client: "It feels more like a three, or even less, at the beginning of the month…probably when I get paid."

Financial Counselor: "Just after you receive your paycheck for the month your finances look okay. But, as the month goes on you are less comfortable. Is that it?"

Client: "Yes, I guess it is. Sometimes, at the end of the month I wonder if I can make it. "

Financial Counselor: "When those time happen, what do you do to meet your financial needs?"

Client: "Use my credit cards."

Financial Counselor: "I give you a lot of credit for facing up to your financial concerns. It takes courage to come here and to start to work on setting things right." "Let's look into the future. If we were talking a year from now how would you like your situation to be different?"

Client: "I'd like to have my credit cards paid off."

Financial Counselor: "Anything else?"

Client: "Yes, I'd like to be less dependent on credit cards to make it from month to month."

Financial Counselor: "How can we work together to make sure that happens?"

Client: "Well, if you could help me get over my immediate needs that would be a start."

Financial Counselor: "Anything else?"

Client: "I think I need to learn to budget so that I don't keep getting myself into fixes."

Financial Counselor: "Okay. So we will work on two things, helping you get past your immediate difficulties and then helping you learn to budget your money. Anything else?"

Client: "I can't think of anything. If we can do those two things I'll feel a lot better."

Financial Counselor: "As you might guess, I've worked with a number of people around similar concerns. I had one tell me, 'I thought I could follow through on what we discussed but I could never do it.' I had another say, 'I knew that I was uncomfortable with my situation but I knew I would follow through.' You know yourself. Does either of these people sound like you?"

Client: "I can see a little of both of those people in myself. I know I have to work at this but sometimes I give up."

Financial Counselor: "That's understandable. I am willing to work with you until you have achieved your goals if you also are willing to work."

Client: "I don't like being stressed out about money. I'll work at it."

Financial Counselor: "Your situation reminds me a little of me when I swim underwater at a pool. If I can see the end of the pool I can hold my breath until I get there. If I can't see the end I give up."

Client: "Absolutely, I'm willing to work if I know things will be better."

Financial Counselor: "I truly believe that that they will." "Now, tell me, when you've overcome your financial difficulties how will your life be different?"

Client: "I know I will feel better about myself and feel less stressed."

Financial Counselor: "Good." "How will you feel if it takes longer than a year to accomplish what we plan?"

Client: "If I can see that we are making progress I'll keep working no matter how long it takes."

Financial Counselor: "I like your answer. You sound committed to changing your financial situation."

Client: "I am."

Financial Counselor: "Once your present concerns are behind you we will be able to work on other financial goals you might have."

Client: "I would like that. Thanks."

RESOURCES

Lee, J. L., Pulvino, C. J. & Perrone, P.A. (1993). *Dynamic Counseling.* Madison: Instructional Enterprises.

Patterson, L.E. & Welfel, E.R. (2000). *The Counseling Process* (5th Ed.). Belmont: Brooks Cole.

Teyber, E. (2000). *Interpersonal Process In Psychotherapy* (4th Ed.). Belmont: Wadsworth.

6 STRATEGIES FOR FOSTERING RESPONSIBILITY

Each of us carries a picture of who we are at the moment, along with another of the possibilities. We're carrying two pictures with us at all times – what we are and what we could be.

Land, G. & Jarman, B. (1992, p.101).

In previous chapters we outlined basic principles of communication, communication skills (verbal and nonverbal pacing), and exploring techniques. In this chapter we discuss impediments to good communication, methods for dealing with client resistance, and advanced motivational techniques.

IMPEDIMENTS TO GOOD COMMUNICATION

A foundation for good communication was laid in earlier chapters. We emphasized principles, positive concepts, skills, and techniques. Also, some communicative processes should be avoided.

Over-Long Statements

Statements that are too long often sound like lectures! There are times when you need to give clients additional information or to correct inaccurate information. However, the most effective professional process is a collaborative problem-solving approach that assumes that both parties are involved and responsible. If you use over-long statements, statements that sound like lectures, there is the danger that you may begin to sound autocratic. Clients may feel belittled or feel that they are being treated with diminished status. As soon as clients begin to feel this way, you may damage the openness and trust necessary for effective financial communication. Consider the following.

Client*:* *I* think that I'm ready to have a will drawn up.

Professional: I was wondering when you were going to get around to that. You know, it's not so bad. I mean, having a will doesn't mean you're going to die. A person in your situation should probably have considered this long ago. And also, … (more talk about the benefits of a will).

Put-Down Questions

We have discussed this issue previously under faulty questions. This type of question is often a rhetorical question, usually spoken with strong emotional overtones of sarcasm, anger, or frustration. A financial analyst who asks, "Why don't you ever pay more attention to your cash flow?" probably isn't expecting an answer. Rather, the analyst is making an emotional statement. A common result of this type of question is that clients will feel defensive and try to justify themselves. While there may be rare occasions when it is appropriate to put clients on the defensive, it is not a good idea to do so by indirectly expressing your emotions through put-down questions.

When counselors are feeling frustrated or angry with clients, they will be more effective by stating their emotions directly. For example, "I get frustrated when you make me entirely responsible for your financial decisions. I believe that I could be more helpful if you would get more involved!" In a congruent manner, this feedback statement tells the client how the counselor feels and points out what the counselor would like. This type of statement, because of its directness and specificity, will raise less client defensiveness than a put-down question.

Speaking In Generalizations

People try to influence one another through generalizations. Most of us have tried this communicative strategy. As a teenager, you may have asked to use the family car and received a definite *no* from your parents. Your response might have been something like, "Why not? Everybody else does!" This kind of statement was probably a strong attempt to convince your parents that they should let you use the car. This sort of generalization *implies* that if they were good parents, they would be like everyone else and let you use the car. The usual parental response to this sort of plea is, "Well, we aren't everybody else!" This exemplifies the fact that people usually are aware when others try to manipulate them through use of generalizations.

The use of generalizations in professional interactions usually is subtle. Statements like, "Well, everyone seems to think this investment is sound" and "Most tax accountants are recommending ..." exemplify this point. These two statements imply that the client should accept what is being recommended because *everyone else* or *most tax accountants* have made similar decisions. A more open and direct approach would be for you to share with the client the characteristics, advantage, and disadvantage of the particular financial investment or tax strategy.

There is a second form of generalization that is equally destructive to effective relationships, the over-generalization. Over-generalizations are usually emotional statements that are meant to put someone down. An example of an over-generalization is, "A simple savings account is never a good way to invest your money!" As with most generalizations, there are usually exceptions that depend upon the attitudes and goals of the client. Words like *never, always, everybody, all,* and *nobody* usually indicates that an over-generalization has been used. It is better to state your feelings and thoughts directly and congruently than to use generalizations or over-generalizations.

Mind-Reading Statements

Statements implying that you know what clients are thinking are called mind-reading statements. Examples of mind-reading are: "You don't listen to what I try to tell you" or "You don't care what happens to your money." An alternative to using mind reading is to remember that clients carry out what is best for them, given the information they have in their representational maps (See Principle 2.9). When you make mind-reading statements, you imply that clients are wrong and should not be thinking as they are. Instead, using feedback, a counselor can label behavior that clients exhibit and state the counselor's reactions directly. For example, "You don't act as if your money is important to you and I don't know what to do to help you." This approach is direct and provides clients with specific information about the counselor's reactions to their behavior.

"You Did..." Statements

The opposite of this statement "You Didn't ..." is also used. These kinds of statements are often used to blame others for their behavior. An example of this type of statement is, "You didn't send me the information you promised!" In this statement, it is obvious that blame is being placed on the recipient of the message, maybe in a highly emotional fashion. Statements like this can do serious damage to an effective counselor/client relationship because they indicate that the counselor was right and the client was wrong. For instance, a counselor may wish to tell clients, "I told you so!" when they fail to follow financial proposals that would have proven more beneficial than the actions they did take. Even though it may be tempting to do so, it is better to avoid using such statements. A more effective approach is to tell clients what the counselor is thinking or feeling. When counselors tell clients directly, they model the openness and honesty they wish to develop in an effective working relationship.

"You Should..." Statements

Because one of the major aspects of professional interactions is recommendation of plans, options, and possibilities, *should* statements might appear to be quite appropriate. However, there are two dangers in using *should* statements. First, clients may become defensive because of a history of experiences with people telling them what they *should* do. This history can help create elements in clients' representational maps that will lead them to automatically respond defensively whenever someone tells them they *should*. The second danger is that when counselors use *should* statements they are making a definite, conclusive statement about what a client ought to do. While this is sometimes appropriate, there is always the danger of suggesting through a *should* statement a course that later proves disastrous. It is usually better to indicate several options to clients and have them choose one. In this way clients make the choice and must accept responsibility for outcomes.

The one exception to these warnings is telling clients what they should do based on sound financial principles. For example, "You should have sufficient cash reserves before you begin speculating in the stock market", or "You should protect yourself with liability insurance rather than taking a chance that nothing will ever happen." *Should* statements of this sort revolve around accepted financial principles and help clients to expand their representational maps so that they can make sound decisions in the future. Obviously, the responsibility for accepting the advice you offer through *should* statements remains with clients.

Defending Statements

Defending statements are often used to pull rank. In everyday communication they might take a form like, "I have a right to talk any way I want" or "Because I'm your father, that's why". This type of statement usually implies that the listener has no right to question the speaker's behavior, statements, or motivations. In professional interactions, statements of this kind can be blatant ("I was only suggesting that plan for your own good!") or subtle ("I was trying to suggest a plan that seemed to fit the goals we outlined!"). While both statements may be absolutely true, statements of this type make you sound defensive.

Remember that communicative interactions are reciprocal. What counselors do or say affect how clients respond and *vice versa*. In the professional process, defending statements may lead to arguments, and may leave the counselor and client feeling that nothing has been settled. It is better to use a direct feedback statement that relates a client's behavior with the consequences being experienced. For example, a client who has persisted in playing the stock market might be told, "I can see the attraction of your investments, but last year you had a net loss of 5 per cent on your ventures. This seems to be out of line with your goals to earn a minimum of 10 percent a year on your money." When clients experience the consequences of their actions, usually they are open to change. By avoiding the use of defending statements, counselors can help clients to face up to the results of their behavior and, consequently, to make better decisions.

Threatening Statements

Threatening statements call for action. For instance, if you tell someone, "If you say that again, I'm leaving," and they say it again, you are faced with a choice to leave or to ignore the threatening statement. In either case, the ensuing action will be detrimental to the relationship and continuing effective communication. In professional relationships, threatening statements are subtle and frequently take the form of veiled warnings. For example, "If you continue the way you are now, you're going to lose your investments!" While it is appropriate to warn clients about possible consequences of their behavior or decisions, it is not appropriate to use threatening statements to control or manipulate clients. Clients intuitively will know when counselors are trying to manipulate them and will become defensive. A break in the relationship can result.

All of the following are impediments to good communication: over-long statements, putdown questions, generalizations, mind-reading statements, *you did* something statements, *you should* statements, and threatening statements. Monitor your communication to keep these types of statements to a minimum. To the degree that you accomplish this end, you will be able to establish trouble-free relationships with clients.

DEALING WITH RESISTANCE

Resistance can be viewed in two different ways. In the first perspective, a person does not do what another wishes and resists change. In the second, a person seems to be closed and displays resistance to anything new. The statement, "Don't confuse me with the facts, my mind is already made up" exemplifies this form of resistance. When confronted with either of these forms of resistance in clients, keep the following in mind. Clients are doing the best they can, using the stored information they have (see Principle 2.9 in Chapter 2). If counselors accept this principle, then they can say that clients are not being resistant, but rather that clients do not have information in their representational maps to act differently.

The practical meaning of communication is the response you receive. This is discussed in detail in Principle 9.5 in Chapter 9. Briefly, this principle implies that what we often perceive to be resistance is, our own inability to communicate in ways that move the client in the direction we think best.

Accepting these principles can lead us to the conclusion that there may not be client resistance. Rather, we might conclude that there are clients with limited representational maps and times when we, as financial professionals, are limited in the number and type of responses we can make in a given situation. From this perspective, a counselor's task is to help clients to integrate new information into their representational maps and to use a wide variety of communicative procedures to assure client acceptance of ideas, suggestions, and information. The following techniques should prove helpful in overcoming either form of resistance:

Using Tentative Qualifiers

In general, people have a tendency to resist *absolute statements.* Absolute statements do not take into account the fact that clients have idiosyncratic representational maps. In addition, each of us has a stubborn streak. We automatically resist direct commands when someone tells us how to behave or think in some situations. If someone tells you in a loud, commanding voice to blink your eyes, a typical response is to refuse. You resist the command. Similarly, clients will resist direct commands about their behavior or how to think.

The first set of communication skills to reduce resistance revolves around statements, suggestions, or advice given in *tentative* ways. This can be done through addition of adverbial qualifiers. Words like *usually, sometimes, often, whenever, might, maybe, probably* can be used to soften communication. If instead of an absolute command to blink your eyes, you hear "Sometime in the next few seconds you *might* blink your eyes," you're more apt to cooperate. The qualifier *might* takes away the command nature of the direction. The qualifier makes the statement consistent with your subconscious knowledge that every few seconds we do blink our eyes. Consequently, you, like most individuals comply with the statement and blink your eyes. As an example of this concept, consider the following client/attorney interchanges and the attorney's use of tentative qualifiers.

Client: I don't want to think about having a will drawn up.

Financial Counselor: I can see that discussing this is difficult for you. You might be ready to discuss the advantages the next time we get together.

Client: I'm not sure my heirs can manage what I want to leave to them.

Financial Counselor: I can understand your concern, yet, you'll probably find some way to get more specific information about their ability in that area.

Tentative qualifiers allow you to make suggestions in a manner that does not put clients on the defensive. Your idea can be communicated and resistance can be held to a minimum.

Using Dilemma Questions

Another set of communication skills that can be applied to reduce resistance revolves around dilemma questions. If you recall, dilemma questions appear to give clients a choice. When examined, however, the ultimate choice of accepting alternatives or of making a choice has been excluded.

Dilemma questions and tentative qualifiers can be combined to make suggestions, give directions, and minimize resistance. For example, "Would you like to make a decision about investing in this real estate venture this week or maybe next week?" When this question is examined, it becomes obvious that the client has not been given a choice of whether to invest but, rather, when she will invest. The addition of *maybe* in the second part of the question also increases the possibility that the client will make a choice.

Dilemma Questions A Financial Counselor May Pose

"Would you like to invest $50, $100, or $200 a month through payroll deduction?

"Would you like to set up a meeting with the consumer credit counselor this week or maybe wait until next week?"

"Would you like to start a gifting program now or wait until after January 1st?"

"Would you like to recommend my services to a colleague, or possibly just bring him with you to our next meeting?"

In all of the above, the client is being faced with a dilemma. A choice of either alternative in each question results in a decision to do *something*. In these questions, clients are *not* given the option of doing nothing.

Using Psychology

Communication skills that employ psychology can be used to reduce client resistance. In popular language, when someone accuses others of "using psychology on me," the message usually being transmitted is that they are using psychology "to make me do what they want me to do." A famous psychiatrist, Milton H. Erickson, says he first learned about this way of dealing with resistance as he was watching his father trying to get a cow to go into the barn. His father was pulling on a rope attached to the cow's halter as hard as he could, while the cow was pulling just as hard in the opposite direction. Erickson reports that he does not know why it occurred to him, but he ran over and grabbed the cow's tail and jerked as hard as he could. The cow bolted into the barn. In order to *resist* the new pull on its tail the cow had to move forward into the barn. (Rosen, S. , 1982).

In financial encounters, we can accomplish a similar effect by using a special linguistic form called *not doing* or *not knowing.* A statement like "You know you *don't* have to talk about anything you don't want to, "gives the client permission to avoid what he may not want to share with you. On the other hand, this statement could encourage the client to think about all the concerns he does not want to share with you, and, because the client has been given the responsibility for sharing, could lead the client to be more open about all his concerns. Consider the following professional statements as examples of this concept:

Statements Employing Psychology To Reduce Client Resistance

"You don't have to plan for every possible financial emergency."

"You don't have to think about retirement until you have your kids through college."

"Obviously, you've thought about how you'd like to distribute your estate."

All of these examples demonstrate the "use of psychology" to encourage clients to think or act. This approach, although effective, should be used carefully and probably should be limited to those cases where *strong* resistance is encountered.

Logical Connections

Finally, awareness of logical connections can be used to overcome resistance. Two thoughts or ideas tied together with logical verbal connectors like *and, when,* and *as* characterize logical connections. For example, "*When* you are doing your monthly budget, you *might* think of ways you can cut corners to find the needed resources to meet your goals." In this example, two ideas are tied together through the use of the word *when* doing a budget and finding additional resources. Also, notice that the use of a tentative qualifier in the second half of the sentence reduces the possibility of resistance. When using logical connections, it is not necessary for the two ideas, suggestions, or directions to be *logically* consistent. Consider the statement: "*When* you are working this week, you might think of other financial objectives that are important to you." In this statement there is no logical connection between working and thinking about financial objectives. However, when clients hear such a statement, it will *seem* to make sense. The suggestion subconsciously will be attended to and help clients, consciously and subconsciously to think about their financial objectives.

ADVANCED MOTIVATIONAL TECHNIQUES

We now move to advanced techniques that can be used to help clients make decisions and, in the long run, to accomplish their goals. These techniques build on a counselor's natural interpersonal inclinations. When used in financial situations, these techniques should be purposeful and controlled.

Using Truisms

A truism is a statement that relates to normal experience and is stated in such a way that when clients hear it, their usual response is, "Oh yeah!" Truisms tap into clients' representational maps in such a way that they recognize the experience, or at least realize that the truism is something they could have experienced.

> **Examples of Truisms**
>
> "You say you can't solve this problem, yet you've solved more complicated ones in the past."
>
> "You say that right now you're financially pinched, sort of like you've said you were when you first started out."
>
> (Said to a client who just purchased a new house) "It probably will be like when you purchased your last house - somewhat difficult at first, but then it continuously will become easier to make payments."

Notice, statements are used that will encourage clients to examine their previous history as a means for generating ideas or as motivation in dealing with present situations.

Using Generic Examples

Generic examples, like truisms, are drawn from normal life experiences. Financial counselors can use generic examples to help clients tap into their own representational maps to understand the point, advice, or information being presented. By using the client's own experience you increase the likelihood that the point, advice, or information being offered will be both understood and accepted. For example, in talking about investing in the stock market, one might say something similar to the following:

> "It's like going to a horse race. There are some long shots and a number of favorites. Also, there are no guarantees a favorite can't lose. On the other hand, even a long shot can pay off. "
>
> "It's like investing in the stock market: It will have its ups and downs, but, if history is any indicator, in the long run, it will be more up than down."

> "Involving yourself in the stock market is like marriage. The more you invest yourself in the process and the more you work at understanding the intricacies, the more likely you are to be successful."

Generic examples can take the form of analogies, like the three above, or of personal examples like the following:

> "I've had a number of clients who have questioned whole life insurance. One in particular decided to buy term insurance and invest the difference in certificates of deposit. That's worked well for him."
>
> "One of my older clients was wondering how to provide for her sister, much like you. She decided to set up a trust fund."

In all cases, generic examples can be used to answer clients' questions, to provide additional information, to overcome resistance, and to motivate. Also, generic examples provide counselors an excellent opportunity to use their professional experiences as a source of financial possibilities for clients.

Using Your Voice

Counselors can employ voice inflection, intonation, volume, and speech rate to make suggestions or to emphasize important concepts. This natural part of the communication process is most effective when counselors *mark* their words. Marking is a process of you highlighting certain words or phrases. This places emphasis on their meaning. Exaggerating voice inflection, intonation, volume, or speech rate does this. People who have developed the use of marking can make suggestions indirectly and seed ideas in the listener. When you walked into the house as a youngster and a parent said your name in a loud clear voice, you automatically knew you were in trouble. Very often when parents want a child to listen carefully, they will *mark* their words by raising or lowering their voices.

This marking of words to emphasize points can be done in many ways. Consider this excerpt:

> "At this agency we try to help you *practice* good money management. Come in and let us show you *what you have* to gain from what we have *learned* about making your money grow."

The words in Italics seem to make sense as they are written. Read the sentences out loud and place emphasis on the words that are italicized. Then read only the italicized words. You will notice that they form a sentence that suggests that you practice the skills and concepts you have learned while reading this book.

Consider this second example:

> "In these times of high inflation it's hard to maintain your ability to buy. We want to *look into* managing your finances to your best advantage. Copies of Everybody's Money are available from our *Financial Planning* staff. Why not let us guide you toward financial independence."

Again, notice that several words are italicized. When you read these words, you will notice that an idea has been seeded to have you *look into Financial Planning.*

The spoken word can be emphasized in the same way as the written word. In talking to a client you might say, "I believe that it is important for you to consider a regular investment program, one in which *you invest* a minimum of *$100 per month."* In this statement, the words *invest $100 per month* are emphasized through voice inflection or volume. Emphasis on these words would seed the idea that the client should regularly invest $100 per month.

The process of using your voice can be used to seed ideas, as above, make suggestions, encourage client actions, motivate new behaviors, or to acknowledge past events. With practice, financial counselors can control a very important communicative skill.

Using Stories

Using stories to teach or illustrate points is a natural process. The use of stories has been one of the most powerful teaching techniques of all the great leaders in history. Jesus taught primarily through the use of parables - short teaching stories. The same is true of Buddha and other great leaders. This normal process can be applied to financial counseling as well. Using short stories to illustrate points can be used for a variety of purposes.

Use Stories To Establish Relationships

Building an effective relationship with clients is central to effective counseling. The relationship should be characterized by openness, honesty, and trust. Counselors can set the tone for relationships by sharing with their clients several short stories about the way they have worked with other clients. This accomplishes several important things. First, it communicates to the clients how the counselor would like to work with them and shares the counselors' working style. Second, counselors can use early story-telling times as a means of client assessment. If counselors carefully watch clients as they relate several stories about different clients in differing situations, they will be able to determine which approaches may be most effective. Consider the following interchange as an example of this point:

> **Client:** I'd like to start a savings program right away.
>
> **Financial Counselor:** I can see that you are anxious to start a savings program, but it's a little hard to jump into this cold, so let me give you some idea of savings programs other clients have established. I had one client who wanted to maximize his rate of return so he went with a two-year certificate of deposit. Another client was more interested in liquidity. She chose to save through regular deposits to her savings account. Still another client found a payroll deduction plan met her needs best. She made deposits into her Pioneer Fund account.

In the above example the counselor must tell the story *and* observe the clients' reactions to each of the three segments. Usually, clients will give some indication of which client story is most like them. Clients will do this nonverbally. They may frown or shake their head *no* to one example, while smiling, leaning forward, or nodding *yes* to another. These actions provide clues as to which approach is most appropriate. If clients do not provide a nonverbal reaction or the counselor is unable to observe differences in nonverbal behavior, all is not lost. The counselor can follow the story with a simple question, "Which of these clients appears to be most like you?" In either case the story can be used to assess the kinds of savings program the client is interested in and assess the client's motivations.

Use Stories To Seed Ideas

There may be times when you notice clients lack information or seem to have their minds made up. Counselors can use stories to seed ideas for them to consider. For example, the counselor might say to a client, "In our discussion of limited partnerships, I was reminded of a friend of mine who wanted to put his money to work with little risk. He, too, considered certain limited partnerships, but then he realized he could get a steady return on his money through triple A rated bonds."

Obviously, in this example you could suggest investing in any vehicle you wish the client to consider. Through this process, you can make suggestions without raising the client's defenses. It is merely a story about some other client. If it has meaning to the present client, then the client will accept the idea. If it does not have meaning for the client, the client will ignore it as an interesting little anecdote.

Use Stories To Suggest Alternative Ways Of Acting

A counselor might tell clients several stories about other clients and their success with particular financial strategies. This will indirectly suggest areas for them to consider. For instance, the counselor might say, "One client I had was concerned about making adequate provisions for his family if he died. He established a trust fund for each of his children and one for his wife." This *story* could be used to indirectly suggest that trust funds are good, as well as to suggest several kinds of trust funds the client might consider.

Use Stories To Motivate Clients

Stories can motivate clients to act. There are two ways of doing this. First, counselors can tell clients stories about some of their clients or people they have known who have made bad decisions and who have had disastrous experiences because they did not plan or did not use their resources appropriately. By implication counselors suggest to clients that if they continue in the same vein, they also will have disastrous results. The danger in telling only disastrous stories is that clients may dismiss them as not being applicable to them.

The second way to use motivational stories is to tell clients several stories about former clients who have had both successes and failures. By alternating or incorporating both positive and negative examples, you can accomplish two things. You can motivate clients to act and you can suggest possible investment ideas. The use of stories to motivate creates a "no lose" situation. If the stories have any meaning to clients, they will isolate the meaning that is right for them. If the story does not tap some part of their representational map, the stories become nothing more than interesting anecdotes. In either case no harm is done.

When stories are used in counseling, clients are given an opportunity to meaningfully identify with characters in the story and apply their own meaning. The counselor does not have to tell clients directly what it is they should or should not do. The counselor can, however, use stories to offer suggestions, make recommendations, and seed ideas. Very often, after clients have heard stories like these, they will return with new ideas about their situation, ideas that were, most often, suggested in the story. The ideas then belong to the clients. Once ideas are *owned* by clients, chances for follow through are increased.

CONCLUSION

There are many ways to communicate. This chapter has examined a number of the more powerful, yet subtle ways of helping clients examine new information or influencing clients to take action in their own behalf. All of the forms presented should be used strategically to foster client self-responsibility. When used in this way, they can insure that clients will achieve their goals and objectives in the most expeditious manner.

RESOURCES

Efran, J.S., Lukens, M.D., & Lukens, R.J. (1990). *Language Structure And Change*. New York: W.W. Norton.

deShazer, S. (1994). *Words Were Originally Magic*. New York: W.W. Norton.

Lankton, S. (1980). *Practical Magic*. Cupertino: Meta Publications.

Land, G. & Jarman, B. (1992). *Breakpoint And Beyond.* New York: Harper Business.

Rosen, S. (Ed.).(1982). *My Voice Will Go With You.* New York: W.W. Norton.

7 DECISION MAKING AND PROBLEM SOLVING

> Creative thinking requires an attitude that allows you to search for ideas and manipulate your knowledge and experience. With this outlook, you try various approaches, first one, then another, often not getting anywhere. You use crazy, foolish, and impractical ideas as stepping stones to practical new ideas. You break the rules occasionally, and explore for ideas in unusual outside places. In short, by adopting a creative outlook you open yourself up both to new possibilities and change.
>
> *von Oech, R. (1990, p.6)*

INTRODUCTION

We discussed communication strategies used to develop and maintain effective working relationships, and strategies that provide the foundation for pacing, exploring, and motivating clients. We now turn attention to another stage of the overall counseling process, ways counselors can apply principles of problem-solving and decision-making to help clients achieve their goals. Specific strategies and tactics can be used to facilitate decision-making and problem-solving; strategies and tactics dependent on concepts of communication presented in previous chapters.

All decision-making and problem-solving strategies have strengths and weaknesses. Their relative merit depends on client needs and client learning styles. People who place a high value on rational thinking or who have an auditory learning style usually select systematic, logical strategies. People who are more kinesthetic or intuitive usually prefer divergent strategies.

Clients may respond better to particular problem-solving or decision-making strategies because of their specific needs or individual learning styles. Therefore, it is important for financial counselors to have a broad repertoire of strategies so that they can adapt to needs and learning styles of various clients.

In this chapter, we will present several decision-making and problem-solving strategies. You should be able to use each, as appropriate, in the manner presented. In addition, you should be able to understand the underlying concepts so that you can adapt, change, or combine various elements to fit needs and learning styles of particular clients.

Decision-making strategies are used when plans and procedures are needed to achieve specific goals. Problem-solving strategies are used when obstacles are encountered that prevent us from achieving goals. Problem solving focuses on how to remove or circumvent obstacles. In practical reality, however, accomplishing goals also often entails removing obstacles. Therefore, processes used in problem-solving and decision-making are very similar and there is overlap between the two.

The effectiveness of decision-making and problem-solving strategies is determined by the degree to which they help achieve specific goals. If the desired goal is reached, we probably would judge the strategy to be effective. If it fails to help us accomplish our goals, we are likely to judge it ineffective. Consider the following example. Two people invest equal amounts of money using identical decision-making processes. If one person doubles his or her money while the other loses, the first person is likely to judge the decision-making strategy as *good,* while the second person is likely to judge the strategy as *bad.* Neither judgment is necessarily true.

The *process* of decision-making or problem-solving must be separated from the *outcome.* Many things in the financial world that can affect outcomes are beyond the counselor's or client's control. Effective decision-making and problem-solving strategies are designed to take into account as many contingencies as possible, recognizing that it is impossible to account for them all. There is always an element of luck or chance that can affect outcomes.

A major problem with judging strategies on the basis of outcome is that if a strategy does not produce the desired results in one situation, it will be dismissed in other situations for which it might be highly appropriate. On the other hand, if a strategy is successful in achieving goals, it may be used inappropriately in another situation. Keep in mind that the value of decision-making and problem-solving strategies is determined by applicability of the process to a particular situation. With different needs or goals, alternative strategies may be more appropriate.

METHODS

People use a number of decision-making and problem-solving methods to achieve goals or to remove obstacles. Dilley (1970) outlined seven basic methods:

Decision Making and Problem Solving
Seven Basic Methods

Follow an accepted rule
Utilize a rational process
Act to gain social approval
Follow intuition
Leave it to fate or chance
Arrange a compromise
Consult an expert

These seven perspectives have stood the test of time. It is as apparent now as it was thirty years ago that when people need to make a decision or to solve a problem, they subconsciously use one or more of these methods. An understanding of the natural decision-making and problem-solving processes clients might use can provide a basis for helping clients to make effective financial decisions or to solve financial problems. Each of the seven methods is described below. Keep in mind that while they are separated for discussion, they can be used in various combinations.

FOLLOWING AN ACCEPTED RULE

People often make decisions by applying what they consider to be a relevant rule to the situation. They may apply the first rule that comes to mind, or review several rules and apply the one that seems to have the greatest power in the specific situation. Clients can develop financial problems by following accepted rules, rules that have become part of our culture or that have been promulgated by advertising to benefit certain industries. Some commonly used "rules" are:

- Buy now, pay later.
- You don't have to wait until you have cash.
- Use your credit. You need a good credit rating.
- Buying on credit allows you to deduct interest and then pay for things with inflated dollars.

- As long as you make the minimum payment each month you will keep your credit rating.
- Travel now, pay later.
- Buy low, sell high.
- Don't put all your eggs into one basket. Develop a broad-based savings plan.

Such "rules" are designed to simplify complicated situations. Following an accepted rule works well in situations that repeat themselves regularly. One of the major limitations of following an accepted rule as a decision-making or problem-solving method is that there may be conflicting rules which apply to the same situation and then one is left with trying to decide which is most appropriate. For example, "Leverage your money" and "You can get the best deals if you pay cash" could both be good advice. However, they directly contradict each other in some situations.

A second major problem with following an accepted rule is that people often use them as mandates rather than as guidelines. Therefore, counselors should not only help clients become aware of the rules they follow, they should also help them become cognizant of the positive aspects of their rules. Finally, counselors also need to caution clients against potential negative consequences of adhering to rules. The difficulty is not in the rules, but rather in their inappropriate use.

UTILIZING A RATIONAL PROCESS

There are a number of rational decision-making or problem-solving strategies. The underlying purpose in using a rational process is to predict possible consequences of various choices or actions. By examining possible consequences, people attempt to narrow their choices to those that have the greatest potential for positive outcomes and the least potential for negative outcomes.

Clients frequently make financial decisions based on their feelings or needs rather than on logical evaluation of information. When clients make decisions that are based on primary needs such as the need for security or status, counselors may fail to understand their motivation and wonder why they are not more logical in their choices. A valuable service that counselors can provide is to encourage clients to identify their needs, help them to understand how their needs relate to their financial behavior and goals, and teach them to understand the value of rational decision-making and problem-solving strategies. A number of such strategies will be described later in this chapter.

Acting To Gain Social Approval

Clients may attempt to identify with people they admire or value. Decisions they make are made to be consistent with those values. The phrase "Keeping up with the Jones'" exemplifies how individuals attempt to conform to others, and how external influence is subtle, yet powerful. Individuals are influenced both subtly and openly to do "as others are doing." One way financial counselors can use knowledge of this process with clients is by using *expert* opinions as a means of generating possible plans of action.

Financial counselors often rely on the considered opinions of experts for financial information and investment strategies. While this use of expert opinion is one way of helping clients to make decisions or to solve problems, clients must remember that they are ultimately responsible for their decisions. Expert opinions never guarantee results. In the final analysis, clients must consider information from relevant sources and then make their own decisions.

Following Intuition

People often act without thinking things through completely. Impulsive buying is an example. A number of sayings or "rules" caution against impulsive or intuitive type buying: "Never shop when you're hungry," "Look before you leap," "Do you really need it?," "Don't buy it just because it is a bargain," or "Don't commit yourself to a particular car!" People also make decisions based on their hunches or feelings. Good poker players often explain their success by saying that they have good hunches. Intuition or hunches are often based on subconscious information, information that is learned over time and leads to the "feeling" that one choice may be better than another in a given situation. Intuitive decision making or problem solving often appears to be impulsive, but may, in fact, be based on solid subconsciously stored and processed information.

There are two things to keep in mind about intuitive decision making or problem solving. First, people often buy or invest impulsively in a manner that can eventually cause financial problems. It is not that intuitive, impulsive buying is wrong. Rather, when a *pattern* of impulsive buying develops, a financial problem is more likely to occur. Of course, it will be a problem only if the results of impulsive actions are negative. If, for example, someone invests in the stock market using "hunches" as an investment strategy and continues to make money, who is to say it is wrong? Most of us, however, would say that they are lucky and would predict that in time their hunches will catch up with them.

Second, intuitive, creative thought usually does not occur without days, months, and even years of hard work. Intuitive, creative decisions that produce good results usually are based on a substantial amount of previously obtained information, much of which may be subconscious. Experience, especially financial experience, increases the probability that intuitive decision making or problem solving will produce positive results. Do not dismiss your intuition or that of your clients. Use of the complementary processes of intuitive and rational methods may increase the probability of generating positive outcomes.

Leaving It To Fate

Any process that involves chance (roll of the die, lottery, and palm reading), luck, or accident belongs in this class. In addition, processes that involve using data that has no known logical connection with the issue at hand also fit this category. People who use their social security number, the numeric representation of their birth date, or their car's serial number as a basis for buying lottery tickets are relying on fate.

Leaving things to fate is a strategy often used by people to solve problems. The old saying "Leave it alone and maybe it will go away" exemplifies this kind of decision-making. People often hope that if they ignore things long enough fate or chance will cure everything. Financial counseling relationships are, of course, based on assumptions directly contrary to this method of decision-making or problem-solving. As a financial counselor, you should help clients become aware of the difficulties that can arise from leaving their financial lives to fate.

Arranging A Compromise

Arranging a compromise is a process that benefits at least two different people or that incorporates aspects of two different processes. In order to compromise, involved parties must give up something. If one party is not willing to compromise, then a different form of conflict resolution must be used. Arranging a compromise is often an integral part of financial counseling when dealing with two or more clients. This is especially true when working with couples.

Consulting An Expert

When people come to you as a financial counselor, they are generally using the method of consulting an expert. They see you as having more information, more experience, and a better understanding of the financial world than they possess. Their expectation may be that, because of your expertise, you will be able to make decisions for them. Consequently, you are obligated to define your role early in your counseling relationship, to share with your clients your perceived areas of expertise, to alert clients to referral sources you are accustomed to using, and to discuss decisions that you can and cannot make in the their behalf. The major danger with clients that choose to "consult an expert" is that they may expect you to make decisions for them. This may be appropriate in situations where someone has been appointed as the executor of an estate or a trust fund. However, in most situations, it is inappropriate to take responsibility for making clients' decisions. It is not inappropriate, however, to use your expertise to generate alternatives from which clients can make choices.

The seven decision-making and problem-solving strategies discussed above describe how people attempt to deal with their finances. No one method is better than the others in all situations. Methods can be combined to produce additional ways that people use to make decisions and solve problems. An implicit goal in most financial counseling is to help people to make their own decisions and to solve their own problems. In this sense, counselors should become experts in decision-making and problem-solving processes. One of the most valuable things counselors have to offer clients is the very process they use to help them. The anonymous quote, "If I give you a fish, I have fed you for a day. If I teach you how to fish, I have fed you for a lifetime" attests to the value of teaching clients a process that will make them more effective in their own right. To do this, counselors should become conversant with many different decision-making and problem-solving processes.

TYPES OF STRATEGIES

Two major classifications of decision-making and problem-solving methods are important in professional financial relationships: rational or logical strategies and intuitive or creative strategies. These two classifications correspond to the way our brain processes information. The left hemisphere tends to process information in logical, step-by-step, rational ways. By contrast, the right hemisphere tends to be more intuitive, feeling, and holistic. Remember, however, that the hemispheres do not operate in an isolated fashion, so that while we may be approaching a problem or decision in a very rational manner, our intuition and feelings are still operative and affect what we do. The following strategies reflect differences in hemispheric functioning. However, in most financial counseling the best strategy is an integrated one, one that uses aspects of both hemispheres.

Rational and Logical Strategies

The key to most rational methods is that they follow a sequential step-by-step format. As clients logically and sequentially move through the steps, there is a progressive narrowing to a decision or solution that can be applied to the situation. We will present five such rational methods.

Rational Problem Solving and Decision Making Methods

Binary System

Systematic Solution Generation

Systematic Solution Evaluation

Time Zero

Force Field Analysis.

Binary System

The Binary System decision-making process has five steps. They are used after the client has determined *what needs to be decided.* This system is especially useful in situations where a client is deciding on making a purchase.

The Binary System steps are:

- Define absolutes
- Define nice-to-haves
- Predict the future by examining the past
- Eliminate "nice-to-haves" and adjust absolutes
- Go with the best, balanced choice

Consider the following example. Mary, a financial counselor, was helping a client to purchase a new car. She asked her client to list all the features that the new car *must* have for it to be considered for purchase. In addition, Mary asked her client to elaborate on any additional features that would make the purchase of the car *more* attractive. Mary helped her client to examine both lists of features, those that were *absolutely* necessary and those that would be *nice to have* but not mandatory. Mary then asked her client to examine each feature and to project how frequently the feature would be used. To help her client to do this, Mary said, "One of the best ways to determine how often something will be used in the future is to look backward in time and to ask yourself, 'If I had that in the past, how often would I have used it?'" By getting her client to look backward, Mary provided a means for helping her client to understand what *probably* would happen in the future. Information gained in this manner was then used to help the client to eliminate alternatives that probably would be little used. Through this approach, Mary helped her client make a balanced choice, one that reflected needs and wants while eliminating alternatives that might be *nice* but not necessary.

Systematic Solution Generation

The brainstorming strategy outlined below incorporates six logical left hemispheric steps. In addition, it also uses right hemispheric processes that rely on intuition.

- Identify a need (or needs)
- Establish a goal (or goals)
- Examine resources
- Brainstorm possible solutions
- Do not censor
- Do not clarify
- Do not assign names
- Use other people's ideas
- Select a solution or combination of solutions
- Evaluate in light of needs and goals

Consider Dana, who went to her financial counselor for help in the development of a savings plan. Dana's financial counselor asked Dana what she hoped to accomplish through a savings program. As a result of the ensuing discussion, Dana realized that she was most interested in preparing for an early retirement and, consequently, she established a goal of having $200,000 committed to savings and investments in the next fifteen- year period.

Dana's financial counselor helped Dana to use this long-term goal to establish intermediate goals, and then helped Dana to examine all of her financial resources that would be used to achieve both sets of goals. In this discussion, the financial counselor focused on monetary assets such as wages, savings, investments, and financial inheritances as well as on personal resources such as motivation, commitment, and willingness to take risks.

After Dana and the financial counselor discussed these resources in detail, the financial counselor helped Dana to *brainstorm* all possible means for Dana to reach her financial goals. This led Dana to consider many ideas, some of which had potential merit, some of which did not. Of the many ideas that were generated, Dana was able to select a savings and investment strategy that allowed her to save and invest on a regular basis, in a manner that maximized her chances of reaching both her intermediate and long-term goals.

Finally, Dana's financial counselor established a systematic means for assessing on a periodic basis the degree to which Dana was meeting her goals. This provided Dana a way to work toward her goals *and* the flexibility to adjust to a changing financial climate.

SYSTEMATIC EVALUATION

The rational decision-making strategy described below incorporates steps and concepts from several other strategies. As with the strategies described above, the method consists of logical steps designed to help clients make the best, balanced decisions.

- Examine needs
- Establish goals
- Generate alternative solutions
- Estimate the costs of each solution in terms of money, emotions, time, effort, social relations, etc.
- Outline the benefits of each solution
- Determine the likelihood of success for each solution
- Consider the seriousness of failure of each solution
- Set a game plan for each solution: If accepted, who will do *what, when,* and *where*

The strength of this strategy lies in its ability to provide a systematic examination of potential alternative solutions. The example that follows demonstrates how this strategy can be applied to a financial concern.

Kelvin inherited $100,000, which he wished to invest. In thinking about possible investments, Kelvin was aware that he had a need for security and, yet, that he was willing to take moderate risks so that his money would appreciate faster than the rate of inflation. With this in mind, Kelvin began to actively think about ways to achieve his financial goal.

He generated a number of alternatives. Some would meet his goal of staying ahead of inflation, whereas others would not. Some entailed high risk, others were relatively risk free. To be systematic in his approach, Kelvin decided to examine all alternatives by applying the strategy presented above.

One of the alternatives that Kelvin considered was to invest his money in a multiple-unit apartment building. It became apparent to Kelvin that this alternative would have a number of *costs*. In addition to the obvious *financial* costs for a down payment, closing costs, legal fees, and insurance outlays, Kelvin became aware of the amount of *time* he might have to commit to overseeing this investment. The *effort* he might have to expend to assure that the investment would be productive, and the *worry* he might have about his undertaking also must be considered.

Kelvin also became aware of the many potential *benefits* of this alternative. He realized that he probably would make an annual profit that would exceed the annual rate of inflation; that his investment, if properly maintained, would increase in value; that he would feel good about owning a multiple unit; and that his investment would be relatively risk free.

Kelvin then rated his chances of being successful with this alternative on a ten point scale, with *ten* being a high degree of success, and determined that his chances of success would be about *nine out of ten*.

Kelvin then decided how serious failure would be. He determined, on a ten point scale in which *ten* would be very serious, that failure on this alternative would be quite serious to his long-term financial plans and, therefore, rated failure as a potential *ten*.

Kelvin did not set a game plan for this alternative because he wanted to find a more ideal alternative, one that had *a high likelihood of success* and a low *seriousness of failure*.

Kelvin then repeated this process for all of the solutions he had generated. Once he settled on an alternative, he made decisions about *who* would do *what, when,* and *where* to initiate action on the chosen alternative.

Time Zero

The Time Zero problem-solving approach was developed by John P. Decker (1978) at Arizona State University as a rational approach for dealing with personality clashes or conflicts. The title, Time-Zero suggests that the time for doing something about a problem is always in the present (now, the time is zero) and that the past, although a source of information, should not be dwelled on. This method has been taught to engineers and other professionals who are in supervisory positions and who are called on to resolve personality clashes. The method is based on an assumption that nearly all personality conflicts between people follow the same basic pattern. Once the basic pattern is recognized, the problem-solving strategy can be used to bring about resolution. This method of problem resolution is important for financial counselors in several ways:

- Supervising employees
- Dealing with fellow professionals
- Helping clients resolve interpersonal conflicts.

When interpersonal conflicts arise, usually a high degree of emotionality is involved. People became angry and feel hurt, depressed, or confused. As they attempt to deal with their feelings, there is a tendency to look for excuses to justify how they feel. Once strong emotions are activated, people tend to generalize and to blame others.

Step 1: Identify Common Errors

The first step in the Time Zero problem solving method is to identify common errors that people exhibit when they become emotionally aroused. The common errors are defined below.

Faulty statement of the problem. People tend to make faulty statements of their problem in one of two ways. The first is to use imprecise words to express both the existence of a problem and to express their feelings. For example, "I'm in trouble with John now" or "I've really got a problem" are statements which express strong feelings but lack any reference to what the problem might be. The second "faulty" reaction is to generalize from the conflict situation. That is, people often use a single conflict situation to make general judgments about their relationships with other people. After getting into an argument about how to invest, one spouse might generalize by saying something like, "He never listens to me and what I want to do. He just bulldozes me into what he wants to do." In this case, the client is expressing a strong feeling and in the process has generalized to every experience of discussing investments. People frequently generalize to justify their strong feelings.

Impulsive explanation. Another way in which people attempt to justify their strong feelings is to place the responsibility for their feelings on others. When people do this, it appears that they are saying that they have a right to feel as they do because others did something that *made* them angry, frustrated, or hurt. Usually, inherent in these forms of explanations is some negative judgment about either the character or the behavior of others. Returning to the previous example, the spouse might give an impulsive explanation such as, "He is just so pushy all the time. He thinks he knows everything and thinks that, as a woman, I'm just dumb when it comes to managing money." Notice that the explanation revolves around making negative judgments about both the character of the spouse and assumptions about the way he thinks. Again, the primary purpose is to blame the other person for the feelings that were activated during the conflict.

Impulsive solution. When conflicts arise, the natural tendency is to want to punish others. Having generalized and blamed others for present feelings, people usually attempt some solution which will "get them even." The punishing and getting even is often self-defeating. That is, the solution of punishing others usually maintains the conflict, intensifies feelings, and often makes the original problem situation worse. Again, returning to the conflict between spouses, "I'll fix him. I'll just spend all my money on something I want, and I won't even discuss investing with him again." The impulsive solution becomes self-defeating in that the conflict may be intensified, and the person is inhibiting herself from making wise investment decisions.

Plea for endorsement. A plea for endorsement can take place in two ways. First, implicitly, through tone of voice and nonverbal behavior clients may ask you to agree with how they have defined the problem, with their impulsive explanation, or with their impulsive solution. Secondly, explicitly, clients may ask for your agreement. For example, "Isn't that right?" or "Don't you agree that it's a bad choice?" or "Isn't that what you would do?" It is important for you to recognize when clients are seeking your agreement so that you do not get forced into a position counter to your beliefs. Once you get forced into agreeing with how your clients defined the problem, accepting their impulsive explanation, or agreeing with their impulsive solution, you will have lost your ability to help them move to an alternative way of solving the problem.

Time Zero problem solving methods revolve around accurately assessing the situation. As you listen to your client who is in a conflict situation, you attempt to identify each of the common errors outlined above. This can provide you with a better understanding of your client and some understanding of the situation. Keep in mind, however, that the four common errors are not produced in all conflict situations. There may be times that clients will define their problem in a faulty way and move directly to some form of impulsive solution without going through, on a conscious level, the blaming involved in the impulsive explanation. Thus, when a client or colleague brings an interpersonal conflict to you, there is potential for any or all of the common errors. After you have listened to or elicited the person's explanations, you can use the six-step process (see Principle 9.4, Chapter Nine) to help him or her resolve the problem.

Step 2: Calm the Person

People usually are in an emotional state when they seek help. Good problem solving involves reasoning. Yet, it may be difficult to be logical when strong emotions are being exhibited. A productive approach to reducing emotional responses and to calming aroused individuals is to use verbal pacing tactics by restating or paraphrasing at the emotional or theme level. This communicates that you accept the individual's emotions and are willing to deal with them. Your purpose at this point is to calm the person so that the two of you can discuss on a more rational level what has happened.

Step 3: Attend To The Present Moment And Identify The Trigger Event

The present moment is time zero, the beginning of the future. People often continue their emotional upset by reliving the past. The more they think about the past and what occurred, the more upset they become. This starts a negative cycle. The more upset they become, the more likely they are to relive old experiences. This, in turn, reinforces the feelings and so on, in a never-ending circle.

This negative cycle limits the ability to think rationally about the situation. People often project past experiences to future imagined encounters with others. They start to imagine future encounters occurring in the same manner as past encounters. This limits their ability to solve problems rationally.

We can help people move to time zero by helping them focus on the trigger event, the one thing that happened which led to the present emotional upset. Usually one or more stimuli bring on a strong emotional response. Your goal is to help the person identify the trigger event in the present conflict situation. For instance, you could ask your client, "What one specific thing happened that led to your present feelings?"

Step 4: Help The Person Decide What To Do Next

In this step, the person moves toward establishing goals. The goals should relate specifically to the conflict situation and to the trigger event. Such goals are most easily stated in terms of what the person wants in future encounters with others. In the example above, you might ask the spouse, "What do you want to happen when you talk to your husband about money?" The client might respond, "I want him to listen to me. I want him to recognize that I have some good ideas too!" At this point, you have successfully moved the client to the present - time zero. You have identified the trigger event and have helped the client decide what is desired in the future.

Step 5: Help The Person Develop A Plan

The plan will vary with the type of conflict, but it often will focus on how the person can respond in future potential conflict situations. In our example above, it might include deciding specifically what the person might say when the next trigger event occurs. For example, "The next time your husband acts that way, what do you think you could do differently?" The client might respond, "Well, I guess I could tell him how I'm feeling." The financial counselor might respond, "What specifically would you say?" At this point, the goal is to develop specific steps that can be thought through and even rehearsed as preparation for future interactions.

In other conflict situations the plan may focus on specific steps similar to those we develop to accomplish other types of goals, such as developing a marketing plan or sales plan. The emphasis should be on specifics regarding *who* is going to do *what, when,* and *where?* It also may be constructive during this step to help the person compare the new plan of action with the old, impulsive process that fostered the conflict.

Step 6: Help The Person To Become Self-Monitoring.

One of the most valuable things we can do for clients is to teach them the very process we used to help them. Of course, this is done implicitly when we use a method such as the *Time Zero* approach. However, we cannot assume that just because people experience a process they have learned it. The method used with a client in one situation probably will be helpful to the client in similar future situations. This is accomplished by discussing with clients steps you have used and how they might be applied to other conflict situations.

Force Field Analysis

The Force Field Analysis technique is based upon three assumptions about people and their problems. First, people can be understood best in relation to their physical and psychological situation. Very few individuals live isolated, totally autonomous lives. Rather, they are in constant interaction with their physical environment and with others in their social context. Those with whom they are involved vary from immediate family and friends to associates at work, individuals from the neighborhood, and people from society at large. The physical and social context is called a *field.* Understanding any person rests upon knowledge of the individual and their field. Second, there are forces within the field that individuals affect and which, in turn, affect them. As individuals grow they are affected by significant others in their lives. Typical adults, for instance, agree substantially with their parents on such basic items as language, religion, politics, and child rearing. This basic agreement between child and parents indicates the effect parents have on their children. At the same time, children affect their parents. For example, parents usually change rearing practices for second or third children as a result of experience with the first child.

Third, forces operating within a person's field can be *positive* or *negative.* This concept is apparent in the statement, "Well, it's no wonder he turned out the way he did. Look at the family he comes from." Such a statement can be made about someone who has trouble with the law, as well as someone who achieves well, graduates from college and takes over the family business. Positive and negative forces exist in all situations. A person's experience and field of interaction determines how the individual will respond to these forces. The Force Field Analysis technique is a way to identify forces and to use them as a basis for generating solutions to the client's problem.

Positive and negative forces interact within a person's field to maintain some degree of balance. Consider a tug-of-war contest. In such an event, if both teams apply equal pressure, balance is achieved. When one team weakens inequality occurs, one team gets pulled across the goal line, and a winner is declared. As long as both teams apply equal force, however, there will be balance and no visible movement. Yet, during this balanced period, both teams will be exerting a considerable amount of energy. The longer the contest goes on, the more painful it becomes. In a similar manner, clients can maintain balance between positive and negative forces in the financial aspects of their lives, but this balancing process can become difficult. When it does, they frequently turn to financial counselors for help.

When people develop financial problems, they may feel as if they are at an impasse, with lack of movement toward problem solution. A client may have positive forces such as a continuous income, savings, and motivation to work through financial difficulties balanced against the negative forces of easy access to credit cards, a number of outstanding bills, and upcoming educational expenses for children. The client might be all right now, but can foresee difficulties in the near future. Desire to break the balance frequently is what brings clients to counseling. An important aspect of the Force Field Analysis technique is identification of positive and negative forces. Once forces have been identified and those amenable to change have been isolated, solution generation focuses on how positive forces can be amplified and negative forces can be diminished or eliminated to achieve counseling goals. There are five specific steps for using a Force Field Analysis in financial counseling.

1. Determine the problem and write a goal statement.
2. Identify positive/negative forces that are impacting the problem.
3. Rank, from most powerful through least powerful, the relative power of all forces.

4. Rate the ranked forces as to possibility of change. Give a rating of *one* to forces that would be easy to change, a rating of *five* to those that would be difficult to change and a rating of *three* for forces that would be moderately difficult to change.

5. Determine *what* will be done by *whom*, *how* and *when*.

In applying this technique, help the client to be as specific as possible about the problem and to identify a goal(s) which is achievable and measurable. Encourage the client to be thorough in generating positive and negative forces. In examining forces, be aware that some forces are more amenable to amplification or change than others. Also, some forces do not need amplification. For example, if the client's motivation to change is high (a positive force), there would be no reason to try to increase it. Finally, in using this technique, it is important that you help the client to work with those forces that are of the highest rank (the ones that have been determined to be the most important) and have the highest rating (the most amenable to change).

Frequently, the process of using the Force Field Analysis reveals a number of areas that need clarification. When this happens it is usually because the original problem and/or goal have not been clearly developed. It is not unusual to do several Force Field processes, each time, developing increased clarity. Consider a counselor working with a client on a problem of negative cash flow with a negative force listed by the client as the easy use of credit cards. The counselor might use a separate Force Field Analysis to help the client understand this force. The second Force Field Analysis could help the client to clarify forces operating to maintain misuse of credit cards. This could eventually diminish or eliminate the negative impact of the credit card usage by providing direction relative to controlling their use. While second and sometimes additional force field analyses may be useful, over diagnosis should be avoided. Clients may become discouraged and lose motivation to work on original counseling concerns.

The Force Field is complete when the problem has been clearly stated, a specific goal(s) has been identified, positive and negative forces have been identified, forces have been ranked from most important to least important and for ease of change; and decisions have been made about *who* will do *what when* to achieve the goal(s).

In all of the rational decision-making and problem-solving approaches described above, emphasis has been on logical thinking. Sequential steps help people to do that. Common to all of the approaches is the stating of goals, the orderly generation of potential solutions, and the evaluation of those solutions. The methods vary in the emphasis they place on kinds and forms of information they use to arrive at meaningful solutions. The difficulty with most rational approaches is not in the methods or processes, but in the people who use them. It is difficult to stay on a purely logical or rational level. We each have values, attitudes, beliefs, and feelings that, at times, disrupt our logic. The saying "Don't confuse me with the facts. My mind is already made up!" exemplifies how values, attitudes, beliefs, and feelings can defy logical, rational thinking. Rational problem-solving and decision-making take effort and time. Often we prefer to do what comes naturally or intuitively. This is not to say that rational approaches are not powerful processes. People would probably make better decisions in their lives if they were more rational, but there are other ways of problem-solving and decision-making that are useful. These other forms can be classified as being right hemispheric or intuitive methods.

Intuitive And Creative Strategies

Rational decision-making and problem-solving approaches proceed in a stepwise fashion, with each step forming the basis for the next step. You cannot start in the middle because the foundations of the previous steps have not been laid. You start from what you know and go straight ahead, following the steps sequentially. For the outcome of rational processes to be effective, each step in the process must produce desired results. Rational approaches are highly esteemed, and rightly so. However, they are not the only way of arriving at solutions.

At times people have "bright ideas" that seem to pop into their heads and that frequently seem to work. Whenever solutions are generated in this intuitive or creative way, you can usually see in hindsight how they could have been arrived at using rational processes. This usually is true, or the solution wouldn't be acceptable or producc the desired effects. In rational methods, we usually begin with certain psychological sets about the problem or situation. These sets then guide our logic and are used as a basis for evaluating both information and the steps used. Intuitive or creative decision-making and problem- solving, however, often disregard previous psychological sets or, at least, use different ones.

It may sound like a contradiction to have intuitive or creative problem-solving methods because they just seem to happen in our experience. Intuitive or creative methods are aimed at blocking our use of subconscious psychological sets and at forcing us to think about the decision or problem differently. They encourage free- thinking. While there are a large number of these intuitive or creative methods we will only describe six of them.

> **Intuitive and Creative Problem Solving and Decision Making Methods**
>
> Brainstorming
>
> Problem Expansion
>
> Problem Reversal
>
> Using Random Stimulus
>
> Making the Problem Worse
>
> Using a Solution to one Problem to Solve Another.

Brainstorming

Brainstorming is a process of free association. An individual can use it, but the process is more productive when used by two or more people. The basic premise of this approach is that ideas stimulate other ideas. Consequently, the general process of brainstorming involves saying or writing down all ideas or thoughts about a problem that come to mind. Ideas generated in this manner may, in turn, stimulate further ideas or thoughts. Keep in mind the following *rules* for brainstorming.

Rule 1: Avoid Censoring

The purpose of brainstorming is to generate as many ideas as possible. Yet, people have a natural tendency to evaluate their ideas before they voice them or write them down. Their assessment is often negative. They might think that the idea would never work in the given situation and, therefore, they tend not to share it. By avoiding the censoring process, individuals can say whatever comes to mind, no matter how relevant they think it might be. Ideas generated in this manner could stimulate others' thoughts about alternatives for the given concern.

Rule 2: Avoid Clarifying

Do not explain ideas or concepts. Clarifying has a tendency to slow down new idea generation. The purpose of brainstorming is to generate as many ideas as possible.

Rule 3: Avoid assigning names

When brainstorming is used with two or more people, there may be an inclination to assign names to specific ideas, i.e., Joe came up with idea X, Mary had idea Y, or Cindy thought of idea Z. Assigning names often slows down idea generation and limits the free reaction to an idea at later stages of brainstorming.

Rule 4: Use Other People's Ideas

Since the brainstorming process uses all available stimuli for generating ideas, one person's ideas or thoughts may stimulate another's ideas or thoughts. Consider the following as an example of this process.

> **Financial counselor***:* Well, Kathy, what thoughts have you had about developing a systematic savings plan?
>
> **Kathy***:* I've been thinking of some of the benefits, but so far I've only come up with the security it provides.
>
> **Financial counselor***:* Do you mean security from worry or security as a nest egg or something else?

> **Kathy***:* I guess I was just thinking about freedom from worry, but your questions make me think about a number of other things I should consider, like how much money do I need to save to feel secure?
>
> **Financial counselor***:* That's good. Let's brainstorm some of the things that a systematic savings plan can provide.

In this example, the financial counselor initially used the brainstorming process informally. In the financial counselor's last statement, you can see a movement toward a formal use of the technique.

Brainstorming encourages free association and, thus, breaks previously held assumptions and attitudes. The process encourages the generation of many possible solutions that subsequently can be evaluated on the basis of problem relevancy and potential effectiveness.

Problem Expansion

The problem expansion method combines two steps to help you get away from standard ways of thinking. The first step is to repeatedly define the problem. The second step requires that you use the brainstorming process to generate solutions for how you defined the problem each time. The problem expansion process can be used through a number of cycles, a cycle being the process of defining the problem and brainstorming solutions.

This process is usually most effective if used through at least three cycles. That is,

1. Define the problem and brainstorm solutions
2. Redefine the problem and brainstorm solutions
3. Again redefine the problem and brainstorm solutions

Very often people discover that no matter how they define the problem, similar solutions get generated in each brainstorming session. This may be the hallmark of a good solution, one that applies no matter how the problem is defined. Following are two examples, one to highlight the process and another to illustrate how this technique might be applied to a financial decision making or problem-solving situation.

Suppose you are driving to an important meeting. Suppose, as well, that you have allowed yourself just enough time to get to the meeting. While driving to the meeting, you discover you have a flat tire. When you look in the trunk for the jack and the spare tire, you notice that the jack is broken.

Given the situation as stated, how would you define the problem? The way you define the problem will affect the kinds of solutions you generate. If you define the problem as getting to the meeting on time, you might call a cab, hitchhike, or call someone you know to come and get you. If you define the problem as one of changing the tire, then you might stop another motorist to borrow a jack, call a service station to have someone come to fix the flat, or drive the car on the flat tire to the nearest service station. If you define the problem as a broken jack, you might try to fix the jack, flag down a passing motorist to borrow a jack; or find some other way of lifting the car so that you can change the tire. You might consider driving the car to a point where the flat tire is sitting in a deep hole or hanging over the edge of the road. Notice that each time you define the problem differently, different solutions result. Let's apply this technique of redefinition and brainstorming to a financial example.

Financial Counselor: Good morning, Ned. What brings you in today?

Ned: Good morning. I think I'm really stuck ...

Financial Counselor:: What seems to be the problem?

Ned: I'm having trouble meeting all of my expenses ... I don't seem to have enough money to go around.

Financial Counselor: Okay ... we can attack this in a number of ways ... let's just generate some ideas. Is that all right with you?

Ned: That sounds good to me.

Financial Counselor: Could it be that you don't have enough income?

Ned: I suppose so.

Financial Counselor:: How might you generate more income?

Ned: I could raise the rent on my apartment units, or I could work more hours at my part-time job, or I could even get a full-time job.

Financial Counselor: All of those are possibilities. Another way to look at your problem might be to cut down on your expenses. How might you do that?

Ned*:* That's a good idea ... I could do more around the apartments myself instead of paying others to do every little thing ... or I could see if I could get a better deal on some of the things I've been buying for the apartments ...

Financial Counselor: Excellent ideas. Now, let's switch the focus one more time. What besides income and expenses might be causing you to feel short of money?

Ned: I think that I've been pretty loose lately ... I've bought whatever I've wanted when I wanted it. I could just be more careful and get my family to do the same.

Financial Counselor:*:* It does sound as though there are a number of things that you could do to get over the difficulty you're in. Where would you like to begin?

Problem expansion forces us to break our initial way of thinking about the problem or decision-making situation by forcing us to *redefine* a number of times. Each new definition will lead to a new set of solutions. Remember, if the same solution seems to be generated no matter how you define the problem, you probably have identified at least one solution that could be effective.

Problem Reversal

Problem reversal, like other intuitive or creative methods, forces us to examine the decision or problem situation from a new or different perspective. To do this, you turn the decision or problem situation around and approach it from the end rather than from the beginning. A simple example will illustrate the process.

Imagine that you were asked to organize a singles tennis tournament at the annual financial institution picnic. One hundred clients signed up for the single elimination tournament - if you lose a match you are out of the tournament. The problem you are faced with is to determine how many matches will be needed to complete the competition. The natural, logical way most people would solve this problem is to create a tournament sheet. You would start with 50 matches from which there would be 50 winners. These 50 winners would then be paired for a second round of matches, and there would then be 25 new winners. At this point, there would have been 75 matches. You would proceed, logically, until you discovered how many matches you would need to declare a champion of the tournament.

Had you started at the end (problem reversal), however, you could have arrived at the answer much more quickly. The champion must win all matches and everyone else must lose. That means that we need as many matches as there are people ... less the one, the person who always wins. That means that we need 99 matches in the tournament. When you read the solution it makes logical sense, but notice that it was determined by proceeding in an intuitive, non-sequential manner. This same method can be applied in some financial situations. Consider Jane's interaction with her financial counselor, Gloria.

> **Gloria:** Jane, you've been trying to get a down payment together for that new house for some time now. How are you doing?
>
> **Jane***:* Not very well. I keep adding to my collection of antique glass and don't seem to have money left over for anything else. I've thought about not collecting for a while, but I truly enjoy the pieces and the process of collecting them. I'm not sure I'll ever have enough money for a down payment on a house!
>
> **Gloria***:* Maybe you already have what you need ... you might be able to use your antique glass as collateral for a down payment loan.
>
> **Jane:** Is that right? ... I've been trying to think of ways of coming up with the money and it may have been right in front of me all the time!

In this interchange, Gloria was able to *reverse* the problem by viewing Jane's antique glass collection as a form of savings, rather than as a drain on revenue. This intuitive perspective could provide Jane an alternative that could lead to solution of her problem.

Using A Random Stimulus

Intuitive or creative decision-making and problem-solving methods help break our normal attitudes and assumptions. Using a random stimulus forces us to do that. Using a random stimulus suggests that we utilize something which, on the surface, does not appear to apply to our decision or problem situation as a basis for generating new solutions. The most common random stimulus used is any word chosen randomly from a dictionary or a book.

The book is opened to any page, and a word is randomly selected. The word is used as a stimulus for brainstorming possible solutions. For example, one of the authors was working with a group of financial institution managers, one of whom mentioned that a major problem in the financial institution was dealing with a large number of clients at peak hours. The clients would stand in long lines and become impatient while waiting their turn. The clients would then take their impatience out on the tellers. A number of solutions had been tried, but none seemed to solve the problem. As a group, the financial institution managers were asked to use the random stimulus method to try to generate possible solutions. One of the managers had a book about Mexico with her. The author asked a manager to randomly open the book. He then had another manager point randomly to a word on the page. The word pointed to was *fiesta*, the Spanish word for a party. The group was then asked to brainstorm possible solutions by applying the word *fiesta* to the problem of long lines of customers. The group generated solutions similar to the following.

Make it a party.

Give out balloons.

Give a prize to the person who had to wait the longest.

Serve refreshments while people wait.

Play video cartoons for the children in one area of the lobby to keep them happy and occupied.

Have "theme" nights, when the tellers would dress up differently, in Mexican, Hawaiian, or Indian costume, for example.

Play music.

Have customers take a number and then go for refreshments or watch television until their number was called.

Greet the people at the door and give them a party favor for coming in on a busy night.

Get a popcorn wagon and hand out free popcorn.

The manager later reported that several ideas generated using random stimulus were combined and tried. The result was that clients expressed appreciation for the thoughtfulness. Clients were less likely to be angry and impatient with tellers, and tellers seemed to be able to keep their composure and respond to clients in more helpful and pleasant ways.

Making It Worse

One characteristic of problems is that when they are unresolved they tend to get worse. Making it worse is an intuitive or creative process that utilizes this concept by amplifying it. In effect, it begins with the question, "How can I possibly make the problem worse?" or "What can I do to make sure we have the worst possible outcome?" Once you have decided how you can make the problem worse or how you can guarantee that you will get the worst possible outcome, the focus is shifted to how you can use this perspective to solve the problem. Consider this example from industry.

> A chemical manufacturer situated in a northern state was having trouble with the reservoir water pumping system. The water, used as a coolant during the manufacturing process, was pumped continuously to and from the reservoir. The pumping station was located in the center of the reservoir, at its deepest point. During the winter the water would freeze and, at times, the pump in the station would also freeze. When the pumping station froze, the plant would shut down until the pump could be repaired. A number of different solutions had been tried, but none was entirely satisfactory.
>
> Finally, one of the plant engineers arrived at a creative solution using the process of "making it worse." In answer to the question, "What could you do to make sure the pump froze?" the engineer decided that the best way to accomplish that would be to pump liquid nitrogen into the pumping station. Liquid nitrogen is used to make dry ice. It freezes very quickly. If liquid nitrogen were pumped into the station, it would freeze into a solid block of ice. If that could be used to make sure the worst possible outcome was achieved, how could it be used to solve the problem? The engineer responded that you could probably pump something else into the station that wouldn't freeze…antifreeze! The solution, then, became very simple. When the cold weather began and there was a danger of the pump freezing, the engineer simply filled the station with antifreeze. The plant no longer had to stop manufacturing because of a frozen pump.

The process of "making it worse" can be applied to financial situations. Consider the following:

> Marion was having difficulty knowing where his money was going. It seemed to him that he should be able to save on a regular basis and, yet, at the end of each month he felt financially "strapped" and unable to save. When Marion asked himself, "What would make my situation worse?" he decided that if he had $100 less in monthly income he would experience increased financial difficulty. To test this idea, Marion decided to place $100 in the bank at the *beginning* of the month and to use this sum only for emergency purposes. Marion discovered that he was able to do what he wanted to do during the month and that he ended the month with no greater financial difficulty than he had before he started setting the $100 aside. After experimenting with "making it worse" by setting aside $100, Marion decided that he could make it on $100 less in spending money and, therefore, to use this approach as a regular form of savings.

Using A Solution To One Problem To Solve Another

There are times that we find solutions to problems by using rational or intuitive/creative means. These solutions, or achievement of desired outcomes in one situation, can sometimes provide a stimulus or means for determining solutions in other situations. In mathematics, for example, frequently a final solution is determined by solving a series of interrelated problems in which the final answer is dependent on answers to previous steps. This process has uses in the financial realm. The following examples demonstrate how this can occur.

> **Example 1:** Ellen wanted to purchase a new automobile without using her savings. To do this, she had to find a way of coming up with a sufficient down payment. When faced with similar situations in the past, Ellen had asked her parents for the money and then paid them back out of her regular earnings. She again considered this possibility, but decided that she would rather find another source of funding. Ellen thought about the *solution* she had previously used, which stimulated her to think of how she could borrow to provide a down payment for her automobile. This process eventually led Ellen to consider borrowing against the cash values of her life insurance policy as a source of funding. Such a "loan" merely reduced the ultimate

death benefit of her policy and didn't really have to be paid back until later or not at all.

Example 2: Rod wanted to build a new house. In order to obtain a construction mortgage, he had to have a 10 percent down payment or prove that he owned the property on which the house was to be built. Rod, therefore, decided to achieve his long-term goal of building the house by first achieving his short-term goal, owning the land on which the house was to be built. To accomplish this short-term goal, Rod reflected on how in the past he used equity in his house as collateral for obtaining a home improvement loan. Consequently, Rod decided to purchase the land for the new house and to use it as collateral for obtaining a construction mortgage.

In the first of these examples, Ellen used the solution from previous financial problems as a *stimulus* for her present problem. By contrast, Rod used the solution of buying the property as a *means* for accomplishing his long-term goal.

CONCLUSION

Decision-making and problem-solving can employ logical, rational, orderly strategies *and* intuitive reasoning to arrive at meaningful solutions. It should be clear that situations differ and that the process used in one situation may or may not be appropriate in another. There are no *right* or *wrong* techniques. The correctness of a strategy is dependent on the outcome it produces. Thus, while a counselor may use what appears to be an appropriate technique with a client, it may not be successful. There are numerous intervening circumstances within any person's field of experience which cannot be controlled and which may be more powerful than the action plan.

As financial counselors communicate with clients, they are expected to determine which strategy is best in a given situation. Their understanding of decision-making and problem-solving strategies enhances their chances of being helpful. Finally, using some form of systematic decision-making and/or problem-solving strategy with clients not only facilitates problem resolution and/or goal attainment, but also teaches clients processes they can use when problems occur. This aspect of counseling is especially beneficial because it builds prevention and productivity into every counseling relationship.

RESOURCES

De Bono, E. (1992). *Serious Creativity*. New York: Harper Business.

Decker, J.P. (1978). *Solving Personality Clashes With Time Zero.* Tempe: Synecology Press.

Moody, P. E. (1983). *Decision Making.* New York: McGraw Hill.

Russo, J.E. & Schoemaker, P.J.H. (1990). *Decision Traps.* New York: Simon and Schuster.

von Oech, R. (1990). *A Whack On The Side Of The Head.* New York: Warner Books.

Wycoff, J. (1995). *Transformation Thinking*. New York: The Berkley Publishing Group.

Section 2

Financial Counseling Applications and Issues

8 FINANCIAL COUNSELING ISSUES

Counseling is many things. It is a technique of informing and assessing. It is a vehicle designed to modify behavior. It is an experience in communication. Most of all, I think, it is a mutual search for meaning in one's life, with the growth of love as an essential concomitant and consequence of the search. To me, all the rest is fairly trivial or down-right senseless without the search for meaning. Indeed, that search is really what living is, and counseling is just a special intensification of the quest.

Dr. Ray Strowig

This quotation now appears on a plaque at the University of Wisconsin-Madison, Department of Counseling Psychology, whereon the names of the recipients of the Strowig Memorial Award are recorded.

INTRODUCTION

This chapter has been developed to provide a discussion of issues that frequently arise in financial counseling. Although this discussion is not inclusive, the presentation should clarify the specific nature of financial counseling and provide the reader with a perspective about the breadth of the financial counseling process.

Definitions

It is important that financial counselors develop a clear and specific definition of financial counseling so that they can communicate to clients what can be expected when participating in the financial counseling process. Following, you will find a definition of financial counseling and a number of related professional encounters that are sometimes erroneously considered to be financial counseling. Pay particular attention to the *primary* purpose for each of the topics presented.

- **Financial Counseling:** Financial counseling is a specific professional intervention that uses clearly defined communication and counseling strategies and tactics to achieve specific client *financial* goals and objectives. The goals and objectives that become the focus of the financial counseling interaction revolve around remedial, preventive and/or productive issues. The process used to achieve financial counseling goals and objectives is interpersonal in nature. Primary responsibility for the *process* that is used rests with financial counselors, whereas the primary responsibility for *focus* or *content* rests with clients.

- **Personal Counseling:** Personal counseling is a professional intervention that applies the principles of communication and counseling to the resolution of *personal* concerns that are not financial in nature. Processes used in this relationship parallel those used in financial counseling.

- **Interviewing**: Interviewing is a process in which one individual uses specific formal/informal and open/closed techniques to gather information from another. The purposes or goals of interviewing are varied and are determined by the individual using the interviewing process. The process of interviewing is central to, and in some situations, identical to the process used in both financial and personal counseling.

- **Loan Granting**: A primary role of financial institutions is the granting of loans. The process used to determine if a client is eligible for a loan usually, but not always, includes the use of an interview. The determination of eligibility is based upon comparison of a client's qualifications with the financial institution's requirements for granting the specific type of loan. This may have been determined through the interviewing process. The failure of a client to receive a loan *could* result in a recommendation that the client seek either personal or financial counseling or both.

- **Budget Counseling**: A financial counselor could determine that a client needs to learn a specific financial skill in order to maximize use of financial resources. Knowing how to budget might be the skill that the client needs to develop. In this case, financial counseling would be used to teach the client a specific skill, one with a clearly defined goal. As can be seen in this example, budget counseling is *one possibility* in financial counseling and could be considered to be a subset of financial counseling.

REFERRAL

In some situations counselors will not be able to handle difficulties that arise. It is possible that a client will have a concern that is beyond a financial counselor's expertise, i.e., a personal issue such as dealing with all the emotions related to a divorce, as well as the financial concerns emanating from the divorce. In this situation it is the financial counselor's responsibility to help clients become aware of other sources of help. These sources of help can come from two distinct sources, i.e., *internal* referral and *external* referral. Examples of each follow.

Internal Referral

Many financial institutions are organized around employees' specialized areas of expertise. A financial institution may have several professional employees, all capable of providing standardized service to clients. In addition, each professional employee may have training in another specialized area. One individual might have specialized training in investments, another in trusts, another in budget counseling, while another in consumer lending concerns. This approach to staff development helps the financial institution provide all services that are relevant, yet makes it possible for individual employees to achieve expertise in one area and not to be overburdened with being expert in all areas. When this approach is used, financial counselors have *internal* referral sources. If, when working with a client, in-depth information is needed about consumer credit issues, the counselor could refer the client to the appropriate person within the institution.

Internal referral also is used in another way. At times the interaction between a financial counselor and a client will be less than perfect. A difference in values, perspective, approach, or attitudes can lead to a poor or non-functional working relationship. When this happens, it is helpful if the counselor can refer the client to another counselor within the institution. In some institutions, public schools for example, this is a standard operating procedure. A benefit of this form of referral is that the client can receive the needed service within the organization. A second benefit is that internal referral is less costly in terms of time and convenience than when referral is made outside the original financial institution.

External Referral

At times expertise needed to help a client can only be found outside the institution. Financial counselors should be able to work effectively with financial counseling issues of a remedial, productive, and/or preventive nature. Yet, in working with clients around financial concerns, other issues may surface. Some of these issues will fall outside the counselor's area of expertise. When this occurs, financial counselors should be aware of *external* sources of referral. These sources may include mental health agencies, pastoral counseling, social work counseling services, counseling for alcoholism and drug abuse, rape counseling, battered women and battered children counseling centers, suicide prevention counseling centers, and anxiety reduction counseling centers. It is the financial counselor's responsibility to know local referral resources.

In both internal and external referral, counselors can act as a liaison for clients. If a referral is to be made, and after receiving consent from their clients, counselors may initiate the referral. At other times, it would be more beneficial for the client to initiate the contact with the outside agency. In either case, counselors can provide information to the referral agency about clients. This sharing of information always is dependent upon client awareness and appropriately signed client releases.

COUNSELOR ROLES: POSITIVES AND NEGATIVES

Financial counselors may *wear many hats* during the course of their employment in an institution. Because of their multiple roles, they may have occasion to work with clients in several capacities. This occurrence can have a positive or negative impact on the financial counseling process. Some of the areas that might be considered follow.

Positive Consequences

The greatest positive consequence of a financial counselor having multiple roles is that the counselor can achieve first-hand experience in a variety of domains within the financial institution. The resulting widespread knowledge can be helpful in counseling by providing counselors and clients more options in the financial counseling process.

Second, when financial counselors operate in multiple roles they are more visible to clients. The possibility that a financial counselor will interact with a client increases as the counselor's roles within the financial institution increase. A relationship developed between the counselor and client in *any* role can facilitate the development of an effective counseling relationship. That is, a client can become familiar with the counselor's style and personality in a non-counseling relationship before counseling starts. This can shorten the time needed within counseling to arrive at meaningful counseling issues.

Third, when financial counselors have a variety of experiences, other professionals view counselors as being more influential. This perspective can be helpful to clients in the short term and in how professionals respond to clients in the future. Professionals that respect a financial counselor's knowledge and expertise assume that clients with whom the counselor works will experience positive counseling outcomes. They will treat these clients accordingly.

Fourth, financial counselors involved in the total organization through a variety of roles have greater potential for acquiring generalized financial institution knowledge. Increased knowledge frequently translates into increased awareness of issues and a better understanding of organizational perspectives. This awareness can result in increased political power. For example, a financial counselor involved in multiple roles would be in a position to observe the need for counseling while participating in other services and examine the impact of the financial counseling program on clients. This unique position, in which a person can be part of the total financial institution offerings through multiple roles *while being* a financial counselor, could be politically powerful, and ultimately, helpful to the financial counseling program.

Negative Consequences

The major negative drawbacks to a counselor maintaining multiple roles within the institution are client expectations, time, and expertise. The first of these, client expectations, refers to the carry-over effect of having worked with a client in another capacity. The relationship previously developed *could* be positive and have a facilitating impact on the financial counseling process. However, it *could* be negative and hamper the counseling relationship. For example, in a previous interaction while performing another role, the financial counselor may have accepted total responsibility for what was done. The client expectation in the newer interaction of financial counseling might carry residues of the previous relationship. The client may expect the financial counselor to accept full responsibility for what is done in counseling, much as they did in the previous interaction. This expectation might be very difficult to overcome.

Second, financial counseling is a time-consuming enterprise. Time is needed for preparation, delivery and follow through. When individuals have multiple roles, frequently they are torn between what needs to be done to complete their responsibilities to those roles and to fully prepare for counseling. One of the two probably will suffer. Finally, being a financial counselor requires initial academic preparation and continuous updating. This is very difficult to do if the financial counselor must do other tasks and learn materials for one or more other roles within the financial institution.

The positive and negative consequences of being a financial counselor while simultaneously filling a number of other professional roles should be examined when one considers becoming a financial counselor. The specific financial institution, the nature of the roles being filled, the financial counselor's propensity for filling many roles, and client demands can all influence whether consequences will be positive or negative in a particular situation.

VALUES, BELIEFS AND ATTITUDES

Among the many things that are important to financial counselors, three of the most significant are values, beliefs, and attitudes. It is through these three variables that financial counselors can arrive at a better understanding of themselves, become more aware of clients with whom they work, and arrive at a basis for their involvement in a client's life. Values, beliefs, and attitudes are cornerstones on which human interaction rests, and as such they provide counselors with a foundation on which to build the counseling relationship.

Financial Counselors' Values

Individuals devise systematic ways of ordering elements in their environment. Those elements that rank as most crucial become most meaningful. Those that are cherished become valued. Values are not inborn, but rather, are the direct result of one's environmental interaction. These valued objects or elements become the driving force for many actions. Nugent (1990, p.262) defined values as "standards or ethical guidelines that influence an individual's or group's behavior, attitudes, and decisions." Some of these standards or guidelines are at the conscious level, others at the subconscious level. Both provide reference points for the individual in the environment. Values can be either specific or general in nature. In either case, values affect a person's manner of viewing the world. They provide a frame of reference for experience and a means for making sense out of new phenomena. Values determine what is seen, provide a meaning for that which is observed, and consequently, provide boundaries for the person's behaviors. Edward Hall (1981) in *Beyond Culture* suggests a continuum of culture from low to high context. Values that are held by individuals from high and low context cultures reveal basic differences. Low context culture members tend to be future oriented, view change as being constant, demonstrate emerging value systems, tend to be goal oriented, and depend heavily on coded verbal messages. Individuals from high context cultures, by contrast, rely on historical precedence of the family or community, demonstrate a stable value system, tend toward a group rather than individualistic perspective, and rely on facial expressions and gestures when communicating. It is true that whenever two individuals interact, misunderstanding can occur. However, as a result of basic value differences, potential for misunderstanding is increased when individuals from high and low context cultures interact.

Individuals are influenced by many different values at any given time. Financial counselors may be influenced by two powerful sets of values - their personal set of values and values derived from the financial institution and membership field in which they work. Usually, financial counselor values and financial institution values will be congruent. There are times, however, when these may be in conflict. An example illustrates this point.

> Jennifer, a financial counselor values a client's right to independent, responsible action. Jennifer's financial institution holds a value which suggests that clients who don't make their loan payments are guilty until they have proven themselves to be innocent. In action, this example might appear as follows: A client asking for a loan, wishing to complete payments in six months, requests that he not have a co-signer for the loan. The client indicates that he is able to make the commitment and make payments, but that he has no way of obtaining an assessment of his financial record. Because of his lack of financial record, the financial institution demands that the client have a co-signer to protect against default of payments. Jennifer, the financial counselor's value might be, "Let's give this person a chance." From her interaction with the client, Jennifer believes that the client is trustworthy and honest, and that he is going to honor his obligation. Yet, the financial institution demand for a co-signer may go against values this financial counselor holds. In this situation, the financial counselor is obligated to abide by the institutional value despite her personal value.

The decision a counselor makes, and the subsequent action that the counselor takes, depends on the counselor's values, beliefs, and attitudes. Consider this example relating to bill consolidation.

> Many financial institutions might have the value that a bill consolidation loan is in the best interests of both the client and the financial institution when a client becomes financially over-extended. However, James, a financial counselor in such an

institution judges that, in this particular case, it would not be in the client's best interest to be given a bill consolidation loan. James believes that the client needs to learn more about daily budgeting and learn to handle the financial situation by talking with creditors directly. In James's mind, the second strategy will help prevent occurrence of another bill consolidation loan in the future.

This is a common conflict in values. The financial institution value and policies are designed to protect investments, i.e., loans, and are aimed at the *overall membership*. The financial institution's values and policies may not be best for a particular client.

Financial counselors are more likely to make appropriate decisions in these and other situations if they are aware of their value structures. To do this financial counselors must ask themselves a number of basic questions:

Basic Values Questions

What do I hold as important?

What do I believe to be true about myself?

What do I want to accomplish in my life?

What do I believe to be true about clients with whom I work?

What do I hope to get out of my interaction with clients?

What needs of mine are being met within the counseling relationship?

Knowledge of one's values provides a more clearly defined reference point from which to view experience. If financial counselors understand their values, decisions they make will be more consistent and potentially more beneficial to clients with whom they work. Because financial counselors are human systems, and there are many parts of a human system, there are many areas of influence on one's values. Although values are an essential ingredient of beliefs that individuals hold and attitudes they espouse, values also are influenced by these beliefs and attitudes. Values, beliefs, and attitudes are inter-linked and interdependent.

Financial Counselors' Beliefs

The power of belief is extremely strong. Napier and Gershenfeld (1973) relate a story that emphasizes this claim.

> A poor Russian laborer's job was to clean out boxcars in a railroad yard. One evening during a break, he slipped into an empty freezer car which was being aired out, piled some straw in a corner, and proceeded to catch a few winks. He was awakened when the door was slammed shut by a yard policeman who had not noticed him in the car. Being philosophical about the plight of his life anyway, he decided to record for posterity the process of death as it slowly crept up on him. There appeared to be no escape unless the guards returned unexpectedly before morning. As the night wore on, the notes he scraped on the wall become less and less coherent, his fingers numbed, and his breath came in short gasps. But he continued to write and hoped that his short history of impending death would be of interest. At some point in the early hours of the morning he scratched his last message: "I can no longer grasp this stick, there is no air to breathe ..."In the morning, when the heavy door was pulled open, he was found dead, lying there still clutching his stick. The temperature inside was 55 degrees, and there was plenty of oxygen".

Williams (1964. p.68) in the *Wisdom of Your Subconscious Mind* shares a story that also attests to the power of belief. Consider the following:

> Physicians had been given permission to experiment on a criminal who had been sentenced to death. The prisoner was told that he would bleed to death. He was placed on a table, his eyes covered and then small incisions made on his arm but not deep enough to cause blood to flow. A small stream of running water was allowed to trickle down over his arm into a bowl and this he felt and heard distinctly. Standing by, the attending physicians were making remarks on the progress of the bleeding and his growing weakness and approaching death. In a short time the prisoner died and he had all the symptoms of cariac syncope from the loss of blood.

Whether these stories are true is less important than accepting that the mind can respond to suggestions from the outside. There are many documented cases to show how suggestibility influences behavior. Hypnosis is a prime example. The key for hypnosis seems to be the ability of the hypnotist to establish a belief within the person being hypnotized that an alternate reality exists. Belief within the financial counseling session is equally as important as it is in hypnosis or in the stories above by Napier and Gershenfeld and Williams. The beliefs that financial counselors hold about clients sets the stage for the impact they will have on clients.

Beliefs can be categorized in a number of ways. For ease of discussion, three central ways will be discussed.

What Is Significant About Clients?

Financial counselors have certain beliefs about people and how they function in life. This set of beliefs is a determinant for how they interact with clients. They may believe that clients are able or unable, dependent or independent, friendly or unfriendly, worthy or unworthy, or helpful or hindering. These contrasts are not intended to be inclusive, nor are we suggesting that financial counselors classify clients as totally one way or another. What we are suggesting is that financial counselors will have a tendency to classify clients according to their beliefs, and will respond to those clients in accordance with their classification. If financial counselors believe that clients are able to perform a certain act, they will respond to clients in a different manner than if they believe clients are unable to perform the desired act.

If financial counselors truly believe that clients are able and capable of solving problems, they will provide some direction knowing that clients could sort through difficulties involved. With this belief, financial counselors would enter relationships to help clients find answers to problems, not to provide answers for them. However, if financial counselors have the basic belief that people are unable, then they would do something very dramatic to affect the lives of clients. Financial counselors would have to intercede in a more active way to get clients to begin movement in a positive direction. In addition, if financial counselors believe that clients are unable, it would be necessary to establish systems whereby clients would continuously be reinforced by significant others in their environment. One basic belief, whether a person is able or unable, can lead a financial counselor to a totally different counseling interaction. It is crucial, therefore, that counselors know their basic beliefs about clients. It is these beliefs which are influential in determining how, when, and to what degree counselors will get involved in the lives of clients with whom they work.

What Is Significant About Counselors?

Clients are one half of the financial counseling relationship. Counselors are the second half. Beliefs financial counselors hold about themselves are of major significance, and can be discussed under three major interrelated categories: skill, information, and personality.

- **Skill:** Financial counselors presumably have beliefs about their capability as helping professionals. Self-awareness and feedback from clients and peers provide financial counselors with an ongoing evaluation of their effectiveness. Although financial counselors might not *feel* as effective as they'd like, they probably have some degree of confidence that they are skillful at their job. In most cases this confidence is well founded; in others it is not. When the counselor's confidence is justified, and they are skillful, clients probably benefit from the counselor-client interaction. When counselors are confident but not skillful clients probably will not benefit from the interaction. What is important for our purposes is that in either case, financial counselors have beliefs about their skill. What they do about maintaining or improving that skill is another issue.

- **Information:** Financial counselors have beliefs that they can or can not comprehend and / or use relevant information necessary for doing their jobs. If financial counselors believe that they are able to gather and use information, they will respond to clients in a different manner than if they believe that they are incapable of utilizing information effectively. In the former case, financial counselors may demonstrate confidence by sharing relevant information with clients. In the latter, financial counselors will probably refer clients to other sources for data. What is important is not whether financial counselors are correct about their beliefs, but whether beliefs held do have an impact upon decisions made on behalf of clients.

- **Personality:** To a significant degree the financial counselor's personality is the medium through which financial counseling occurs. Different financial counselors hold different beliefs about how they can employ personality characteristics most effectively to influence their clients. Some financial counselors, for instance, believe that modeling is very important for client learning. Using this belief as a basis, financial counselors will demonstrate ways they think clients should behave. If the financial counselors' actions are congruent with their personalities, clients will get the message, "Oh, so that's how I'm supposed to be." If financial counselors are inconsistent, clients will probably perceive them as being untrustworthy. From a modeling perspective, these financial counselors may be serving as horrible examples!

Other financial counselors, with different beliefs about the impact of their behavior on clients, may use an interactive approach that builds on clients' characteristics and not on those of the financial counselor. Modeling, if it occurs, would be of secondary importance.

What has been addressed so far under the subtitle of *Personality* is of secondary importance. What is centrally important is that the beliefs financial counselors hold will influence the theory they espouse, the approach they use in sharing theory, and whether the focus of the interaction will be on client behavior as a reflection of financial counselor behavior. All of these financial counselor choices result from counselor personality characteristics and beliefs.

What Is Significant About The Counseling-Client Interaction?

The effectiveness of financial counseling is dependent on beliefs about the potential of the counselor-client relationship. Three central beliefs are of prime importance.

The one-one relationship is central to client change. The concept that a one-one counselor client interaction will help clients change attitudes, behaviors, beliefs, or, in some instances, their basic values is the foundation on which financial counseling rests.

Two people can work together for the benefit of one person. A second belief financial counselors hold is that counseling provides a unique opportunity for two individuals to work together for the purpose of *helping one of those individuals.* The belief that two people, engaged in a special relationship, can be more potent than one individual working alone ascribes a degree of power to the interactive process. Belief that change occurs *as a result of* the interaction is central to many counseling theories.

The counselor's belief system impacts how counseling will occur. Finally, the particular strategies that financial counselors employ are dependent on beliefs they hold about themselves, clients, and the process of change. One financial counselor may believe that the most efficient way to motivate a client is through modeling. Another may think that reinforcing behavior is more appropriate. A third might believe that helping clients gain insight about their problems is the most beneficial approach. All approaches can be beneficial, although some may be more expedient than others with certain clients. All approaches are built on the belief that the financial counselor-client interaction will make a difference in the lives of clients.

The issue of *belief* is of great significance in all areas of counseling, but it has particular significance in financial counseling. A crucial question that financial counselors must ask is: "Am I counseling a *person* about financial problems or am I discussing *financial problems* with a person?" Which area does the counselor focus on, the *person* or the *task* at hand? As an example, if one were a financial counselor focusing on the person the counselor might spend nine-tenths of the time with the person helping the client understand needs, wants, desires, and ways to actualize those needs and desires. Only one-tenth of the counseling time would be focused on financial matters. A subject oriented counselor might spend a great deal of time, as much as nine-tenths of the total counseling time, dealing with financial matters and only one-tenth of the time helping the client relate those financial matters to the client's personal life. What the financial counselor believes to be important would determine which way the counselor functions.

Financial Counselors' Attitudes

Financial counselors' attitudes represent another level of functioning dependent upon the previous two levels (values and beliefs). Values provide the consistent foundation or reference point against which we judge experience. As a result of the continuous comparison of experiences with our value structure, we form certain beliefs. Beliefs become reasonably stable and place restrictions on how we define reality. An attitude is usually based upon a firmly entrenched belief system.

In financial counseling, four attitudes have particular significance. First, financial counselors benefit from entering relationships with the attitude that through the interaction, clients will make strides forward, that they will be able to make appropriate decisions, that they have the capability of accepting responsibility, and that they will change and grow as a result of counseling. Without this attitude, financial counselors may accept undue responsibility for what occurs within relationships; may prevent clients from taking steps that will be necessary for growth and adjustment; and may hamper hard decision-making processes that clients must undertake.

The second attitude that benefits financial counselors is that they are capable of providing sufficient help for clients. Financial counselors have to believe that clients will gain through their interaction. In addition, they have to exhibit the attitude that they are knowledgeable individuals, and that they have information and skills that will help clients.

The third important attitude is that the process of financial counseling is sufficient to provide clients with help that is needed. Financial counseling is not a simple task. It is not *a quick and easy* means for helping clients solve problems. Financial counselors must enter the relationship with the attitude that if they use skill, knowledge, themselves, and time effectively, then clients will solve their own problems. This attitude must convey a respect for clients and for themselves. In addition it must convey a deep respect for the process that is employed.

Financial counselors can develop an atmosphere conducive to growth and development of clients. This can occur when counselors demonstrate self-awareness and the capability of sharing insights with their clients.

EXPLICIT AND IMPLICIT PROMISES

In establishing a financial counseling program, financial institutions develop and communicate messages to their membership about what the service of financial counseling is or will be. In some instances, these messages are stated directly, while in others they are implicitly or informally presented. It is important in any professional offering to be clear about what the service will provide, to work from explicitly stated financial institution goals, and, whenever possible, to identify those offerings that are implicitly stated. Following are a number of explicit and implicit promises that could be made by a financial institution regarding financial counseling.

Explicit Promises

The most obvious explicit promises might be that you will provide clients assistance in remedial, preventive and/or productive counseling. Specifically, you might advertise that you will, through financial counseling, help clients better meet their financial obligations by employing budget counseling, consumer credit counseling, or by helping them to learn financial problem-solving and/or decision-making skills. More specifically yet, you might state that financial counseling will help clients balance their checking accounts, meet their monthly obligations in a timely manner, or save for retirement. Statements posted at the financial institution or printed in flyers or newsletters could attest to any of these explicit promises.

Implicit Promises

By the very nature of these promises they are harder to classify and usually much harder to detect. Some clients will be aware of them, others will not. Examples of implicit promises include promises that financial counseling will *make* the client a better person, a more responsible individual, a better community client, or a more responsive institutional client. Financial counseling may attempt to help the client become all of these, but cannot guarantee that any of them will occur. An implicit promise could lead a client to believe that financial counseling will guarantee achievement of these and other goals and ensure their eventual success.

CONCLUSION

This chapter has touched on a variety of issues that are central to the development and success of a financial counseling program. Some issues discussed can be addressed directly, others must remain in the consciousness of those individuals who want to ensure the success of a financial counseling program.

RESOURCES

Hall, E.T. (1981). *Beyond Culture*. New York: Doubleday.

Napier, R.W. & Gershenfeld, M.K. (1973). *Groups: Theory And Practice.* (Instructor's manual). Boston: Houghton Mifflin Company.

Nugent, F.A. (1990). *An Introduction To Professional Counseling.* Columbus: Merrill Publishing Company.

Williams, J.K. (1964). *The Wisdom Of Your Subconscious Mind.* Englewood Cliffs: Prentice-Hall.

9 THE COUNSELING RELATIONSHIP

Linda entered the counselor's office and said, "Mr. Brown, may I shut the door?" Mr. Brown said, "Sure, Linda, shut the door." Linda did and sat down. She started to cry. She cried for about five minutes and Mr. Brown said, "Linda, can I help you?" Linda said, "No, Mr. Brown" and continued to cry. She cried for twenty-five minutes longer, looked up and said, "Thank you Mr. Brown," got up and left the office.

INTRODUCTION

Effective counseling relationships do not just happen; they are based upon important principles and develop through orderly stages. These stages can be identified and promoted by the use of appropriate strategies. The principles underlying the strategies include:

***Principle* 9.1**: The purpose of counseling is to influence and motivate clients toward acceptable goals.

***Principle* 9.2**: Six strategic tactics exist in an ideal counseling relationship: openness, realistic expectations, structure, power, confirmation of differences, and mutual involvement.

***Principle* 9.3**: Counseling progresses through four stages: initiating, exploring, understanding, and acting.

***Principle* 9.4**: Specific counseling relationships have specific developmental stages.

Principle 9.5: In counseling the practical meaning of communication is the response you get.

Principle 9.6: When there is consistent and accurate feedback during the counseling process, clients will become increasingly responsible for themselves.

Principle 9.7: Counseling relationships adhere to ethical guidelines.

Building effective counseling relationships is both a science and an art and, consequently, has characteristics of both. From a scientific perspective, effective counselors use strategies to maintain an objective posture, building toward goals through the development of effective interpersonal relationships. Effective relationships are orderly and sequential, with stages of the process building upon one another. In addition to scientific elements, effective counseling incorporates a high degree of art. Art refers to the unique and creative ways individual counselors apply scientific elements to each client relationship.

This merging of scientific and artistic elements is analogous to the painting of a picture. Although there are scientific principles for mixing a color palette and applying paint to the canvas, art in painting comes from the unique way artists apply paints to create images. The same is true in counseling, counselors artistically use scientific principles.

PRINCIPLES

◈ Principle 9.1: The purpose of counseling is to influence and motivate clients toward acceptable goals.

All counseling approaches have the general purpose of influencing and motivating someone toward acceptable goals. Acceptable goals may be established by the client, the financial counselor, suggested from an outside source, or even, required by an outside agency. The form and amount of influence attempted will change with the unique purpose of the counseling relationship, but influence and motivation are at the core of all counseling relationships.

Communication is reciprocal. Communication by one person has an effect on the type of response that will be made by another. Because of the reciprocal nature of communication, one cannot *not* influence. Whether we intend to or not, the way we communicate or the manner in which we choose to respond has an effect on the way people respond to us.

In financial counseling, the influence we exert results from this reciprocity, as well as from our desire to influence the client toward specific goals. Influence varies along a continuum from a direct attempt to convince a client to act differently, as in remedial financial counseling, to providing an atmosphere in which a client can explore feelings and values about themselves and the use of financial resources. In the direct strategy, the goal of influence is to convince a client that behavior needs to be changed. In remedial financial counseling, the counselor usually deals with clients who are financially overextended. Frequently, these are clients who have made irresponsible decisions about their money. In remedial financial counseling, the purpose of influence is to convince clients to make responsible financial decisions. In productive financial counseling or planning, the purpose of influence may be directed more toward helping clients discover financial goals that are consistent with their values, e.g., financial security vs. risk-taking, or saving money for future education vs. allowing children to earn their own way. While counselors' specific goals may vary, their underlying purpose remains constant. They attempt to influence.

The primary method financial counselors use to influence clients is *control of information*. Information can be controlled on two fronts. Counselors can control the process of information dissemination and they can control content of information. In reality, content and process overlap; they are separated here only for discussion. Financial counselors are primarily responsible for process, and clients are primarily responsible for content. While content has impact on process and *vice versa,* the focus of the financial counselor's strategies for influence should be on process, influencing how information is used. Clients, on the other hand, focus on content: the information necessary for understanding, problem solving, goal setting, and decision making.

It is entirely possible for a financial counselor to control a process and help clients move toward problem solving or decision making without knowing any of the information a client is using. For example, a financial counselor might conduct a planning seminar for a group of clients. During the seminar the financial counselor could guide clients through a planning process that included the following steps.

Step 1 Clients complete a net worth statement.
Step 2 Clients write several financial goals for the next six months.
Step 3 Clients list possible ways for achieving the goals.
Step 4 Clients make a choice among the various alternatives.
Step 5 Clients develop a personal plan to implement chosen alternatives to achieve goals.

In this manner a financial counselor could help a number of clients at the same time. Each client would supply necessary information and develop an action plan, while the financial counselor would have no knowledge of individual content used. In this type of seminar the financial counselor controls the process and clients control the content.

FOCUS ON PROCESS

The financial counselor's primary strategy is to control the process of interaction as a means for exerting influence. The remaining principles in this chapter deal with this concept.

◈ Principle 9.2: Six tactics exist in an ideal counselor relationship: openness, realistic expectations, structure, power, confirmation of differences, and mutual involvement.

Effective counseling usually incorporates most, if not all, of these six dimensions. Although each of the tactics is discussed separately, they are interactive.

Openness

Openness refers to individuals' willingness to share information about topics under discussion and about personal aspects that relate to the purpose of the relationship. One way of understanding the concept of openness is through the metaphor of the Johari window (see Figure 9.A). The Johari window was originated by Joe Luft (1969). He originally used a four-pane window as a way of expressing areas and degrees of openness appropriate in communicative relationships. We believe his conceptualization has as much relevance today as when it was conceived.

	Known to Self	Not Known to Self
Known to Others	**Public**	**Blind**
Not Known to Others	**Private**	**Hidden**

Figure 9.A

Here's how the Johari window is interpreted:

- **Public Area:** In normal communication, the nature of information dealt with is in the *public* area: information that is known to both persons. This is the type of information that we share readily with others.

- **Private Area:** The *private* area contains two differing types of information. The first type of information relates to things about oneself, such as values, beliefs, fears, and feelings that are shared only with certain people or under certain circumstances. The second type of information contained in the *private* area relates to reactions to others during the communicative interaction. We have feelings, judgments, and ideas about others that we are aware of but may not share.

- **Blind Area:** Each individual has a blind area. The area consists of feelings, judgements and ideas others have about the individual. As the name "*blind*" indicates, the individual is unaware of these perceptions.

- **Hidden Area**: The information contained in the *hidden* area relates to deeper subconscious processes that are not readily available to the individual or to others as they communicate. We can become aware of information in the *hidden* area through dreams, either night dreams or daydreams; in moments of emergency; through free association; or through therapy.

Openness in counseling refers to the counselor's willingness to share with a client information from the counselor's *private* area and the client's willingness to share information from the client's *private* area. Information from the counselor's *private* area that is most appropriate to share in financial counseling relates to judgments, ideas, and reactions to the client. There are times when it also may be important to share beliefs, values, and judgments about financial issues relevant to the purpose of the counseling relationship. Counselors also may wish to create an atmosphere in which clients are willing to self-disclose information. Open communicative relationships can be depicted as follows (see Figure 9 .B):

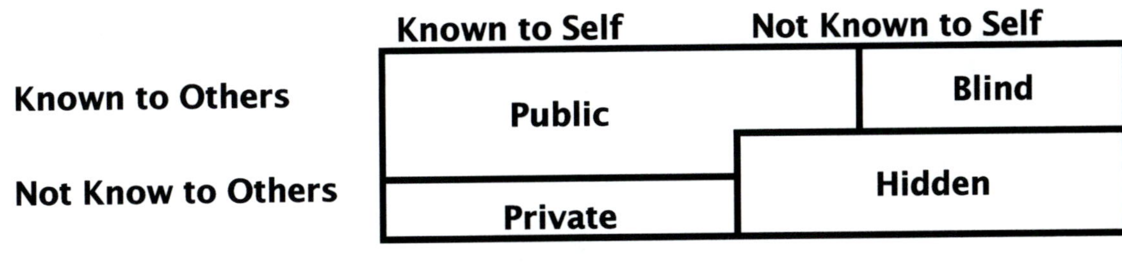

Figure 9.B

Notice that as one person shares information from the *private* area, this area gets smaller, and so does the *blind* area. This occurs because as people share their feelings, reactions, and judgments about other people, each becomes more aware of things that were previously known only to the other. Notice also that as the self-disclosure continues, the *public* area becomes larger. This is the nature of open relationships.

Realistic Expectations

There are two aspects of realistic expectations to keep in mind.

- Judgment about whether goal expectations are realistic or not depends upon a number of factors in the relationship. In any given situation, counselors need to exercise knowledge and experience to determine if specific goals are realistic.

- Some clients may expect the counselor to take complete control of their financial situation and to make all the necessary decisions. This may be applicable if the counselor is setting up a bill consolidation loan to be managed by the counselor or the financial institution. On the other hand, it is unrealistic for clients to expect that counselors will make decisions for them. In either case, effective financial counselors spend time at the beginning of their working relationships to clarifying role expectations. This tactic prevents misunderstandings.

Structure

Effective counseling follows a structure appropriate to the setting and goals of the relationship. We referred to such a structure at the beginning of the chapter when we discussed the scientific and artistic nature of effective relationships. There is an underlying structure to effective counselor relationships that will be discussed in Principle 9.3.

Power

The concept of power underlies tactical influence, the underlying purpose of all financial relationships. Power stems from various sources, including the counselor's appearance and communicative style. Counselors have power that stems from their general counselor expertise and specialized information and knowledge. Also, a counselor's ability to control decision-making and problem-solving processes for the client's benefit is a source of power. Effective financial counselors use their sources of power to control relationships and influence clients as a means of helping them achieve their goals.

Confirmation of differences

No two people are alike. Counselors and clients typically differ about financial values, beliefs, and attitudes; willingness to take financial risks; and financial goals. Effective financial counselors recognize these differences, help their clients to understand what they are, and help clients to use their understanding to make personally relevant choices.

Although counselors need to share with clients their best judgments, they must recognize that a client's goals, and subsequent choices, will be related to the client's qualities, values, and beliefs. Conflict may arise between counselors and clients when client goals are unrealistic, given their values and beliefs. For example, clients may wish to become financially independent in a short period of time but want only "safe" or "guaranteed" investments. In such a situation it is appropriate for counselors to point out discrepancies by giving appropriate feedback. However, counselors should avoid trying to persuade clients to assume greater risk. Confirming differences and adjusting to them builds trust necessary for effective financial relationships.

Mutual involvement

This tactic relates to realistic expectations. Effective counseling occurs when counselors and clients actively attempt to promote the relationship while planning for and achieving goals. Underlying this concept is the issue of dependence. When clients become too dependent upon counselors, allowing counselors to make all of the clients' decisions, counselors become totally responsible for clients' goals. If counselors' suggestions do not produce results clients desire, then clients think counselors are "at fault" for failure. Trust in the relationship can be diminished. The key to effective relationships is to get clients involved so that there is mutual responsibility for setting goals, developing plans to achieve them, and for follow through.

The six tactics of an ideal counseling relationship are interrelated. As openness develops in the relationship, likelihood increases that expectations will become more realistic and differences will be acknowledged and accepted. Finally, the degree of mutual involvement is related to the degree of openness. As counselors and clients become more self-disclosing and both of their *public* areas become progressively larger, mutual involvement usually results.

◈ Principle 9.3: Counseling progresses through four strategic stages: initiating, exploring, understanding, and acting.

Effective counseling does not happen magically. It is through knowledge of the four strategic stages that counselors increase their ability to control the process.

Initiating

A client's perception of friendliness, threat, and responsiveness are influenced by initial moments of the interaction. Initial criteria of friendliness are not hard to meet. A smile, a firm handshake, direct eye contact, and a warm greeting all communicate an interested attitude. Small talk, even about the weather or recent newsworthy events, helps reduce the tension associated with beginning or renewing a counseling relationship. The purpose of *small talk* is to help counselors and clients relax and to create a readiness to begin.

Counselors may not see themselves as threats to clients. After all, they want to help clients make the best use of their finances or help people overcome financial problems in their lives. But, to some degree, counselors are intruders in clients' lives. Counselors will be an unknown entity until the counseling relationship is firmly established. Financial issues are a personal matter and talking about them may pose a threat to clients. Consciously or subconsciously, clients want to know certain things about the financial counselor. Will this person think I have made foolish decisions with my money? Will the person understand what I want? Will this person try to "sell" me something? How do I know this person can be trusted? These and other questions pose a threat for clients as they initiate counseling. It's up to counselors to be non-threatening.

Finally, counselors should be responsive and listen well, especially at the beginning of a relationship. Counselors can use a variety of communication strategies to demonstrate that they are good listeners. Active listening can demonstrate to clients that counselors are interested in them, that they appreciate the feelings they reveal, and that they want to assist them in whatever way is appropriate.

People have differing motivations for initiating counseling relationships. Financial counseling can vary on a continuum from "strictly business" to close, personal friendships. People do not always start counseling with a particular motivation. Counseling relationships develop over time and, based on the experience between the people involved, move along a continuum. The degree of initial openness and friendliness counselors and the clients express sets a tone for a continued relationship. During the early stages, each person constructs a picture, consciously or subconsciously, of the other person. Even though this picture is continuously subject to change, the picture is used as a basis for continued communication. As people communicate, they may discover that they have certain interests in common and, as a result, become more interested in each other. The more similar counselors and clients are in interests, values, and beliefs, the more likely the relationship will move along the continuum toward personal friendship.

There are times when the client initiates the counseling relationship. At other times, the counselor may have initiated the relationship. Counselors should be aware that clients may use *small talk* appropriate in initiating an interview or relationship as a way of avoiding exploring important issues.

BEWARE THE TOO FRIENDLY

It is neither possible nor desirable for you to become personal friends with all clients. Although clients may wish the relationship to develop beyond "strictly business" to friendship, counselors must stay focused on the initial goal or purpose. If a counseling relationship does develop into a friendship, it may be more difficult for the counselor to remain objective when dealing with counseling issues.

Exploring

Once the counseling relationship has been initiated, either as a new relationship or as part of a continuing relationship, the next strategy is to explore important issues relating to the client's needs, purposes, or goals. There are two aspects to exploring, planning, and problem solving. The two aspects are not mutually exclusive.

When the general purpose of the counselor relationship is *planning,* the focus of exploring is on needs and goals. Client goals can vary from complex issues that involve a great deal of exploring to immediate decisions about financial issues that involve very little exploring.

Exploring in the planning situation may involve acquiring additional information from or for the client. For example, in helping a client plan for retirement the counselor needs to know everything relevant to the client's financial situation, needs, and ultimate goals, information that comes from the client. On the other hand, the client may want more information, information that the counselor needs to research and then share with the client. This is information the counselor would have to gather for the client. In essence, counselors have to be able to gather information within and outside the relationship, and to use both types on behalf of the client.

In a situation where the general purpose is *problem solving,* the financial counseling relationship takes on characteristics of remedial counseling. The following questions are helpful in problem-solving situations.

- ***Is the presented problem the real problem?***

  Many times clients may not reveal the real problem until they are comfortable with counselors and believe that they can be trusted. In addition clients may withhold real problems, not because of lack of trust, but because they cannot identify the real problem.

- ***Is the presented problem a solution to some other problem?***

  An effective way of looking at problems is to view them as solutions to other problems. In the financial arena, it seems likely that there are few financial problems that aren't solutions to other things. It is difficult to imagine someone spending more than they have and not knowing that this process will cause them financial problems. If this were such an obvious connection, then why would clients do something that seems so self-defeating? It is usually because clients use money to solve some other problem or to meet some other need, like "trying to keep up with the Joneses." In this type of situation, clients may have high status needs and purchase items to fulfill those needs. Eventually they may become financially overextended. The real problem, in this situation, is the client's use of money to gain social approval.

▶ ***What type of problem is it?***

Some possibilities might be a conflict of personal values, lack of planning, unrealistic goals, or lack of information.

▶ ***Who owns the problem?***

Counselors should make sure the problem is the client's problem. If it isn't, then it changes the counselor's role to that of a consultant in helping the client influence others.

▶ ***What solutions has the client tried thus far?***

Knowing this gives the counselor information about the client's problem-solving and decision-making processes and tells the counselor what *not* to suggest. This will avoid a response that begins with, "Yes, but...." If counselors suggest a solution the client has tried before to no avail, clients may become defensive and resist other good solutions.

▶ ***What financial and personal resources does the client have?***

Financial resources relate to the client's financial worth, while personal resources speak to the client's use of personal potential to achieve stated goals. Clients may have personal resources that they have not used to solve the presented problem. For example, a woman may not think she has financial management skills. This same woman may have been managing all of her family's finances or managing the finances for a church group. The client may have been using many of the skills in her personal life that would help her achieve the goals she identified while working with the counselor.

Answers to these questions are important in the exploring stage of counseling relationships. The purpose of the exploring stage is to gather information necessary to move to the understanding stage.

Understanding

This strategic stage of the financial counseling relationship occurs when the counselor and client generate plans for either goal achievement or problem solving. Plans that are generated depend upon financial goals. Emphasis during this stage should be on strategies for generating at least three possible alternatives for the identified goal or problem. There are a number of ways that alternatives can be generated.

- The financial counselor may suggest alternatives.
- The financial counselor can encourage the client to generate alternatives.
- Both counselor and the client can generate alternatives.

By encouraging generation of alternatives, counselors teach clients that there are several possible solutions to problems. This increases the possibility that clients will find a meaningful solution. Clients than can be encouraged to make choices based on alternatives that best meets their needs. By following this process, clients are more likely to become responsible for counseling outcomes. Also, by encouraging clients to generate alternatives, to examine possibilities, and to make choices, clients learn the process of problem solving. This prepares clients to deal with future problems and reduces the possibility that clients will blame counselors for alternatives that are unsuccessful. If the understanding stage proceeds as expected, there is a natural evolution to the final stage.

Acting

During the action stage counselors or clients carry out alternatives chosen during the understanding stage. A necessary part of the action stage is the ongoing evaluation of how well the alternatives are working to either achieve the established goals or to solve existing problems. If evaluation results indicate that goals are not being achieved, then counselor and client can return to earlier stages of exploring or understanding.

A primary reason why alternatives fail to produce desired results is that information gathered during the exploring stage may have been incomplete or not appropriate for the situation. The possibility also exists that the counselor and the client moved to the understanding stage too quickly. It usually is better to error by spending too much, rather than too little, time in the exploratory stage. It is extremely important that the counselor and client are certain that they have discussed all pertinent information. In the long run, delaying generation of alternatives until all information has been discussed is helpful.

◈ Principle 9.4: Specific financial counseling relationships have specific developmental stages.

Financial counseling relationships vary according to their purpose. While the four basic developmental stages discussed under Principle 9.3 underlie most counselor financial relationships, there are some that have specific developmental stages. Several are outlined below to indicate how the broader developmental stages need to be adapted to specific purposes.

Financial Planning Model

The financial planning model has six stages.

1. Gathering Data

Accurate, pertinent data is the essence of financial planning. There are two kinds of important data: quantitative and qualitative. Quantitative data is the usual factual information of the client's financial situation: data relating to assets, liabilities, income, and expenditures. Qualitative data is the basis for understanding the client's representational map about issues which affect financial planning: money values, financial goals, financial decision-making style, learning style, general and financial risk taking, social and psychological needs, and family relationships.

2. Establishing Client Objectives

Using both quantitative and qualitative data, the financial counselor helps clients establish realistic objectives that are an outgrowth of the client's experiential maps and stated goals.

3. Processing And Analyzing Information.

The financial counselor must be skilled in processing and analyzing two types of information. The first, of course, is technical information. Based upon a definitive understanding of economics and the nuances of time and its influence on the value of money, the financial counselor must be able to provide clients with realistic insights about technical information like financial statements, legal contracts, stocks, bonds, mutual funds, investment contracts, and real estate issues. Appropriate advice, however is equally dependent on the second required area of knowledge - knowledge about clients. Most would agree that one financial plan would be inappropriate for all clients' needs or that one financial plan would meet an individual client's needs for all time. People are different and people and times change.

4. Recommending A Total Plan

Before financial counselors can recommend a total financial plan, they must take precautions that most viable alternatives have been explored; that proposed choices are indeed appropriate to the client's constraints and goals; and that all information concerning the client's needs and goals have been explored. Once financial counselors are satisfied that all significant possibilities have been examined, they can recommend a total financial plan. This stage, the recommendation of a plan, is central because at this point the client is given the integrated data the financial counselor brings to the client's situation. The goal of this stage is to bring the client's experiential map together with a financial plan, a plan designed specifically to meet the client's needs and developed to achieve the client's objectives.

5. Implementing The Plan

Once the plan is recommended and accepted by the client, implementation can occur. Implementation usually occurs in one of two ways. In situations where the financial counselor has expertise and appropriate credentials, the financial counselor can implement the plan directly. In most cases, however, the financial counselor must be able to work in a liaison capacity with other financial planning counselors, accountants, insurance agents, brokers, and attorneys.

6. Monitoring the plan

The final stage is a continuous process of evaluation and subsequent modification to assure that the financial plan, as devised and implemented, continues to operate in the client's best interests. When significant changes occur in either the marketplace or clients' lives, the six-stage model automatically recycles to the first stage, *Gathering Data.*

Financial Counseling Model

Financial counseling, like financial planning, usually has six stages. The major difference between the two models lies in focus or goals. Financial counseling emphasizes remedial, preventive, and productive issues, whereas financial planning focuses almost exclusively on clients' productive goals. The six stages of financial counseling are as follows.

1. Building A Relationship

The financial counseling relationship depends upon the counselor's

a) skill in using strategies to convey a positive attitude to clients.
b) awareness of clients' financial situations.
c) concern conveyed in a helpful and beneficial way.

The underlying purpose of financial counseling is to help clients help themselves to solve or prevent financial problems. "If I give you a fish, I have fed you for today; if I teach you how to fish, I have fed you for a lifetime." This old adage incorporates the underlying purpose of financial counseling. The effective financial counseling relationship is characterized by four core conditions of congruence, empathy, warmth, and trust.

Congruence refers to the financial counselor's consistency, genuineness, and honesty. Congruent communication requires that both verbal and nonverbal behaviors are consistent.

Empathy is the financial counselor's ability to put him/herself into the client's frame of reference and to understand the client's representational map as the client understands it. Empathy includes sharing this understanding with the client in an objective way. The financial counselor should bring a detached logic to bear on the financial problem.

Warmth includes the financial counselor's friendliness, openness, and consideration.

Trust is critical in financial counseling. It is based on the client's belief that the financial counselor is working in the client's best interest. Trust results from the financial counselor's ability to genuinely demonstrate openness, congruence, empathy, and warmth.

2. Diagnosing Needs And Setting Goals

Diagnosis is a systematic attempt to understand clients and their financial situations. A good diagnosis is a description of a client's problem which includes essential details of the problem, its history, and possible causes. The basis of effective diagnosis can be found in answers to the questions raised in the exploring stage (discussed under Principle 9.3.).

Goal setting is the logical strategy that flows from diagnosis. Goals in financial counseling revolve around two major areas. The first, *process goals* state how the financial counselor intends to help clients. The second, *outcome goals* specify what clients will be doing differently with their finances as a result of the help received in financial counseling.

3. Generating Alternatives

In financial counseling it is important that the counselor conveys an attitude that gives clients the potential for accomplishing their own goals. One way of doing this is to use a strategy to help clients generate their own alternatives. Financial counselors may suggest some possible solutions. However, clients are more likely to carry out alternatives they have discovered for themselves. Helping clients generate their own alternatives serves another broader purpose. If an alternative does not work, clients must take personal responsibility and not blame the financial counselor.

4. Choosing A Plan Of Action

Once possible solutions are generated, the financial counselor helps clients to evaluate alternatives in light of diagnosed needs and established goals. Effective financial counselors can pose pertinent questions as a primary strategy in this process. For example, "What are the costs and benefits of each alternative?" (Costs and benefits refer to more than just finances. Costs and benefits include effort, emotional stress, social factors, time factors, psychological factors, and even physical considerations.) "What could possibly go wrong if an alternative is used?" "What is the potential impact if the alternative does not work? Answers to these and similar questions help clients and financial counselors narrow down alternatives that may best meet diagnosed needs and goals.

5. Implementing the plan

At this stage, the emphasis is upon action. The client and financial counselor must do something to carry out the alternatives chosen to solve the problem. This is usually accomplished by answering another set of strategic questions: Who does what, when, how, and where? Responsibilities are assigned and schedules are established to carry out the plan.

7. Evaluating The Plan

In financial counseling there are two areas for evaluation: process and outcomes. When evaluating process, financial counselors are concerned with the problem-solving process used during the previous six stages and are concerned that clients learn a process they can use to help themselves in the future.

Of course, financial counselors also evaluate outcomes. Did the client actually carry out the plan and solve the problem? In both forms of evaluation, there may be need to recycle through some of the stages until both counselor and client are satisfied that mutual goals have been accomplished.

GOAL IS SELF RELIANCE

Financial counseling differs from financial planning in terms of client self-reliance. Unlike financial planning a goal of financial counselors is to work themselves out of business. That is, if they do their work effectively, clients will no longer need them and will be able to solve their future problems because they have learned a process they can apply by themselves.

.

◈ Principle 9.5: In counseling, the practical meaning of communication is the response you get.

As discussed previously, communication between counselors and clients is a reciprocal relationship. What counselors say to clients will affect the response they receive from clients and *vice versa*. On occasion, a communicator's intention or motivation appears to be independent of the response elicited. For example, most of us have said something we thought was innocent. Yet, we may have received a response of frustration or anger. Our original intention was to engage in conversation, but the response was inconsistent with this intention. This experience has taught us that the practical meaning of the communicative interaction is the response of the second person, not necessarily what we had intended. The response becomes the focus. An example from everyday life might clarify this principle.

A couple's young son is not behaving according to expectations. The child is not spending an appropriate amount of time studying, is not cleaning his room, and is not helping around the house.

In this situation, the parents may use a lecture approach. They may sit down and talk with the child and explain their expectations, explain why it is important, and try to motivate the child with a "pep talk." Much to their chagrin, they find that their child continues to act in the same way. They again talk with the child, but this time they express their anger and frustration. The child continues to act in the same way. The parents try again, with more anger and frustration and, maybe even a few four-letter expletives! The child still does not change. In this situation the parents continued repeatedly to try the same tactic (talking). Each time they received an identical response. The practical point of this principle is that if you aren't getting the response you want, then try something different. The frustrated parents might try using *time-out* or deny the child some privilege. By varying their inputs the parents are more likely to elicit an appropriate response by the child.

There are two underlying assumptions in this principle. The first is that counselors have some idea of the type of response they want from clients. The second is that counselors have a variety of communicative skills to produce different responses. They should have several approaches for explaining the same concept. To help counselors achieve this end, a number of strategies are presented and discussed in detail in the text.

◈ Principle 9.6: When there is consistent and accurate feedback during the counseling relationship, clients will become increasingly responsible for themselves.

Communication is a process of making informational outputs and receiving informational inputs. Feedback is a special class of interactive information processing. Technically, feedback is a specific kind of input people use for correcting their informational outputs. Feedback is simply a process in which some of a person's informational output is returned to the person as part of new informational input. Feedback is an essential tactic in information processing because it allows people to become more self-directing, or responsible for themselves. When people receive feedback about their outputs relative to their goals, they can make appropriate corrections to achieve their goals.

The simplest mechanical example of a self-directing feedback system is the automatic thermostat. When a thermostat is set at a specific temperature, a goal is established. When the temperature in a house falls below the prescribed temperature, the thermostat provides feedback to the furnace through an electrical signal. The furnace responds, turns on, and supplies heat to the house. When the temperature reaches the desired level, the thermostat gives feedback to the furnace that the goal has been achieved, and the furnace turns off. This simple mechanical system will continue to achieve its goal until a mechanical or electrical failure destroys the feedback process. The thermostat is a self-directing system. We can say that the thermostat is *responsible* in the sense that it continues to achieve its goal to control the temperature in the house without any input from the outside.

People operate in a similar manner. When they receive feedback they become more self-directing and responsible for themselves relative to their goals. Feedback can be positive, negative, constructive, or destructive.

Positive feedback provides information to people that their behavior is consistent with their goals, thus encouraging them to continue behaving in ways that will help them to achieve their goals. Positive feedback may also tell people that they have achieved a goal and allows them to establish new goals.

Negative feedback operates in a restricting manner, tending to keep people within the limits prescribed by their goals. Negative feedback provides people with information that their behavior is not consistent with goals. In effect, it provides people with information about how far they are from achieving their goals.

Feedback is *constructive* if it is used to help people measure whether their behavior is helping them to achieve their goals.

If feedback is used to discourage or belittle people, it is *destructive.*

Obviously, financial counselors should make a concerted effort to use constructive feedback and encourage their clients to do the same. Much of effective communication between counselors and clients relies on the transmission of feedback. Keeping the following points in mind will help you to provide appropriate feedback.

- Focus feedback on behavior rather than on the person.

  Making a statement like, "You aren't very responsible with your money." focuses on the person and makes a judgment about him or her. On the other hand, making a statement like, "When you use your credit cards you seem to spend more than you realize!" focuses on the person's behavior. The concept to keep in mind is that people can change their behavior more easily than they can alter the qualities we judge them to have. Besides, our judgments may not be accurate.

- Focus feedback on immediate situations.

  Feedback not closely related to behavior is less useful. As discussed above, the purpose of feedback is to help people achieve their goals. Feedback such as, "You never seem to think ahead," focuses on a judgment made about the person and on some indeterminate time. It might be better to say, "You don't seem to be thinking of what will happen if you choose that alternative." Even with feedback, behavior from last week or last month cannot be corrected. You cannot change the past. But with feedback you can have an effect on the present.

- Consider the amount of feedback the receiver can use at one time, rather than the amount of information you have or want to share.

  There are times when you have accumulated a great deal of information about a client, information that might be helpful if the client knew about it. However, clients can deal with only a certain amount of information at one time. This is especially true if the feedback you wish to share with clients is negative. Don't overwhelm clients with large quantities of feedback at one time.

- Focus on the feedback's potential value for the receiver, not on the value or release it provides you.

  Feedback, especially negative feedback, can be misused when it is merely a way of venting emotions. Feedback should be offered to help to clients.

Feedback is an essential process in communication. It is the process that helps people to become more self-directing and responsible. Effective feedback can help clients achieve their goals without causing them to feel bad about themselves, their choices, or their behaviors.

Principle 9.7: Counseling relationships adhere to ethical guidelines.

Counselors are hired by financial institutions to perform an important service. Within that service, counselors are obligated to abide by rules and regulations which govern financial transactions. Counselors also have responsibility to clients who seek help. They have responsibility to colleagues within the financial institution, and indirectly they have an obligation to the society at large. And lastly, but equally important, counselors have responsibility to themselves.

Ethical Adherence to Rules and Sanctions

Financial institutions have *Standards* that they invoke. These standards usually deal with financial and institutional policies and procedures, league or affiliation mandates, and state and federal requirements. Financial counselors must be aware of rules and regulations from all of these sources. Financial counselors also are faced with making decisions and providing services that are not entirely financial in nature; they must be aware of psychological and social constraints. In order to be knowledgeable in this second category of responsibilities, counselors must go beyond financial institutions to obtain an ethical base for judgment.

There are a number of sources that provide this base. The National Education Association (NEA) developed a comprehensive code for counselors in schools. Gray (1963) in a book entitled, *The Psychologist In The Schools,* states that the management oriented NEA code stresses such practices as going through channels, adhering to conditions of a contract, and maintaining desirable relationships with patrons. Concepts included in this code are over thirty years old. Yet, they are not dated and definitely have application within financial institutions. A current source, by Alle-Corliss and Alle-Corliss (1999*), Advanced Practice In Human Service Agencies* highlights ethical and legal boundaries for counselors working with individuals or families. Emphasis in this source is placed on ethical and legal considerations regarding diversity, confidentiality, dual relationships, and decision-making models.

An important ethical consideration relates to information and how it is used. Counselors should be aware of procedures for requesting and releasing information. This responsibility has ethical and legal implications. Counselors have an obligation to protect the privacy of clients. All records maintained must be held in strictest confidence. Any release of records must be done with the client's approval. Obviously, conversations about clients should be held to a minimum. Gossiping about clients should never be done. Counselors concerned with the professional, ethical, and legal information are referred to Patterson's (2000) text,

The Counseling Process. Counselors can further their understanding of ethical and legal foundations for counseling from reading any of the sources suggested above.

Ethical Responsibility to Clients

Additionally, it is important for counselors to maintain desirable relationships with the institution's patrons. The American Psychological Association (APA) presents an ethical code for counselors. The APA code suggests that counselors are responsible primarily to clients and ultimately to society. These basic loyalties guide all of the counselor's professional endeavors. Counselors are expected to respect the integrity and guard the welfare of all clients with whom they work. Also within the APA code, it is stated that ultimate allegiance is to society and that counselor behavior should demonstrate an awareness of social responsibilities. Although financial counselors usually are not psychologists, they have a dual responsibility to clients and society and are advised to use the intent of these codes as guidelines for counselor endeavors in financial institutions.

Ethical Responsibility to Colleagues

It is important that counselors are aware of appropriate channels for solving problems that emerge from counseling. Failure to do so can lead to internal strife and possibly legal complications. It is obvious that counselors have to adhere to conditions of all personal and institutional contractual arrangements. Legal ramifications of not adhering can be dramatic. Relationships are the core of counseling in any institution. Counselors are advised to accept the responsibility for developing and maintaining relationships within and among institutions that foster their clients' counseling goals.

Counselors are in a position of responsibility. Waiting for a situation to arise before responding in a responsible manner is unwarranted. Counselors should be prepared before an event occurs to know strategic ways to respond. In order to do this, it is suggested that financial counselors and/or management within a financial institution prepare guidelines which deal with a number of common situations and how they should be handled.

One of the counselor's prime areas of responsibility is in regard to maintaining client confidentiality. Counselors should not either directly or indirectly lead a client to believe that counseling will be confidential if, for any reason, it will not be. It is the counselor's responsibility to tell clients which elements will be held in confidence and which will not.

Most counselors would agree that data about clients should be kept in confidence, and yet there are occasions where sharing may be appropriate. Institutional guidelines might address how data will be shared, if it is to be shared at all. Who will it be shared with? Under what conditions will it be shared? Will the client know that data are to be shared and with whom? Are there procedures that will allow the client to release information? When and how will a counselor refer a client to an agency outside of the financial institution: for pastoral counseling, for psychological counseling, for alcoholics counseling? These are just a few of the questions and issues that might be addressed in prepared guidelines. Institutional personnel should be made aware of these guidelines, so that the procedures counselors follow will be known. Personnel will know the type and amount of data that they can expect to receive and they will know the limits of confidentiality that counselors must maintain.

Ethical Responsibility to Self

Beyond these guidelines, counselors have a more subtle set of responsibilities. The first of these is the responsibility that counselors have to themselves. Counselors should try to maintain physical and psychological health. It's important that counselors learn to leave trials and tribulations of the job at the office and not carry home problems that occur within confines of the counseling relationship. For counselors to be effective, they must be alert and able to attend to every client. This will not happen if they are physically or mentally tired. On certain days counselors may be incapable of facilitating client growth or change. On these occasions counselors should either postpone meeting with clients or refer them to other counselors.

A second responsibility that counselors face is to be aware of their own limitations. Counselor limitations can occur on many fronts. They can have physical limitations, skill limitations, knowledge limitations, and data limitations. No counselor can be helpful to all clients. Counselors must remember that their purpose is to help clients, not to help themselves.

A closer look at each of these limitations may prove beneficial. If too many clients are seen in one day, a counselor may get tired, be less attentive, and be less helpful than she would be if the number of counseling contacts were limited. It is wise to set up counseling schedules so that counseling can be interspersed with other types of activities.

Counselors should participate in educational opportunities, which will help update their counseling skills. Practice, with feedback, is a beneficial way to develop and maintain counseling skill. Knowledge is constantly changing, with new information continuously becoming available. Consequently, it is important that counselors have opportunities to read and discuss new materials that could have an impact on their development.

Counselors should be aware that they might not be able to interact effectively with all people. They should be aware of interactions that pose them difficulties, situations where they can not feel comfortable. They also should be aware of situations in which clients are uncomfortable. In these situations counselors must recognize limitations and refer clients.

Finally, counselors should not encourage a belief that they can accomplish more than they are capable of achieving. The ethical responsibility for clearly stating what can be done through financial counseling must be made eminently clear to clients.

RESOURCES

Alle-Corliss, L. & Alle-Corliss, R. (1999). *Advanced Practice In Human Service Agencies.* Belmont: Brooks Cole Publishing Company.

Gray, S.W. (1963). *The Psychologist In The Schools*. New York: Holt, Rinehart, and Winston.

Luft, J. (1969). *Of Human Interaction: The Johari Window*. Palo Alto: Mayfield Publishing Company.

Patterson, L.E. (2000). *The Counseling Process.* Belmont: Wadsworth/Thomson Learning.

10 COUNSELING: BASIC STRATEGIES

A student, upon graduation from high school, made an interesting statement. He said, "In high school I was considered to be a very serious, no-nonsense kind of guy. My reputation became hard to live up to. I couldn't wait to go to college far away from my home town so that I could be who I really wanted to be."

INTRODUCTION

This chapter discusses essential strategies that have significant influence on financial counseling. Identifying client characteristics, goal setting, specifying objectives, generating potential solutions, establishing action plans, and implementing plans is discussed first. These are the six core strategies within the counseling process. Communication skills, discussed in subsequent chapters, are needed to assure that these strategies are accomplished in a manner that is efficient, thorough, and in the best interest of clients.

Focus is then turned to application of eight conceptual *frames* first developed for the text *Dynamic Counseling (*Lee, Pulvino and Perrone, 1993) .

BASIC COUNSELING PERSPECTIVES

Identifying Client Characteristics

Identifying client characteristics is a systematic process used to understand clients and their situations. The result of this strategy is a detailed description of a client presenting an underlying concern. The focus of this description varies with types of concern clients bring to the financial counselor. As mentioned earlier these concerns vary along the continuum of remedial to productive counseling. A good description will include some or all of the following: essential details of the concern, its history and if appropriate, possible causes, client resources (personal as well as financial), and other individuals involved. Identifying client characteristics begins with a client statement of need.

There are two sources of information used during this strategic process. The first source is clients themselves. The perspective from which they see situations, how they respond to the them, and how they feel about the situations all provide vital information. Clients' perceptions may not be accurate. Nevertheless, their perceptions govern their behavior and provide a starting point for counselors. A second source of information comes from clients' life situations and is usually verifiable from significant others in their lives. This information includes demographic information such as location of home and employment, amount of income and indebtedness, and number of dependents.

Perhaps the most important thing to remember during this identification process is to be aware of the obvious. At the beginning, the most obvious problem is the immediate need clients' report. However, most problems have several layers. The upper most is usually termed "the presenting concern." It is this initial concern which brings clients to counselors for help.

Counselors should be aware that clients frequently present problems, which are relatively superficial in nature. They are not trying to deceive the counselor, but may be testing to see if the counselor can be trusted. This action is not necessarily done on a conscious level. Clients may not be aware that they are concealing central issues. They do this, however, because trust has not been established in the relationship. The initial moments of interaction are crucial. If counselors respond in open and caring ways, clients are more likely to discuss central issues. This will occur only if counselors allow clients sufficient time and opportunity to discuss and discover real issues.

Counselors must be aware that time is important in the early stages of the counseling process, i.e., building a relationship and gathering information. Counselors should not attempt to move too quickly. Clients usually want to feel listened to and understood before focusing on trying to solve a problem or establishing productive goals. A cursory gathering of information or immediate acceptance of presenting concerns can lead to premature solution generation, which in turn can lead to client frustration when solutions generated prove to be ineffective. Despite this caution, counselors must be aware that spending too much time gathering data about client issues also can be dangerous. Clients may feel overwhelmed by problems that surface and may withdraw or give up. Also, clients sometimes use this strategy themselves as a means of avoidance. Continued sharing and presentation of detailed information can be a way of avoiding change or for accepting responsibility for doing something about one's problems. Counselors should be aware of this possibility. Finally, information should be relevant to the concern. The mere generation of detailed information will not guarantee a solution.

While gathering client information is a critical step, counselors should not use this strategy to impose favorite definitions of, and solutions for, client concerns. Counselors must remember that all clients are unique and problems presented by one client are different than those presented by another. Solutions used with one client may, or may not, be appropriate for another. While gathering client information, counselors should be open to their clients and aware of what they are saying, so that defining client concerns is accurate and relevant.

The information gathering process may go through several steps. The initial step is to deal with the presenting concern. A second step is to deal with the real concern which may be the same or different than the presenting concern. Finally, when sufficient information has been developed, there is a natural progression to establishing goals. An example may show how these various steps happen within the counseling process.

The Case of Casey

Casey enters the counselor's office and says, "I'm having a little trouble, but $300 will get me out of it... my credit's good." On hearing this, the counselor has an option of accepting the client statement as the full information about the concern or taking additional time to gather additional information. If the counselor accepts the opening statement, the counselor might say, "All right, your credit is good and $300 seems like a reasonable request. I'll start processing the papers. You'll get your $300 and you can be on your way."

By contrast, the counselor might use more time to gather additional information about the client and obtain a detailed description of the presenting concern by saying something similar to, "You say you're having a little trouble. Let's talk about that for a moment." This approach provides Casey an opportunity to discuss what has led him to the statement that "I'm having a little trouble." In the process of doing this the counselor provides an opportunity for establishing a relationship in which trust can be developed. It is conceivable that by using this more open ended tactic Casey will get to a point where he can more openly discuss factors which underlie his need for $300. A more definitive statement of Casey's trouble thereby can be determined.

Providing clients an opportunity to talk about their opening statements in greater detail and establishing proper counseling relationships helps clients to go beyond presenting problems. It can lead them to understand factors that underlie their problem. In Casey's situation, it may be that $300 is not the need, but rather, a short-term solution to a problem. Conceivably, Casey could be having difficulties managing his money. The way the counselor might help most is to help Casey develop a systematic way to budget his money over a longer period of time. The counselor would not come to this solution if he responded to Casey's initial statement as being totally representative of Casey's needs. In general, counselors must consistently press for detail in what clients present. In this way, they can help clients understand their difficulties, can best utilize themselves as resources in helping clients resolve those difficulties, and educate clients in ways of preventing difficulties from recurring.

Goal Setting

Establishment of appropriate goals and objectives is a logical consequence of gathering relevant information. Needs that clients bring to a counselor can be explored and clearly defined. However, it is a counselor's task to convert these needs into appropriate goal statements. The types of goal statements that any counselor makes are dependent upon two specific elements.

Element One: The Counselor's Needs. The first of these elements is the counselor's personal theory about growth and development. Any counselor will have implicit or explicit beliefs about how people change, what things are meaningful in their lives, what kinds of knowledge clients must have to make changes in their lives, and ways that they can intercede on behalf of clients. These elements are general and usually cut across all clients.

Element Two: The Client's Needs. At another level however, clients enter the relationship with very specific expectations and needs. Counselors must be able to deal with their own professional beliefs and attitudes *and* clients' expectations and needs. Counselors have the responsibility of tailoring their approach to individuals. To accomplish this counselors must address two different kinds of goals, *process goals* and *outcome goals*.

Process Goals: Counselors must provide the best possible environment for working with clients. Process goals are established to provide conditions in which clients can grow, develop, and learn new behaviors. A relationship with the client, one that is characterized by congruence, empathy, warmth, acceptance, and trust is needed for this to occur. The task of establishing a facilitative counseling relationship is a counseling process goal and is the counselor's responsibility.

Outcome Goals: Outcome goals specify why clients have sought counseling help. Usually these goals are presented in a vague, ill-defined manner, or may not be introduced as goals at all, but rather as client needs. A counselor's task is to help clients conceptualize ill-defined, vague goals or needs in precise terms. Precision is needed so that counseling strategies can be effectively designed and implemented. As an example of vague goals, consider the following client statement: "I'd like to understand how to spend my money more wisely." In working with this goal, a counselor must help the client detail specifically what is meant by "to understand." Through mutual discussion of this goal, the client and counselor might arrive at a goal statement: "to budget and account for my financial expenditures for six consecutive months." The second goal is much more precise because the client now knows exactly what will be gained from the counseling relationship. The client will learn how to do something very specific, i.e., to budget and to account for expenditures.

Specifying Objectives

Once generalized goals have been established, specific counseling objectives should be established. These objectives can then serve as the focus of counseling.

Robert Mager (1975) in his book, *Preparing Instructional Objectives,* outlined various characteristics of clearly specified or stated objectives. These characteristics can be adapted to the counseling process. In this adaptation, a counseling objective would describe an intended outcome and not be a description or summary of content or process. A characteristic of a usefully stated objective is that it is stated in behavioral or performance terms. It should specify what clients would do as a result of counseling. It is important to note that this is distinct from specifying *how* the objective should be accomplished. In defining useful objectives, terminal behavior is specified in advance. The kind of behavior that will be accepted as evidence that the client has achieved the objective should be stated early in the counseling process.

At times it is important to describe the conditions under which the expected behavior will occur. The client should have a clear idea of what behavior, enacted for what percentage of time, will be considered to be acceptable behavior. In talking about objectives with a client, a counselor is advised to use verb phrases that clearly communicate what the client will be doing when the objective is accomplished. For instance, "to write, to list, to name, and to construct" are all definitive and descriptive of what the client will do, whereas "to understand, to believe, to have faith in, to appreciate" are vague and intuitive. Statements of the first kind can be measured objectively. It is possible for a counselor to see that the client has written, listed, named, and constructed something. It is more difficult for a counselor to know if a person understood, believed, had faith, or appreciated something.

Counselors should help clients strive for specificity in objectives and help them to do away with vague phrases.
Client statements should incorporate all three of the following conditions.

1. *Performance:* A good objective states what a learner is expected to be able to do;
2. *Conditions:* An objective describes the important conditions under which the performance will occur;
3. *Criterion:* A good objective describes the criterion of an acceptable performance by describing how well the learner must perform in order to be considered acceptable (Mager, p. *21).*

Clearly stated client objectives might be: "I will increase my income by January 30th," "I will decrease my living expenses by June 15th of next year," "I will adjust by debt payments so that by June 15th my payments will be $100 less per month than they are now." Each of these statements is stated in a way that it is directly measurable by both counselor and client.

Generating Solutions

Once information gathering and goal setting has been accomplished, solutions must be found to achieve goals and objectives. At this juncture, it is crucial that counselors establish the attitude that clients have potential for satisfying their own needs or accomplishing their goals. One way that counselors can establish this attitude and convince clients that they do have this power is to foster the client's responsibility for generating solutions for problems. Counselors can ask clients to identify solutions and possibilities for solution they have tried in the past. By focusing on the clients' generation of solutions, client confidence can be enhanced and can lead clients to believe they have control of their destiny. If, by contrast, counselors immediately start listing possible alternatives, clients quickly learn that solutions for their problems are outside themselves and that their fate is in the hands of others. This attitude will not be beneficial for clients in the long run, nor will it be beneficial to counselors.

Possible solutions can come from a variety of sources. If the information gathering strategy has been successful and realistic goals and specific objectives have been stated, solutions may be quite apparent. The most effective preparation for generation of solutions is the information gathering process. Often, when clients have a full understanding of the problem and elements contributing to it they will *know* what needs to be done. In like manner, counselors can utilize their resources more effectively if clients' problems are specifically outlined. Effective information gathering provides clients and counselors a basis for solution generation.

Emphasis should be on generation of a number of possible solutions rather than on finding a single *perfect* one. Generation of a number of alternative solutions allows clients to practice commitment and responsibility within the counseling relationship. There is no one *right* way to solve a problem. Rather a variety of ways can produce desired outcomes. Generation of a number of possibilities helps clients to learn a process for making choices. This lesson can be extremely valuable.

What Constitutes A *Good* Solution?

First, a good solution is related directly to the problem or goal. Often clients generate solutions that are not directly related to the problem. A client might state the problem as "paying my present obligations and learning how to budget" and then generate an alternative such as "to go on a payroll deduction plan for Savings Bonds." While buying Savings Bonds might be laudable, it is not directly related to paying present bills and learning how to budget.

A second characteristic of a *good* solution is that it specifies what the client will do. In contrast to this, clients and counselors could generate solutions that require responsible action of individuals other than the client. When this is done, however, clients avoid responsibility for solving their own problems or achieving their own goals. While solutions of this kind may effectively solve problems, clients soon learn that, "If I have a problem and I take it to a counselor, the counselor will solve it for me." The result can be that clients will fail to learn to be responsible for their behavior. The best solutions are those that require clients to accept responsibility for their actions and clearly define the behaviors that will be exhibited.

A third characteristic of *good* solutions is that they are simple. This does not mean that solutions lack sophistication, but rather that they require a minimum of client effort to comprehend and/or carry out. Complicated, involved solutions usually will not be carried out. Clients will continue old familiar behavior rather than attempt complicated new ones. There is a simple principle to keep in mind, if the new solution requires substantially more effort than previous behavior, the new solution usually will not be carried out.

Finally, *good* solutions utilize client strengths. Emphasis should be on using positive client personal and financial resources. Building upon the positive maximizes the possibility of success, while preventing client discouragement.

Up to this point we have suggested that counselors should help clients or provide the structure necessary to help clients generate alternatives for their problems. This was suggested to assure that clients learn to accept responsibility for solving their own problems. However, after clients have had ample opportunity to generate plausible solutions, it is appropriate for counselors to offer additional solutions. It is also appropriate for counselors to give clients new or additional information that may relate to their problems or goals. When this is done, these concepts should be kept in mind:

Adapt Information and/or Solutions To Clients

Financial counselors often deal with very large dollar amounts. Many clients don't relate to such sums. For example, consider a counselor attempting to explain to a client how important time is when dealing with money. The counselor could use sophisticated language dealing with large amounts of money. "You see if we take $10,000,000 and put it in a certificate account just over night, we could make $2,000 or $3,000 in a 24 hour period." Very few clients who seek counseling can understand figures of this magnitude. Very few people, including the counselor, will ever really experience having $10,000,000. Using examples like this can lead to confusion. While the counselor may understand the principle involved, the client may hear nothing more than "ten million dollars," and fail to comprehend the principle. A more appropriate explanation of the importance of time might be the following. "A shoe store owner deals with shoes as his commodity. When he buys shoes from the wholesaler and places them on his shelf, he establishes a retail price. If he keeps those shoes on his shelf for several months, he does not lose any money. Our money does not work that way. When we take money and place it on the shelf, so to speak, its value stays the same. Time works against us. The longer our money is on the shelf, not working for us, the more money we lose because it is not earning anything and because of inflation. Time becomes very important. The quicker we can get our money into a savings program, the more it can work for us in earning interest. So, while one day of leaving shoes on the shelf will not affect the shoe owner's earning power, one day will affect how our money will work for us."

Adapting information and solutions to a client requires that the counselor use language and examples that clients can understand. Also, solutions will have to be adapted to the specific needs and goals of each client. For example, a bill consolidation loan may provide a solution for one client and not for another. For one client the loan might be used to pay all of his present indebtedness. For another, the loan could provide for part of the indebtedness while the client would be responsible for paying off certain debts from regular income. Counselors should treat each client as unique and tailor solutions to this uniqueness.

Offer Several Possible Solutions Or Forms Of Information

As discussed before, clients should be given a choice among a number of alternate solutions. When clients are given choices, and make decisions as to which solutions to use, they become responsible for carrying their solutions out and for results. This responsibility is the clients', not the counselor's. Counselors, by fostering development of a number of possible solutions, help clients build commitment and responsibility.

Help Clients To Become Good Judges Of Potential Solutions

Clients need to learn to evaluate potential solutions so that they can make rational, adaptive decisions. In the short run, allowing clients to do this may extend the time needed for counseling, but in the long run, it will build trust in the relationship. Trust will become increasingly important as clients attempt to carry out possible solutions. If trust has been built, clients are more likely to accept and carry out the counselor's solutions by making them their own.

Help Clients To Become Their Own Solution Generators

When clients become effective solution generators, they will no longer need counseling services. If counselors introduce clients to solution generation techniques, clients will learn ways to become independent. For example, counselors could teach clients to use the technique of brainstorming. Brainstorming is a simple technique for generating possible solutions that emphasizes quantity and delays critical analysis. Clients' concerns can provide a focal point for practicing this technique within counseling.

Once clients have developed solution generation skills, explored possible solutions for their problems, and examined a number of possible alternatives for achieving their stated goals/objectives, counselors and clients should establish a system for analyzing alternatives (possible solutions) in light of stated goals. One way of examining alternatives is to examine the level of difficulty. An alternative that is difficult to undertake may not be appropriate. By contrast, an alternative that is easy for clients to initiate would be more appropriate and more likely to be successful.

The entire list of alternatives should be rated on their *ease of enactment.* By doing this, and then looking back across the list of all alternatives, clients can make meaningful decisions as to which alternatives would be easiest to implement.

Alternatives isolated from the overall list should then be viewed from other perspectives. With each alternative, clients should decide *what* must be done, *how* to initiate action with each alternative, *when* the best time to initiate action is, and *who* should be involved in each alternative. The questions of *what, how, when* and *who* should be asked for every alternative that is considered. At this point, counselors should help clients choose alternatives and put them into action. Counselors must emphasize that the choice process is not infallible. It is possible that choice of alternative(s) will not be appropriate. If success does not occur there will be an opportunity to try again. A counselor's responsibility is to serve as a sounding board, to discuss pros and cons of alternatives chosen, to elaborate on relative merits of alternatives, and to share an opinion as to why certain alternatives may be more likely to result in success. Counselors should attempt to help clients make the best possible choices, realizing that there are no guarantees in this kind of endeavor.

Establishing Action Plans

Counselors and clients must proceed successfully through early strategies of the counseling process, - building a relationship, diagnosis and goal setting, and generation of solutions, before they are able to choose plans of action that lead to problem resolution or goal attainment. If counseling has proceeded satisfactorily, there will be a number of possible plans of action. Also, if the counselor has followed rules for determining *good* solutions, *what, how, when* and *who* necessary for goal attainment will have been specified and will then provide a plan for action. The decision as to which plan or combination of plans is to be implemented should be made as quickly as possible. If making a decision is prolonged, the client may become frustrated, confused, and lose motivation. The counselor should press for a decision and at the same time address several important issues relevant to each potential action plan.

▶ What time, effort, and resources will be required by the client and/or counselor to carry out the action plan?

What financial resources does the client have? The answer to this question is very important when attempting to plan for financial solutions. However, the client and counselor also should consider additional forms of client resources. What is the client's motivation for change? What attitudes does the client have? What skills or experiences can be brought to bear on the problem? Are there additional client resources that should be considered? Answers to each of these questions are as important as knowing the client's financial status.

▶ How much effort toward reaching a solution can be expected from clients?

When clients come to counselors for help they expect that their problem will be resolved with a minimum of effort and involvement. Usually, if clients had their way, the counselor would solve their problems for them. Counselors should guard against this natural tendency. They should examine each action plan to determine how much additional time and effort will be required of clients and/or themselves. Action plans, which require unreasonable effort on the part of clients, will probably be unsuccessful. Action plans, which require undue time and effort on the part of counselors, run the same risk. Counselors must be realistic about how much time and effort they should expend on behalf of clients. However, before action plans are eliminated because of the time, effort and resources required, clients and counselors should examine answers to the following questions.

▶ What will action plans produce for clients?

In addition to primary problem resolution or goal attainment, action plans will usually produce side benefits for clients that must be weighed against the time, effort and resources required. A consolidation loan action plan, for example, may solve the immediate financial problem but may not produce beneficial side effects (e.g., client may not learn how and why the problem originally developed). On the other hand, a consolidation loan coupled with budgeting training may solve the client's present financial problem and enhance the client's budgeting skill. In such a case the side effects may outweigh the time, effort and resource requirements.

▶ What is the possibility of failure if the action plan is implemented? How critical would failure be?

While many action plans look feasible on paper, they may have a high probability of failure. A consolidation loan with repayment through payroll deduction will probably not result in default. On the other hand, suppose payroll deduction is not possible. What assurance is there that a previously unreliable client will make payments on the consolidation loan? Obviously, possibility of delinquency increases. Clients and counselors should be aware of failure possibilities and build in safeguards.

Action plans that have a high probability for failure should, of course, be eliminated from serious consideration. In conjunction with failure potential, clients and counselors should examine the seriousness of failure consequences. While one failure may lead to bankruptcy, others may lead only to momentary setbacks. In all cases, critical effects of failure should be examined.

Implementing Plans

Once plans of action have been chosen, only implementation remains. Implementation, of course, is the responsibility of clients. However, counselors can be involved during this step. Counselors should provide support during implementation, in relation to the extent of client change required by a specific action plan. Support can take several forms. Counselors can schedule interviews with clients to evaluate how things are going. Such follow-up interviews allow counselors to provide feedback to clients relative to carrying out action plans and resolving original counseling concerns. They also provide counselors with an opportunity to reinforce learning that took place during the counseling process. A second form of support could be friendly telephone calls in which counselors ask clients how things are going and whether they have encountered any unexpected difficulties. Finally, counselors could write clients letters reminding them of what took place in counseling and offer help if problems occur as action plans are carried out. Contacts of this sort should always be positive in nature. Even if clients have not carried out entire action plans, positive feedback concerning what *has* been accomplished can be a powerful motivator for continued effort.

FRAMES: A NEW VIEW OF COUNSELING STRATEGIES

We have discussed general principles and concepts in strategies of information gathering, goal setting, specifying objectives, generating solutions, and establishing action plans and implementation. There are no *right* uses of these strategies. The *correctness* of any strategy is dependent upon the outcome it produces. Thus, while a counselor may use what appears to be an appropriate strategy with a client, it may not be successful. There are numerous intervening circumstances within any client's field of experience which cannot be controlled and which may be more powerful than the action plan.

Finally, using some form of systematic solution generation strategy with clients not only facilitates problem resolution and/or goal attainment, but also teaches clients a process which they can utilize when new problems occur. This aspect of counseling is especially beneficial because it builds prevention and productivity into every counseling relationship.

Another approach to counseling is breaking the counseling process down into specific stages or *frames*.

In this approach, counseling is conceived as consisting of eight frames. Bateson (1972) introduced the term *frame* as a way of conceptualizing human activity. A frame can be thought of as a moment in time in which the counselor's focus is in a particular direction. The term frame is similar to the frame on a picture or painting. The frame focuses attention on what it surrounds. To frame is to put a border around something of interest with the understanding that the frame is used for convenience of discussion, not because it is a discreet part of reality. Life is a continuous flow. Yet, by breaking the flow into discreet events, portions or aspects of life can be examined. The border, or frame, focuses attention on a moment in life. Much like a snapshot, this framing process allows counselors to focus on one event or moment in time. This focusing process is helpful. Use of frames allows counselors a process for interrupting the natural flow of life while providing a strategy for helping clients to achieve their goals.

Lee, Pulvino, and Perrone (1993) in *Dynamic counseling* suggest that the aim of counseling is to help clients control their behavior and to focus their attention. They believe that these general goals can be accomplished through application of eight specific frames, frames that order the counseling process while focusing the counselor's attention.

The eight frames to be discussed are

- Blending,
- Reframing
- Setting Goals
- Identifying and Creating Exceptions
- Prescribing Action,
- Experiencing
- Using and Transforming Personal History
- Future Pacing.

Each of these frames can be used separately or they can be arranged in combinations. There is not a particular order to the use of frames. Yet, the first frame, the Blending frame, usually is used in the initial stages of counseling.

The above eight frames are presented as a means for strategic intervention. At times, words like blending, reframing, or future pacing are viewed as being communication *tactics*. The difference between the dualistic use of these words is understood in terms of the counselor's intentions. When the words are used to structure counseling they are *frames*. When they are used otherwise they are primarily communication techniques.

Blending

The focus of the blending frame is on joining the client's world. To *blend*, counselors must hear the inner meaning of what clients communicate, observe their non-verbal behaviors, and reflect their observations through their subsequent response to clients. Through blending, counselors will gain a better understanding of clients' concerns and be in a better position to communicate that understanding back to the client. Sometimes clients want only to be heard, to be understood, or have their feelings, fears, or anxieties accepted. It is important for clients to have their stories heard. Blending is the process that allows this to happen. It is dependent on the counselor's ability to listen to the client's verbal and non-verbal messages, explore the nuances of what is communicated, and to focus the conversation. Sometimes blending and acceptance is all clients want or need.

Reframing

Reframing is a process of showing someone how the data they are using for their formulation of *reality* can be used to support an alternate *reality*. It is usually agreed that we do not deal with reality *per se*, but rather with interpretations of reality. If one reflects on the political process this clearly can be observed. Republican and Democratic politicians have a knack for seeing identical data in totally different ways. In this situation, as in all others the individual ascribes meaning. Counseling deals with this aspect of *knowing*. Reframing breaks the illusionary frame inherent in any world image, and thereby reveals that what appeared unchangeable can indeed be changed and that there exists alternate realities. What turns out to be changed, as a result of reframing is the meaning attributed to the situation. Counselors can use the process of reframing to help clients see alternate realities by helping them focus on counter-balancing desires or positive feelings. This helps clients mobilize their energies toward positive outcomes. At times, reframing of presenting problems or feelings is all that is necessary. Consider the following interchange between a therapist and a parent who has brought his daughter for therapy.

Parent: I would like you to hypnotize my daughter and change her.

Therapist: Change her?

Parent: Yes, she is the most stubborn person in the world. She is sixteen and about to leave home. I am afraid of what will happen to her. She is far too stubborn.

Therapist: I see. Your daughter has a mind of her own. She sticks to her ideas. She demonstrates tremendous tenacity and persists when she believes she is correct.

Parent: Yes, that is true.

After a few minutes of thought about what the therapist had said the Parent looked the therapist in the eye and said, "Thank you, I don't think we'll be needing your services." He took his daughter and left.

This example demonstrates reframing. The therapist listened to the parent and determined that the parent viewed an aspect of his daughter's behavior as being negative. The parent used the word *stubborn* to describe his perception. The therapist understood the behavior described by the parent but *reframed* it by presenting the "flip-side", by labeling the behavior as *tenacity*. The therapist emphasized the positive aspects of a behavior that the parent had previously only seen as negative. Once the behavior had been reframed, the parent no longer sought therapy for his daughter. The parent did not want his daughter to lack *tenacity*!

There are times when counselors need only to reframe a client's experience to help them. At times, problems can *magically* disappear when defined as an asset. At other times, reframing can be used in conjunction with other frames to help clients reach satisfactory counseling goals. In all situations, reframing builds on a basic assumption that every life event is an opportunity.

Setting Goals

Financial counseling is a goal directed activity. In this interpersonal activity emphasis is on how clients will behave once counseling is completed. When goals are desirable, meaningful goal setting can have a dramatic impact on clients' present behavior. The counselor's task is to help clients establish goals that are meaningful for them and under their control. When such goals are achieved, clients' self-concepts, self-esteem, and sense of self-efficacy usually increase.

Goal setting, as a counseling strategy usually is successful when goals are under the client's control, when they are stated positively in the client's language, and when they specify what the clients will be doing differently at the conclusion of counseling. When counseling goals lack this degree of specificity responsibility in the entire counseling interaction is hampered. Lack of properly stated goals can inappropriately place responsibility for outcomes on the counselor, client satisfaction with counseling is difficult to achieve, timing of closure is difficult to determine, and evaluation of counseling is impeded.

Identifying and Creating Exceptions

Exceptions to most problems exist or can be created. Counselors can use awareness of exceptions to help clients to see alternate possibilities for dealing with their concerns. The key in this frame is to help clients identify exceptions to their concerns and to help them understand how they can contribute to making these exceptions occur. By helping clients foster exceptions to their concerns, counselors help clients gain control of their behavior. This increases the probability that exceptions will happen with increased frequency. Obviously, the more the exception to a problem occurs, the less the problem does. Therefore, making exceptions happen moves the client closer to achieving established goals.

It is natural for clients to attend to negative experiences and to minimize positive experiences. By focusing on exceptions, counselors can bring to light the reality that there are more exceptional times than times in which problems occur. Consider the following:

Client: "I'm always strapped financially."

Financial Counselor: "All of the time?"

Client: "Yes, all of the time."

Financial Counselor: "Can you think of any time in the past year when you weren't?"

Client: "Well, I was during the holidays and at income tax time."

Financial Counselor: "I can understand that, but can you think of when you weren't?"

Client: " After the first of the year until about April 15th I was okay. Then, June through November was okay.

Financial Counselor: " What was different about those times?"

Client: " I didn't have to deal with large expenditures like gifts and taxes."

Financial Counselor: " It sounds like the financial difficulty occurs two times year and that for most of the year you are okay." " Is that true?"

Client: "Yes, I think it is true."

It would be appropriate and helpful for the counselor to follow this conversation with ways the client could extend the exceptional times, times when he was not being strapped financially, into those times of the year when he was. Through role-playing, visualization, reframing, or planned experiences the counselor could help the client learn how to make *exceptional* times occur more frequently, even in the face of adversity. While doing this, the counselor must retain a positive perspective and encourage the client to do whatever possible to assure positive exceptions in the future.

Prescribing Action

Helping clients view their personal worlds in new and different ways may be therapeutic. However, designing ways clients can gain insight or reformulating their experience in alternate language does not necessarily change the experience or provide a basis for change. Words of wisdom do not change clients' lives, unless the words are put into action. For many, *experience* may indeed be the best teacher. The nature of the prescribing action frame is to fill the void between words and experiences. In this frame, counselors purposefully plan and prescribe experiences designed to help clients achieve their goals. More specifically, planned experiences provide a set of actions, actions that are eventually under clients' control. Although experiences can be drawn from any source, one of the most obvious behavior prescriptions results from identifying exceptions. The behavior clients use to make exceptions happen can be prescribed. The exception for a client who says, "I never set money aside" might be *except* for his children's birthdays. The counselor could help the client to identify what he specifically did in preparation for his children's birthdays and then *prescribe* that he do exactly the same thing at the end of every month.

The above example demonstrates a *direct* prescription designed to alter the client's behavior. Action prescriptions also can occur when clients learn desired behavior *indirectly*. The advantage of indirect learning is that resistance is reduced and acceptance is facilitated. An example from a University Counseling Center demonstrates an indirect prescription. A male student who was a major in accounting stated to his counselor that "There are no good woman on campus." Discussion of the client's statement led his counselor to conclude that primarily the client was shy about approaching women he didn't know. From the counselor's perspective, the client's statement reflected the client's defense against having to approach women. As a basis for helping, the counselor discussed with the client what the client meant by a *good woman*. A *good woman*, by the client's definition was a woman who was an upper class student and who was available for dating. The client did not believe there were any woman on campus that fit both categories. The counselor challenged the client by stating that information was needed to support his claim that, "There are no good woman on campus." The counselor suggested that the client use his interest in numbers to arrive at meaningful data. Together, the client and counselor created a short questionnaire to be used to solicit information from women on campus about their year in school and aspects of their dating behavior. Once the questionnaire was completed the client used it as a basis for interviewing fifteen women on campus. Results of his interviews did not confirm his original hypothesis. The client then told the counselor that he thought the fifteen respondents were not a representative sample and that a larger sample was needed. His counselor agreed. The questionnaire was then used as the basis for interviewing fifty more women. Case closed.

Let us examine the above from the perspective of *action prescriptions*. The counselor prescribed the exact behavior that was central to the client's problem, he was afraid of approaching women. The treatment consisted of having the client do what he was afraid to do. He *directly* interviewed the women. *Indirectly* he learned how to overcome his shyness. In order to complete the questionnaire the client had to approach women, initiate a conversation, and then query them about their dating behavior. He not only learned about their dating behavior, but more importantly, he learned that he could approach women he did not know and start a conversation with them. In fact, he approached sixty-five women! This experience, for this client, was very beneficial. It probably was more beneficial than if the counselor had used a totally verbal counseling strategy.

Experiencing

It was pointed out in the previous discussion that *experience can be a good teacher*. This frame is built specifically on that belief. It may be appropriate to use a behavioral or attention focused experience during counseling. Depending on the specific need, there are a variety of ways that this can be accomplished. Relaxation exercises can be used to help stressed clients. Physical centering exercises can be used to help clients to become alert to their environment. Visualization exercises can be used to discover and transform underlying problems or to rehearse needed behaviors. Role-playing can be used to practice behaviors. All of these approaches can provide relevant direct experiences.

Clients benefit most when counselors use experiences to augment counseling discussions. Consider a client who has difficulty in approaching creditors about his financial situation. The counselor could discuss the issue, reframe it, and/or examine and use exceptions. In addition, the counselor could have the client *visualize* talking with a creditor. The counselor could take the role of the creditor and *role-play* an upcoming conversation with the client. The counselor could reverse the *role-play* and ask the client to take the role of creditor while the counselor plays the role of client. The counselor could ask a colleague to interview the client in advance of the actual interview with creditors. All of these experiences can lead to clients' insight and provide clients an opportunity to practice behaviors before they count.

Personal History

The majority of stored information is not conscious. This stored information is important because it creates a running story about one's life and provides the basis for how one behaves and thinks about him/herself. Stored information is in two categories, content and instruction sets.

An individual's actual experiences provide the content. Typically, content is unchangeable. However, counselors can help clients to move their focus of attention from negative experiences to positive experiences and help clients to alter how they think about negative experiences.

Instruction sets are comprised of how a person thinks about events and their learned problem-solving and decision-making styles. Directly or indirectly individuals develop methods for achieving goals or for fulfilling their needs. Counselors can help clients to use functional instruction sets or to modify those that are dysfunctional. Counselors can help clients make explicit their problem solving and decision-making strategies. This provides a basis for applying previously learned skills to present problems. Often, clients are unaware of previously acquired skills that can be applied to current situations or they are unaware of how they solved problems similar to the present problem in the past. For example, the leadership and organizational skills learned as a class officer in high school can be applied to other leadership tasks, e.g., organizing a hospital volunteer program, organizing a book-parent program for the local elementary school, or organizing the company's annual picnic. When counselors detect that clients' problem-solving and decision-making instruction sets are inefficient, counselors can be helpful by teaching specific problem-solving and decision-making approaches.

There are times when the counseling focus must deal with past events because stored information is affecting present behavior. A general classification of cases exist in which previous experiences that vary from early childhood physical or sexual abuse to military experiences continue to be activated and interfere with clients' present lives. In such cases, focusing on the future has diminished effect because past experiences have a high valence of power. Basic information can not be directly changed. However, counselors can help clients to unearth the basic building blocks of their self-understanding. These basic blocks are at two levels; *encapsulated units* of experience and *theme nets*.

Encapsulated Units

Encapsulated units of experience are content materials that contain a story line with elements of all are senses, e.g., a person's memory of significant life events. Such units of underlying can be activated by a variety of stimuli. The smell of a particular perfume or after-shave lotion can activate memories of first love. A particular look on someone's face can activate a negative response. The sound of someone's voice can activate thoughts of someone from the past. These encapsulated units of experience are part of one's personal history and essential in the stories they build about themselves. They can not be changed.

While this type of information may be important for counselors and clients to recover, it is only recovered as part of the process of transforming the information or in using it differently as content within instruction sets.

Theme Nets

When encapsulated units of experience are repeated or when similar ones are experienced a *theme net* may develop. Consider the following array:

Encapsulated Unit of Experience 1: Parent praises child for a good report card but wonders why all grades are not A's

Encapsulated Unit of Experience 2: Grandmother makes child sit quietly at a family party to keep clothes looking perfect.

Encapsulated Unit of Experience 3: Child has performed well at a piano concert but the teacher points out all the little errors of fingering and tempo.

From this litany of encapsulated units of experience the child develops a *theme net* that is, "I have to be perfect." A theme net such as this can be activated throughout the individual's life. Getting good grades in college might not be enough. They have to be perfect. Doing a job well may not be enough. It has to be done perfectly. Cleaning the house has to be done perfectly. Keeping a budget has to be done perfectly. Theme nets can impact all aspects of an individual's life.

Counselors can help clients identify *theme nets* and to discover meaningful underlying *encapsulated units of experience*. By helping clients examine these elements clients can learn to deconstruct significant theme nets. Deconstruction is the process of going backward from the identified theme net to determine the nature of underlying encapsulated units of experience. Once this is accomplished the client faces a choice; to continue reacting as before or to change to a more positive way of behaving.

Counselors can introduce deconstruction by enlisting clients to cooperate in trying to understand how past events might have influence on present behaviors. Consider the following counselor statements to a hypothetical client with a theme net of needing to be perfect:

> "I think it might be helpful to identify specific times in your life when being perfect was the logical thing to do."
>
> "I'm wondering when you might have seen others being perfect as a way of pleasing people and what that meant for you."
>
> "Describe a situation for me in which you felt it was important to be perfect."

To follow up on client responses to questions like these the counselor can then objectify the effects of the experience with clients. Questions of who, what, when, where, why, and how can be used.

> "Who do you have to be perfect for?"
>
> "What impact has trying to be perfect had on you?"
>
> "How do you think about yourself as a result of trying to be perfect?"
>
> "Why is it important for you to keep trying to be perfect?"

Questions similar to these help clients understand their encapsulated units of experience and theme nets, while helping counselors get insight into the client's problem. These questions also provide counselors information needed to bridge from the *Personal History* frame to other frames. For example, the client's response to questions might allow the counselor to *reframe* what was stated. It might suggest a needed *experience*. It could lead to a discussion of the client's goals and *goal setting*.

Personal History can be limiting to an individual. Most individuals are relatively unaware of the limitations imposed. However, the student quoted on the first page of this chapter was aware of how his high school behavior created a standard that he felt he must live up to while in high school. He was very aware that by going to college far away from home he would be free to behave in a manner that contrasted with how he had in the past. This student's statement reveals a hope of overcoming shackles of his personal history.

Counselors can help individuals gain an understanding of ways personal history might be limiting. Consider the client who makes the statement, "I can't do that, I've always done it this way". This statement is indicating adherence to a standard emanating from personal history. Since individuals have a natural tendency to resist change, this adherence is typically at an unconscious level. Counselors can help clients overcome this natural resistance by helping them examine similarities between current situations and past events and by assisting clients as they learn new goal oriented ways of responding.

By knowing a client's personal history the counselor can gain a greater appreciation for the client's motivation, know more about the client's problem solving and decision-making skills, or learn about aspects of the client's content that are amenable to deconstruction and change.

Future Pacing

Future pacing may range from development of an elaborate plan about what needs to be accomplished at some distant point in the future to simply rehearsing a behavior that will be used after counseling. Future pacing has two primary steps.

Step One: Clients are encouraged to imagine some time in the future when a problem similar to the present problem might occur.

Step 2: Clients are encouraged to discuss and/or imagine how they might apply a specific action to achieve goals that have been set. The key to success is in helping clients transfer to future events what they have learned about themselves and their ability for problem solving and decision-making.

Future pacing can be stimulated in several ways. Counselors can help clients explore events before they occur through pointed questions. Examples include

"How will you keep these actions going?"

"What will you do differently in the future to keep the solution working?"

"Tell me how you plan to apply what we have discussed in the next two weeks."

"I am curious about how you are going to apply what we talked about?"

In addition to questions, counselors can use *role-playing* to help clients experience how they want to behave in the future. This activity prepares them for the future and indicates to them what they have to know and do in the present to achieve that future.

Finally, counselors can use *visualization* to focus clients on a future time when they will be acting in a manner consistent with the counseling goals that they have established.

Movement Between Frames

The eight frames presented are independent. They all can be used alone. However, financial counseling is most effective when frames are used in concert. Usually, counseling starts with the *blending* frame because it is this frame through which the counselor learns about the client and builds a working relationship. From this point forward any number and/or combination of frames can be used.

RESOURCES

Bateson , G. (1972). *Steps To An Ecology Of Mind.* New York: Ballantine Books.

Lee, J. L., Pulvino, C. J., & Perrone, P. A. (1993). *Dynamic Counseling*. Madison: Instructional Enterprises.

Mager, R. (1975), *Preparing Instructional Objectives.* (2nd Edition). Belmont" Fearon Publishing Company.

11 COUNSELING INTERVENTION STRATEGIES

You cannot help men permanently by doing for them what they **could** and should do for themselves.

Abraham Lincoln

INTRODUCTION

The illustrative cases that follow are intended to demonstrate the use of strategies, tactics and tact that are possible when counselors approach financial counseling from a strategic perspective. The situations reflect the diversity of ideas presented in this text. Presentation of strategic ideas is not in a specific sequence. Each should be viewed as a separate entity with its own message.

INTERVENTION STRATEGIES

The following strategies can be used in all forms of financial counseling. Specific use depends upon client needs and financial counseling goals. As you explore the strategies, keep in mind that several strategies may be combined when working with a client.

Budgeting

One strategy available to financial counselors is the process of *budgeting*. When used in counseling, it should be used to satisfy a specific client need. As such, it should be used to achieve a specific goal and to satisfy specific client objectives. For some situations and with some clients budgeting is an ideal strategy. With other clients it may not be the strategy of choice. Consider the following case.

Client: I'm having trouble keeping track of where my money goes...It seems like no matter how much I make, I can't make ends meet.

Financial Counselor: Which money, specifically, are you talking about?

Client: Well, my monthly salary... I just don't know where it goes.

Financial Counselor: Okay, I see... and when you say, "I can't make ends meet", what do you mean?

Client: I guess I mean that at the end of the month the money needed to pay my bills is larger than the money I have.

Financial Counselor: I thought that was what you meant, but I had to make sure I understood you correctly. What would *you* like to do about this problem?

Client: I'd like to get a handle on how I spend my money. Can you help me do this?

Financial Counselor: I believe so... that is, if you're willing to put some time and energy into it.

Client: I sure am... I've been worried about this for some time.

Financial Counselor: Okay...First, it would be helpful if we could get some idea of what you spend your money on. To do this I'm going to ask you to keep track of how much you spend... and where it goes. To start with, you'll have to identify a number of items - who you owe money to, how much you owe, what your insurance and seasonal expenses are, and what your monthly expenses look like... I've got a number of forms you can use to make this easier... Once you've got them filled out we'll have a clearer picture of your financial situation. Then we'll be able to work on a strategy for doing something to get your expenses in line with your income... Will you be willing to follow through on this?

Client: I'm willing to give anything a try...

Financial Counselor: Good...Well, let me explain some of these forms...

In the above situation, the use of budgeting was an appropriate strategy because it met the client's need to identify expenses and to get the client's financial situation under control. Within this strategy, the financial counselor used a number of verbal strategies. The counselor used clarification to make sure the client was understood. A questioning tactic followed to get the client to accept responsibility for what was going to occur and finally the tactic of a direct, specific question was implemented to make sure the client was committed to doing something about the dilemma.

Identification of Financial Condition

Inherent in the above discussion of *budgeting* is the awareness of one's financial condition. At times, *identification* of the client's financial condition can be viewed as a strategy. A strategic approach in this identification could be to use counseling relationships to discuss specific elements. This would rely on the verbal interchange to uncover or discover the financial condition.

Other strategies could be used. For instance, Waddell (1987) created a self-scoring questionnaire in which clients can respond to 25 specific questions, answers to which can provide the client and the financial counselor with an idea of the client's financial condition. Questions on this scale ask about issues such as rent payments, use of credit or cash for payments, how frequently one is worried about financial issues, and use of savings accounts. The responses can be scored to indicate if: (1) financial problems exist and corrective action is needed; (2) severe problems exist and immediate corrective action, including financial counseling is recommended; or (3) extremely severe problems exist that demand immediate corrective action with financial counseling being essential. This strategic approach is more specific with a definite outcome. A third strategy might be to incorporate Waddell's scale with counselor discussion. A fourth might be to encourage the client to identify all elements of the financial condition as was done in the budgeting example above. Choice of a specific strategy will be dependent on what the counselor is trying to accomplish, the time available for helping the client, and the client's willingness to invest energy into the process.

Identification of Financial Attitudes/Values

It is appropriate in financial counseling to help clients identify their financial attitudes or values. One might ask, "What is the most efficient way to do this?" Choice of approach will depend on issues such as the reasons clients sought counseling, time available to the counselors and/or clients, tactics financial counselor choose to employ, and client's commitment to the process. In selecting a procedure, be aware that the counseling process is relevant in most situations.

Financial counselors can use this strategy with most clients under many conditions. However, there might be times when the financial counselor believes it would be appropriate for the client to accept greater responsibility or that employing other strategies would be a more efficient use of time. In these cases, strategies can be employed that use independent means for helping the client identify financial attitudes or values. A number of self-assessment inventories have been developed for this purpose. One, developed by Waddell (1987), is particularly appropriate. In his schema, a number of important financial attitudes are identified and assessed. For example, his assessment package addresses attitudes toward savings and debts, credit, spending habits, financial progress potential, financial values, financial satisfaction, and money usage. Use of this assessment package can be accomplished independent of the counselor and can provide clients with valid information about their attitudes and values.

For many clients, a useful counselor strategy is to use a three-step approach. Financial counseling (phase one) can be used to prepare the client for phase two, independent use of instrumentation such as Waddell's assessment. After the client has responded to the assessment package the financial counselor can follow up (phase three) with a discussion of the meaning and potential implications of what has been learned. In general, financial counselors can use counseling and/or outside stimuli like an assessment package or prescribed readings in a strategic manner. Specific choice of strategy must depend on what the counselor is trying to achieve with the client.

Using Clients' Resources

Clients have resources. A meaningful counseling strategy is to identify and utilize client's resources. For instance, as resources a client may have savings, a steady job, motivation to get ahead, a supportive family, a good reputation, a solid credit history, and/or willingness to work hard. One financial counseling strategy might be to use the client's financial resources to help the client achieve goals. A second strategy might be to use the client's desire to get ahead as a motivator for specific behavior change, whereas a third strategy might to incorporate the client's willingness to work hard to overcome financial difficulties. It is obvious that different goals may dictate the use of different resources. By being aware of *all* of the client's resources, the financial counselor can be most helpful to the client and have the greatest possibility of choosing an appropriate strategy.

Shifting Responsibility

One of the implicit goals of counseling is to help clients to be responsible. Achievement of this goal assures that once financial counseling has been terminated, clients will be able to face financial difficulties with greater confidence and make better decisions. In helping clients to develop responsibility, counselors must be aware of how clients try to avoid accepting it. This can be seen in the following counselor-client interchange.

Financial Counselor: Jim, it's good to see you again...What brought you in today?

Client: I've run into a little problem...and...uh...I'd like for you to give me some ideas of what to do.

Financial Counselor: Tell me what the problem is.

Client: Well, my oldest kid wants a car to get back and forth to school and he wants me to provide the money...what would you suggest?

Financial Counselor: It sounds like your oldest would like you to buy the car...but... you don't sound so sure that you want to...

Client: I'd like him to have a car...but right now isn't a good time for me...what should I do?

Financial Counselor: So, you'd like to see him get a car, but financially it would be difficult at this time...is that it?

Client: Yup,...that's right...I'm stuck.

Financial Counselor: Jim, tell me what you've done about this concern.

Client: Well, so far nothing...other than to come to see you.

Financial Counselor: I see, you seem concerned about the problem...but really haven't done anything specific yet. What could you do?

Client: Get a loan.

Financial Counselor: Anything else?

Client: I suppose I could take it out of savings...but I really don't want to do that...

Financial Counselor: Um hmm...so, you could take out a loan... or take the money out of savings...you don't sound like you have your heart in either of those possibilities. Can you think of anything else?

Client: I guess I could talk with my son...

Financial Counselor: If you did, what would you say to him?

Client: I guess I'd explain my financial situation to him...

Financial Counselor: (Tactfully) You say, "You guess you'd explain your financial situation to him". Why are you so hesitant?

In the situation presented above the client seemed to want the financial counselor to solve his problem for him. The client's early statements were all aimed at avoiding responsibility: "What ideas do you have?" " What would you suggest?" or "What should I do?" The financial counselor opted to use a strategy that indicated understanding of the problem, but one that did not accept the client's responsibility. The financial counselor responded in such a way that the client was forced to accept increased responsibility for generating possible solutions and for examining the value of each. In employing this strategy the financial counselor attended to the client's verbal and non-verbal messages and responded in a caring tactful manner. By using this strategy, the financial counselor could help the client to become increasingly responsible and prepare him to discuss his financial situation with his son.

Role Playing

Financial counselors can provide clients an opportunity to practice behaviors in a psychologically safe setting before they are used outside the financial counseling environment. In the example above, the father may have been embarrassed that he could not afford to purchase an automobile for his son and hesitant to approach his son about his dilemma. The financial counselor could help the client to deal with this situation by providing him an opportunity to practice what he would say to his son. The strategy that is employed is termed *role playing*. An example of how this strategy would be used in a counseling session follows:

Financial Counselor: You appear to be hesitant to talk to your son about your financial situation...

Client: Yeah...I am...I feel like I'm letting him down...I'm not sure that he will understand...

Financial Counselor: Do you want to talk with him about your feelings?

Client: I'd like to...but... I don't know where to start.

Financial Counselor: Would practicing with me what you might say be helpful?

Client: You mean right now?

Financial Counselor: Sure, make believe that I am your son. What would you say to me?

Client: Todd...I know you would like a car to get back and forth to school...

Financial Counselor: Yeah Dad, I sure would...

Client: I'm a little strapped financially...I don't think I can buy one for you...

Financial Counselor: I see...how will I get to school?

Client: Oh... I think we can work something out...

And so on...

Once this *practice* runs it course, the financial counselor can talk with the client about the client's feelings and thoughts and about ways to refine what the client wishes to communicate. The process of *role-playing* provides clients an opportunity to practice their verbalized message. In addition, it provides clients an opportunity to react to responses provided by the counselor. This second aspect can help clients realize that they can control their emotions and thoughts. This realization can provide clients the necessary impetus to initiate discussions.

Teaching

Teaching is as a strategy that has many applications in counseling. Peters and Farwell (1967), in their text *Guidance: A Developmental Approach*, suggest that counselors accomplish their jobs through enactment of six different roles. They believe that counselors interact with clients directly through counseling, group work, and teaching and indirectly work in their behalf through program planning, evaluation, and consultation.

Financial counselors frequently have the opportunity to use teaching as a direct intervention strategy. For example, a typical goal for clients is to save more effectively. One strategy for helping clients to accomplish this end is to use individual financial counseling to provide the necessary motivation for saving. Another strategy might be to have clients participate in a financial awareness seminar to discuss ideas for developing a savings program. A third strategy could be to *teach* clients a number of specific elements that will facilitate savings. In doing this, a financial counselor could use any source of information that was specific and appropriate to the task. One source of information is Waddell (1987). Waddell suggests *twelve key tips for saving*. His list includes items such as making automatic payroll deductions into a savings account, using a *zero based* checking system, and designating one week a month as frugal week, a week in which only necessities are purchased. By providing relevant information, such as Waddell's, and an opportunity to discuss that information, counselors can teach clients about any appropriate topic.

Confrontation

Clients frequently enter financial counseling with unrealistic expectations, little awareness of how they are perceived by others, or an inadequate understanding of their strengths and weaknesses. In these situations, financial counselors can provide clients a mirror of realism that is frequently lacking in their lives. To provide clients an honest appraisal, financial counselors must be able to *confront* in a manner that facilitates. Egan (1990) provides a useful definition of this strategy. He suggests that confrontation is an interpretation that "causes another person to admit to, reflect upon, examine, question, or change some particular aspect of his behavior" (p.107). This definition gets to the heart of financial counseling, i.e., to help other persons to see themselves in a different, possibly more realistic light, thereby providing them an opportunity for growth or change.

To do this within the financial counseling relationship, financial counselors must be able to recognize their own feelings and provide feedback about those feelings to the client. This must be done in a caring, purposeful, and tactful manner. Consider the following vignette as an example of this strategy.

Client: Well, we do budget ourselves…but at the end of the month we just don't know where our money went...

Financial Counselor (said tactfully): On the one hand you say that you budget yourself and then you tell me you just don't know where your money went. That seems to be a contradiction. Which one is true?

Client: Um hmm, maybe we don't budget everything.

Financial Counselor: You don't budget everything? What is it that you don't budget?

Client: We decided not to worry about budgeting on the weekends. We figured that we needed some time to just relax. You know, you can't be tight all the time.

Financial Counselor: So, on weekends you don't worry about where the money goes...and then at the end of the month you wonder where it went. Is that correct?

Client: Yeah, I guess so.

Financial Counselor: At one level you tell me that you'd like to get your finances straightened out. Yet, on another level...you say you just have to relax...and relaxing is not worrying about money. What do you think about all of this?

And so on...

In the above vignette the financial counselor uses confrontation to help the client to understand the inconsistency of his thoughts and actions. This strategy is particularly effective if the financial counselor and client have formed a relationship in which trust has been established and the client knows the counselor is working in his behalf. The manner in which the financial counselor voices confrontation is important. The confrontation should be direct, purposeful, and reflective of what the client has said. Judgement, by the financial counselor, is not warranted or needed.

Using Anecdotes

An anecdote is a short story which illustrates a point and teaches a concept that is deemed important. In financial counseling, anecdotes can be used strategically for diagnosing client concerns, seeding ideas, suggesting alternate solutions, or motivating clients toward action.

Diagnosis

When financial counselors use anecdotes for diagnosis, they should be particularly attentive to the client's reaction(s) to the anecdote. For example, a financial counselor talking with a client about starting a savings program may encounter resistance. Instead of pursuing the idea of savings directly the financial counselor could use an anecdote in the following manner.

> **Financial Counselor** (while watching the client closely): I've had a number of my family that have viewed savings in different ways...I had one uncle who didn't believe in financial institutions of any kind...he always kept his money at home. Another uncle believed the only way to go was the stock market. On the other hand, my dad thought government bonds were the best. My mom always figured you couldn't top the security of a financial institution. I was struck by the fact that all of them wanted the same thing but they all had different ways of achieving their goals.

While sharing this anecdote, a comparison of the client's reaction to savings with the financial counselor's own family, the financial counselor should be aware of which part of the anecdote draws the most positive reaction from the client. If the client's reaction can not be determined after a short period of time, the financial counselor could say,

> **Financial Counselor:** I'm curious about your reaction. Would you agree with any of my family?

Seeding Ideas And Suggesting Alternatives

An anecdote similar to the one used above could be used to seed ideas or to suggest alternatives. If you examine the financial counselor's statement, you will see that four different possibilities were provided. If a client was attempting to think through a particular concern, e.g., about savings, then the financial counselor's statement might be appropriate. It could get the client to think about the four possibilities as presented. If, on the other hand, the client had decided to start a saving program but was uncertain about how to do it, the counselor might say something similar to:

> **Financial Counselor:** I've had a number of clients face this same dilemma. One solved it by using payroll deductions, another by saving all his change and then

depositing it at the end of the month. Still another wrote a check to her savings account when she paid her monthly bills. Would any of these methods work for you?

Motivating Clients

Anecdotes can be used strategically to move clients to action. An example may show how this can be accomplished.

Prospective Customer: I'm going home to think about it, if I decide to buy, I'll come back..

Automobile Salesperson: Hold it a second, another customer was in the other day and decided to go home and think about it. When he came back, the car he was looking at was gone!

Obviously, the motivation to buy was being emphasized by the salesperson. Although financial counselors are not in the business of selling, this strategy is useful in financial counseling. Consider the following interchange.

Client: I'm not sure I can get the paper work done by next Monday.

Financial Counselor: I can understand that next Monday is pretty quick, but the last time I had a client miss the deadline the IRS came down on him real hard. It cost him a bundle!

When anecdotes are used to motivate, three elements become important. First, to motivate, the financial counselor should help the client to look toward the future. By painting a visual or verbal picture, the financial counselor can help the client to see what *could* transpire. This prepares the client for action and provides a goal to be achieved. Second, the financial counselor should help the client anticipate what will be needed to achieve the goal. This may entail specifying the exact steps that will lead toward the goal and discussing those events that could impede the process. Finally, the financial counselor must encourage the client to initiate the first step and be prepared to provide emotional support and reinforcement for the client's actions.

Acting as a Liaison

Many of the strategies discussed to this point are useful to financial counselors in their direct work with clients. In certain situations, however, financial counselors can work indirectly on behalf of clients. Financial counselors can use their position in the financial institution to help clients access other professionals or services within the financial institution or community. For example, a financial counselor might have a client who is in need of consumer credit counseling. The financial counselor could help the client initiate this process, providing names of resource people who are knowledgeable in this area, or possibly, contacting professional acquaintances on behalf of the client. In another instance, a financial counselor could help a client contact creditors by providing names of professional associates or by initiating contact with these associates. The way financial counselors choose to become involved usually depends on clients' specific goals and objectives. In some situations a direct intervention might be most appropriate. At other times, helping clients accept greater responsibility may be preferable. In either case, acting as a liaison is a strategy that frequently will help clients achieve their short or long-term goals.

Using Silence

A simple, useful and powerful strategy that is available to financial counselors is *silence*. There are times in financial counseling when the strategy of silence is *truly golden*. One of these times occurs when the financial counselor wishes to provide clients time to think about particular issues. In this situation, silence usually is preceded by a specific financial counselor stimulus. For instance, a financial counselor might say to a client, "We've talked about a number of possible alternatives. Which one of them do you think would be the best for you in your current financial situation?" An immediate response by the client usually would indicate insufficient thought. In this situation, the financial counselor should be silent until the client responds. If, after a significant period of time, the client has not responded, it is appropriate for the financial counselor to break the silence. In this example, the financial counselor might say, "It seems like you are having difficulty in seeing how these alternatives fit you." The financial counselor again could use silence, or could ask the client a specific question that requires an answer. Which approach the financial counselor elects should be determined by observing the client's nonverbal behavior.

Another time that silence is appropriate is when the client verbally or non-verbally has demonstrated a desire to reflect on a particular feeling. A client might say, "It's been real hard seeing my way through this..." and then stop talking. In a situation in which the financial counselor perceives a heavy emotional component in the client's statement, silence is appropriate. Silence allows the client to examine his feelings in a psychologically safe environment.

A third time that the strategic use of silence is appropriate is when the financial counselor wishes to help clients accept greater responsibility for their behavior. For example, the financial counselor might say, "You seem to want me to make that decision for you..." and then remain silent while the client reflects on the statement. Subsequent discussion can focus on the client's response. Finally, silence can be used strategically to change the pace of an interaction. By slowing the rate of response, the financial counselor can change a *very* dynamic interchange into a reflective one. This may be helpful when the financial counselor believes that a client is using verbiage to avoid *thinking* about an issue that *needs* thoughtful consideration.

Modeling

A strategy that frequently is overlooked by financial counselors is modeling, or the power of influencing by using one's own behavior. The client rarely overlooks this process. Clients usually are very aware of the financial counselor's verbal and non-verbal actions. They are aware of these actions both consciously and unconsciously. From the conscious perspective, a client might be aware of the financial counselor's demeanor, politeness, soft style of communicating, or ability to easily arrive at meaningful conclusions. Also, the client unconsciously might be aware that the financial counselor is honest, prepared, or from a negative perspective, unconcerned, detached, or non-empathic.

Knowing that the client is attending to both verbal and non-verbal actions presents the financial counselor with a strategic means for influencing the client. For example, if a financial counselor would like the client to respond in a straight forward, honest manner, one of the best strategies to achieve this end is for the financial counselor to be straight forward and honest with the client. This is accomplished in a number of ways. First, by being congruent in verbal and non-verbal communications, financial counselors demonstrate honesty, i.e., by saying *yes* with words as well as *yes* with gestures, financial counselors communicate consistency. Second, by following through on what they have promised, financial counselors establish that they are trustworthy. Third, by maintaining confidentiality that is either implicitly or explicitly promised, financial counselors communicate honesty. Fourth, by refusing to accept as their own an idea or value that is counter to their true beliefs, financial counselors can enhance their credibility. Finally, by willingly using self- disclosure, financial counselors demonstrate openness and sincerity. The impact of these behaviors is not lost on clients. They will view their financial counselor as being honest, and because of the power of modeling, get the message that this is *how I should behave in financial counseling*.

Many messages can be communicated through the modeling strategy. Honesty is but one example. A strategic, purposeful use of modeling can enhance the financial counseling process.

Adding Visual Dimensions

Since individuals learn in different ways, it is important for financial counselors to have a variety of strategies in their professional arsenal. Some clients are visual learners. For this population, auditory communication about certain topics or concepts may be difficult or, in rare circumstances, fruitless. An example may demonstrate this point. Consider the following financial counselor client interchange.

> **Financial Counselor:** I think I figured out a way to solve the problem. What you might consider is to borrow against the face value of your life insurance. You could then use the money you borrowed to pay your mortgage payment, leave the value of the money you borrowed in your savings account and then, through payroll deductions, pay back the money you borrowed from your life insurance.
>
> **Client:** What? I really don't understand...could you show that to me on paper?

Some clients might understand the suggestion as presented by the financial counselor. Obviously, this client did not. For this client, it appears it would be helpful to *see* the solution. The financial counselor could draw it out on paper. In this approach, details of the suggestion could become visible to the client. A second approach could be to use visualization in a more abstract form. The financial counselor could help the client visualize the process. The financial counselor could ask the client to visualize himself going to his insurance agent to borrow against his life insurance policy and see himself taking the borrowed money to the financial institution to pay his mortgage payment. Finally he could picture himself opening a payroll deductions program to pay back the money he borrowed from the life insurance. Also, he could be helped to visualize that his savings account was not diminished in size.

Visualization is not for everyone nor is it good in all situations. Yet, for many people, visualization is a powerful strategy.

Uses of Visualization

Visualization has a number of uses. First, visualization is an excellent way to get clients to project into the future. Through visualization, clients can gain a clearer understanding of their goals, come to an awareness of those elements that might impede their progress, and help them to establish means for overcoming difficulties before they occur. Second, visualization can be used to help clients abstractly experiment with alternatives. They can be helped to envision using alternatives and picturing *what might happen*. Through visualization refinement of alternatives can take place within the financial counseling process. Third, visualization can help clients learn to control their emotional responses to specific events. One of the situations in which this strategy is employed is in helping individuals to prepare for an event that promises to have a high level of emotion. A graduating student that is about to have a first job interview can benefit from practicing the interview through visualization. A new manager about to make her first presentation to the board can practice, through visualization, the delivery of the message. A teller can prepare to ask the manager for a raise by using visualization to rehearse the request.

In all of these examples, visualization is a means for examining what might happen before it happens and for practicing responses before they are needed. Visualization prepares the client for feelings that will be aroused when the event does occur. Also, it allows the client time to understand aroused emotions and to learn how to control them.

Using Quotations

A quote is defined as being, "that which is quoted or cited; a passage referred to, repeated, or adduced (Webster, 1959 p.695). Consider the following statements made by a counselor.

1) A client told me, "Putting money into my savings account at the beginning of the month is the best thing I ever did."
2) I overheard a guy say, "Entering financial counseling is the best thing I ever did."
3) One of my managers told me, "The most productive service we have is financial counseling."

These statements are examples of quotations, statements that convey a message about another's thoughts to the listener. Through statements made in this way, a message can be transmitted to the client, but because they are attributed to others, no resistance to them is triggered. In the above statements, the counselor does not have to defend himself for the thoughts of the client, the guy he overheard, or the manager. Yet, messages each of these people conveyed would be heard by the client. Statements adhering to this form are very useful in financial counseling. They can be used strategically to share information, stimulate thought, motivate, and provide feedback. Consider the following examples.

Example 1

Client: I really can't push myself to get started...I'm not sure I have the talent to do it.

Financial Counselor: Um hmm, I can understand your hesitation...it's hard to start something so new...yet...I overheard one of your co-workers say, "If anyone could do the job, you were the guy." He also said, "you could pick things up faster than anyone he knew."

Example 2

Client: I'd like to do it...but...I don't know where to begin.

Financial Counselor: That's interesting because I just heard Jim say, "If I was faced with that job the first thing I would do is contact the superintendent. He knows the job inside out."

Example 3

Client: I think I'll just pay it out of my savings account.

Financial Counselor: That is one possibility. In talking about a problem similar to yours, one of my clients said to me, "Just take out a piece of paper and list every possible alternative before you settle on one." He obviously didn't want to sell himself short.

In all three examples, the financial counselor conveyed a message in an indirect manner. The advantage of using this strategy is that the client can be presented information that does not warrant a direct response. The client can hear and appreciate the message. Yet, because the message is indirect, the client does not have to defend his reaction and, consequently, will be less likely to resist it.

Limitations

The major limitations of using quotations are threefold. First, the financial counselor must develop confidence in using this strategy so that the message can be delivered comfortably. Second, the strategy is most beneficial when financial counselors practice with it to develop an effortless, spontaneous delivery. This practice will enhance content creativity and delivery flexibility. Third, this strategy should be viewed as an auxiliary strategy. It is very useful but can lose effectiveness if used extensively.

Using Attitude Change and Behavior Prescriptions

Psychological theory emphasizes two different ways to help people change. The first of these is to help individuals to change their attitudes toward their previous actions. Theoretically, when attitudes change, behavior change will follow. A number of financial counseling strategies are built on this basic premise. Helping people to talk about their concerns, to discuss the difficult elements of their lives, to verbally explore ways of affecting change, and to verbally reinforce new ways of behaving are all examples of such strategies. In many cases, these attitude approaches are effective. In some situations, however, attitude change approaches are ineffective. The second approach begins with changing behavior. This theoretical position suggests that if behavior changes, attitude changes will follow. Subsequent changes in attitude will reinforce changes in behavior and assure that the new behaviors will continue. Consider the following examples that demonstrate both approaches.

Attitude Change Example

Client: I've been spending too much. Everything I see, I want.

Financial Counselor: It's like you have no control over you're spending. Do you have any idea what's behind this?

Client: I don't know. I think it might be the way I tell myself that I'm as good as anyone else.

Financial Counselor: That is an interesting observation. For the sake of discussion let's assume it to be true. If it were true, what else could you do, besides spending money, which would tell yourself that you are okay?

Client: I guess I could start by telling myself just that...I'm okay!

Financial Counselor: Great! That's a beginning. Let's explore situations when you tell yourself that you are not as good as others...then we'll focus on ways you can build on all of your positive qualities. How does that sound?

Client: I'm willing to do that.

This interaction would continue with the financial counselor attempting to help the client identify specific situations in which the negative feeling occurred. Then the financial counselor would institute an attitude change strategy for helping the client identify positive qualities and then learn which quality could be used in each situation. The attitude change that would be sought would be to help the client realize that previous actions that were perceived to be uncontrollable, i.e., the spending of money to achieve equality with others, was indeed controllable by applying personal qualities such as patience, self awareness, and insight.

If this attitude change strategy is effective the client will know, when faced with feelings of inferiority, that the situation can be controlled by using one of many positive qualities. The client will have more positive thoughts *and* cease spending money to achieve equality with others. The client's attitude *and* behavior will change.

Behavior Prescriptions Example

In this approach, the financial counselor starts from the perspective that a change in the client's behavior will result in a corresponding change in attitude. With this in mind, examine the following financial counselor-client interchange.

> **Client:** I can't seem to get myself to save any money. If I have anything left at the end of the month, I blow it.
>
> **Financial Counselor:** Exactly why does this bother you?
>
> **Client:** Well, I'd like to have a regular savings program...and...I'm just not doing it.
>
> **Financial Counselor:** Okay...you'd like to save...and...you are not presently doing it. What about the part you said about "blowing it"? Does that bother you?
>
> **Client:** A little.
>
> **Financial Counselor:** A little?
>
> **Client:** I wouldn't feel so bad about blowing it if I *also* saved every month.
>
> **Financial Counselor:** So, blowing it would be okay *if* you *also* saved. Is that it?
>
> **Client:** Yeah, that's true.

Financial Counselor: Okay, let's work on this. First we'll have to look at your monthly expenses and income...then work on the concern we've just discussed. Alright?

Client: Sure.

After examining monthly expenditures and income the financial counselor made the following suggestions to the client.

Financial Counselor: In most months you spend about 90 percent of what you make. That leaves you about 10 percent of your income. This 10 percent has been what you've been blowing each month.

Client: Yeah...it has been helpful to see that.

Financial Counselor: I'd like to suggest a new way of behaving...one in which we will talk about for the next few months...

Client: Okay, what do you have in mind?

Financial Counselor: Every month, as soon as you get paid I would like you to place 8 percent of your paycheck in a savings account...then pay your regular bills. At the end of the month...if you have money left over...do what you want with it.

Client: So...make regular payments to myself, right?

Financial Counselor: That's the idea.

An approach like the one initiated above has numerous benefits. First, the client could start a regular savings program, one that should increase a sense of security and enhance the ability to respond to future financial situations. Second, the client will learn, through the behavior change, that what happens to money can be controlled. Third, the financial counselor recognized that *blowing* money at the end of the month seemed to be important to the client and, consequently, allowed the client to continue this behavior. However, the financial counselor did help the client, through a specific behavior prescription, to limit the amount of money that was used for this activity. Through this element the financial counselor helped the client realize that aspects of two worlds could be achieved, savings *and* an opportunity to be free with discretionary income. Finally, the financial counselor established conditions for a change in the client's attitudes about self, the ability to save, and the ability to be self -monitoring. All of this was accomplished by prescribing a specific behavior change, i.e., by putting eight percent of the client's income in a savings account before other bills were paid.

Reinforcing and Extinguishing Strategies

In financial counseling, specific behaviors can be identified that move clients' toward their goals or impede their progress. Financial counselors are in a position to recognize these behaviors and, if the financial counseling relationship is sound, enhance development of positive behaviors and decrease occurrence of negative behaviors. Strategies for reinforcing and extinguishing behaviors are discussed below:

Reinforcing Strategies

Reinforcing strategies are appropriate if they are used to help clients to achieve goals. The purpose for using such strategies is to encourage, reward, or motivate clients. The financial counselor should keep several basic principles in mind when using these strategies:

1. Reinforce performance, not the client. Focus reinforcement on the behavior, not the person.
2. Reinforce with a response that is most appropriate for the behavior in question. Make reinforcements specific to the behavior. General, non-specific reinforcements lack credibility and can be detrimental to the financial counseling process.
3. Use interpersonal reinforcement. Use social aspects of the financial counseling relationship to provide reinforcement. Do not use reinforcements as *bribes* for behavior change.
4. Timing of reinforcement is important. Reinforcement that occurs closer to the behavior is more powerful.

5. Strength of reinforcement should be determined by importance of the behavior. Relatively more important behavior should receive relatively greater reinforcement.

The following example illustrates the concept.

Client: The last time I was in I mentioned how difficult it was for me to save any money.

Financial Counselor: I remember. How is the plan we discussed working?

Client: Really very well. It was hard at first, but now I put 8 percent of my income in my savings account. I don't really think about it...I feel quite good about what's happening.

Financial Counselor: That's great! Sticking with the plan on a regular basis is the key! I'm also glad to hear that you feel good about it. You should. You've done a nice job.

Extinguishing Strategies

At the other end of the continuum we find extinguishing strategies. Financial counselor use these to help clients overcome, diminish, or eliminate negative behaviors. There are a number of ways to use extinguishing strategies.

First, financial counselors must determine elements that help to maintain negative behaviors in a client's life. Negative behaviors can be *useful* to clients and, consequently, be self-maintaining. For instance, a client might spend money very freely and end up in financial difficulty. What might maintain such a behavior? The financial counselor would be advised to ask the question, "What does the client *get* from spending the money?" One answer might be goods or products. Another could be more friends. Still another could be to feel good. Any or all of these could serve to reinforce a negative spending behavior and help to maintain it. In order to know the best way to extinguish a behavior, the financial counselor must know everything about maintenance characteristics and then use this knowledge to remove reinforcing conditions.

A second approach is to withhold *reinforcers*. Parents do this on a regular basis. Consider the 16-year-old high school student who wants to borrow the family automobile to go out on a date. His parents' response is, "If you keep your room clean for three straight weeks we'll let you take the car." The positive reinforcer, using the family auto, is withheld until the unwanted behavior, a messy room, is extinguished. Most readers are probably saying, "Yeah, the room will be clean until after he gets the car. Then it will return to normal!" To some degree this is true. Withholding of a reinforcer can work if the reinforcer is *important* to the individual, but usually is not as effective as positive reinforcement. It will not necessarily change the teenager's attitudes about cleaning his room. He suddenly will not want to have a clean room. But, if getting to use the car is *always* contingent on a clean room, the teenager will gradually develop a set of behaviors that are more likely to lead to the desired outcome-getting to use the car. Also, in financial situations, frequently it is unethical or illegal to withhold reinforcers for which clients qualify.

It is sometimes possible to extinguish a behavior by reinforcing an opposite behavior. For example, a client may have two behaviors that are counter to each other. Consider the client who spends money freely, wants to stop this behavior, and wants to retire in five years. To retire the client may need to save on a regular basis. By reinforcing the behavior of saving, the negative behavior of lavish spending could be extinguished. That is, spending could be extinguished if positive reinforcers were appropriate in strength, timing, and relevance to the client.

Finally, a method of extinguishing behaviors that is used in psychological situations with some success is called *implosion*. In this approach, a massive exposure to noxious stimuli without injurious consequences is used. The idea behind this approach is that if the behavior that is to be extinguished can be made sufficiently noxious, the individual will refrain from the behavior in the future. A story about a 10-year-old boy exemplifies this approach. This 10-year-old was tempted to smoke a cigarette. His father happened to discover him in the process. To the boy's initial pleasure but eventual chagrin his father encouraged him to smoke a number of cigarettes within a short period of time. The expected end result was a very nauseous 10-year-old. The strategy of implosion worked with the boy. To this day he has not smoked another cigarette. Although this approach to extinguishing certain behaviors worked with the 10-year-old, it has limited use by financial counselors. One way that it can be used, however, is to help clients to push a behavior to its logical extreme. This can be accomplished through the process of visualization. The client can be prompted to visualize his behavior at its absolute worst and be led to understand its potential negative consequences. By using implosion in this manner the counselor can help the client understand what might happen if a change of behavior does not occur.

It usually is preferable to reinforce a positive behavior than to extinguish a negative behavior. In most situations results will be faster and longer lasting. There are times, however, when a combination strategy can be used in which undesirable behaviors are extinguished while desirable behaviors are reinforced. The situation described above in which the client wanted to retire in five years is a good example of when the combination strategy would be appropriate. The client could be reinforced to save for retirement while the client's penchant for spending could be extinguished using any of the extinguishing strategies presented. This combination should prove to be more effective than if either reinforcing or extinguishing strategies were used alone.

Being Unpredictable

We have discussed a number of important issues about the financial counseling relationship and process. One of the issues that has been highlighted is the nature of the relationship between financial counselor and client. One aspect of this relationship is that the financial counselor should be viewed by the client as being someone who is intent on being helpful, i.e., an individual who is both caring and resourceful. A second aspect is that the financial counselor should be viewed as being congruent in the counselor's presentation of self. The financial counselor should present the client a consistent image, one that the client can learn to expect and count on. Both of these aspects are important in the development and maintenance of the financial counseling relationship.

Despite the importance of the two important financial counseling aspects highlighted above, the financial counselor must be able to be strategically *unpredictable* in the financial counseling relationship. In order to understand why this is important, it is necessary to understand the basic psychological principle of *orientation*.

Orientation is defined as the "determination or sense of one's position with relation to environment or to some particular person, thing, field of knowledge, etc." and, "awareness of the existing situation, with reference to time, place, and the identity of persons" (Webster, 1954.pp.592). The principle of orientation becomes important in two very important ways. First, in financial counseling the client will be oriented to a particular situation. That is, financial counseling is contextual. Clients have concerns within certain specific contexts and within specific time frames. Financial counselors must be aware of how these contextual elements influence their clients. Consider the following interaction.

Client: I can't pay for everything. I just can't make ends meet!

Financial Counselor: You sound like financially you are at an end.

Client: That's exactly how I feel.

Financial Counselor: I can't quite tell if you are saying that you can't make ends meet *now* or if you think you won't *ever* be able to make them meet.

Client: Well, right now I feel that there won't be an end...but...usually I can see my way clear.

Financial Counselor: I see...a second thing isn't clear to me...when you say that you can't make ends meet. Is this a result of something specific that has happened...or a more general situation?

Client: Usually I can handle my bills...but...my oldest daughter needs braces...all of a sudden I can't see where the money is going to come from.

Financial Counselor: Okay...normally you are okay...but your daughter's braces have added an expense that has moved you out of the normal situation. Is that right?

In this situation the financial counselor has helped the client to clarify two elements of orientation. First, the issue of *timing* of the difficulty was examined and, second, the issue of *normalcy* was investigated. The financial counselor could follow this line of discussion to further isolate specifics of the concern and eventually to work out an action plan.

The principle of orientation can be used in a second way, a way that provides the foundation for *being unpredictable*. Initially clients *attend* or *orient* to the financial counselor. Eventually they come to expect the financial counselor to act and interact in specific ways. This is helpful, but if carried to an extreme, can become a hindrance to effectiveness of the financial counseling process. In general, clients attend closely until they *know* what the financial counselor will do next. Once clients can anticipate what the financial counselor will do or say under specific conditions, they no longer *attend* or *orient* to the financial counselor. In essence, they tune the financial counselor out. When this happens, the financial counselor has lost effectiveness in affecting change in the client's life. One way to prevent this from occurring, and to focus the client's attention, is to activate the orientation principle by *being unpredictable*. Being unpredictable, is built on the notion that if clients don't know what to expect, they will pay attention. It also depends on using a variety of intervention strategies. The following financial counselor-client interaction demonstrates this concept.

Client: The last time I was in you told me what to do about my budget...that worked pretty good.

Financial Counselor: Good... I'm glad that what we talked about was helpful. What brings you in today?

Client: Well, I figured that you solved the last problem...so...I wondered what you'd do with my latest concern.

Financial Counselor: What might that be?

Client: I'd like to add on to the house...also...We haven't had a vacation in a long time. I'm wondering how to do both. What do you suggest?

In the above interchange it is obvious that the financial counselor has established an expectation in the client's mind, the expectation that "If I have a financial concern, the financial counselor will tell me how to solve it." The financial counselor could do *what is expected* and provide the client a potential solution for the problem. This, however, would reinforce the expectation, encourage the client to continue to use this approach for personal problem solving, and keep responsibility for solution generation on the financial counselor. However, the financial counselor decided to be strategically *unpredictable*.

Financial Counselor: I can't think of a thing...but...I bet you can.

Client: What do you mean?

Financial Counselor: Well, you've been thinking about it for awhile...and...I'll bet you've thought about a lot of possibilities. Am I right?

Client: I guess I have thought about some.

Financial Counselor: Good...what are they?

Being unpredictable *does not* infer a strange or unconventional response. It *does* infer doing something different than expected. In the case presented above, the financial counselor merely changed the client's expectation by responding in a different way than the counselor had in the past. This oriented the client to the present situation and established that the client primarily would be responsible for generating solutions to the problem. This was a change from past client-counselor interactions.

CONCLUSION

This chapter highlighted a number of financial counseling strategies. Financial counseling is a unique relationship with unique demands. Consequently, it is important for financial counselors to have a wide variety of strategies for a wide range of client concerns. The manner in which financial counselors use these strategies will be dependent on the client, the concern being dealt with, the financial counselor's goals, the client's needs, and the financial counselor's counseling philosophy. It should be noted that strategies presented above are representative of financial counseling strategies but are not inclusive. The reader is referred to the reference section of this text for additional strategic approaches.

RESOURCES

Egan, G. (1990). *The Skilled Helper* (4th Ed.). Pacific Grove: Brooks Cole.

Peters, H.J. & Farwell, G. (1967). *Guidance: A Developmental Approach* (2nd. Ed.). Chicago: Rand Mcnally.

Waddell, F.E. (1987). *Get Control Of Your Money For Control Of Your Life*. ISBN 0-9615923-2-X.

12 DEVELOPING A FINANCIAL COUNSELING PROGRAM

> ...if one has been sitting in a particular seat and someone else occupies it, one can notice a fleeting irritation. There is the remnant of an old urge to throw out the interloper. The interloper knows too, because he will turn around or look up to say, "Have I got your seat?" at which point you lie and say, "Oh no, I was going to move anyway."
>
> Edward T. Hall (1981), *The Silent Language*

INTRODUCTION

In this chapter we detail development of a financial counseling program. In Section I we explore physical conditions that influence communicative interactions and importance of the counselor's personal appearance. We also examine related variables of time, sound, use of auxiliary personnel, and use of clients' records. In Section II, focus is on specific elements important in development of a financial counseling program. Significant aspects of this process are examined in detail.

SECTION I

PHYSICAL AND HUMAN CONSIDERATIONS

Physical Environment

Physical environment, although not the most crucial variable in counseling, is important. An atmosphere that is comfortable, that allows for privacy, and that uses space in a non-threatening manner can help counselors communicate more easily with clients. The following are some of the basic elements that are important in this regard.

Location

Where counselors meet clients can be influential in determining the counselor's effectiveness, the client's comfort, and what can be accomplished. Placement of the counselor's office within the institution will have an indirect affect upon client attitudes. Consider the following example from a high school setting:

> Jim, a student, sought out the school counselor's office. He wanted advice on how to resolve a conflict with his parents over his plans after graduation. In this particular school, one entered the counseling office by passing through the principal's waiting room. On his way to the counselor's office, Jim walked past students who had been sent to the principal for disciplinary reasons.

In this example, it is quite possible for Jim to be influenced negatively by the location of the counselor's office. He could easily think that the counselor represented the same kind of authority as a principal because of the proximity of the two offices. (Although this *might* be true, in most school counseling situations this would be an inappropriate assumption.) As a result of Jim's assumption, the counselor would have to overcome defensiveness on Jim's part that could be detrimental to the success of their counseling relationship. The point is, the location of one's office can be *influential.* Walking too many flights of stairs, searching down long corridors for the right office, or meeting in an open area near the receptionist, all may have a negative effect that must be overcome by the counselor.

THE POWER OF THE PLACE

In the professional world, offices in the mainstream of traffic and corner offices confer the greatest influence. In the corporate world, offices that are higher in the overall structure and are larger confer the greatest power. Financial counselors should be aware of the "influence" or "power" the location of their office carries and, if they have a choice, be careful in establishing where they locate.

Remember that all locations have potentially positive or negative aspects. In the example above, the counselor's office may be "bad" because it has potential for establishing inappropriate student expectations. Yet, it may be quite "good" from other perspectives, access to records, access to other professionals, or convenience for staff. It is important that both positive and negative aspects are considered and that choices maximize positives while diminishing negatives.

To do this, two sets of needs must be considered: the psychological comfort of clients and the counselor's professional needs. In general, clients feel psychologically safe in a variety of settings and will adapt to different financial counseling atmospheres. In some situations, however, clients will feel less comfortable in a "foreign" environment and will be more reserved in their communication. Counselors can be aware of this possibility and, whenever it is convenient, provide clients an opportunity to meet in a place where they are psychologically comfortable.

The counselor's needs for outside resources must be taken into account, as well as clients' needs for psychological safety. Whenever possible, attempts to satisfy both conditions should be made. On those rare occasions in which both cannot be satisfied, it is better for the counseling relationship if counselors forego their needs and strive to meet client needs for psychological comfort.

Space

In Chapter 3 we presented a number of social implications of space and how interpersonal positioning influences what is communicated. One of the principles discussed in Chapter 3 was Principle 3.7: *Communication is constantly being influenced.* One of the primary influences on communication is the interpersonal use of space. We'd like to build on our understanding of this influence by relating it to how counselors arrange and decorate their offices. The floor plan counselors use to organize office furniture, the colors and texture of furniture they choose, and their use of evidence that attests to their professional competence are all important in establishing an atmosphere that will facilitate communication. Although shape and positioning of office furniture are often overlooked as variables in communication, both are very important.

One of the primary influences of space lies in the *power* that is conveyed in certain spatial configurations. Power, as used here, is defined as being, "possession of control, authority or influence over others or the ability to act or produce an effect." A number of examples can be used to exemplify this form of *power*. Parents usually sit at the *head* of the table; teachers stand a the *front* of the room; ministers, priests, rabbis, etc. stand in *front* and *above* the congregation; and administrators usually have *larger*, more *lavish* offices than other employees. Power is conveyed by all of these examples.

Power to influence is a central ingredient of the counseling process. In financial counseling, the primary goal is to influence the process so that clients can achieve resolution of their financial problems. The financial counselor has a number of sources of power, e.g., knowledge, experience, title, physical attractiveness, and use of physical space. Knowing how to use all of these is important. Each of these is discussed in this text. At this point, however, we will concentrate on the *power* of space.

In examining furniture floor plans, three elements should be kept in mind; the shape of the furniture, seating arrangements, and general positioning of the furniture in the room. In general, round, square, and oval tables or desks can be used to create atmospheres of equality. By contrast, rectangular tables or desks are more likely to create differences in status.

In Figure 12.A, both individuals have positions of equal *power* because neither person is sitting at the *head* of the table.

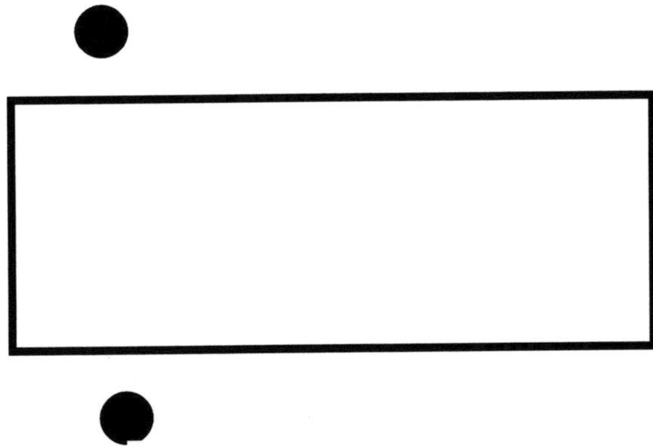

Figure 12.A

By contrast, in Figure 12.B, the individual sitting at the end of the table has more *power* than people sitting at the sides of the table. The *power* that occurs is a result of the end person's positioning, which allows that person to establish and maintain eye contact with all other individuals at the table, a difficult task for the rest of the people at the table.

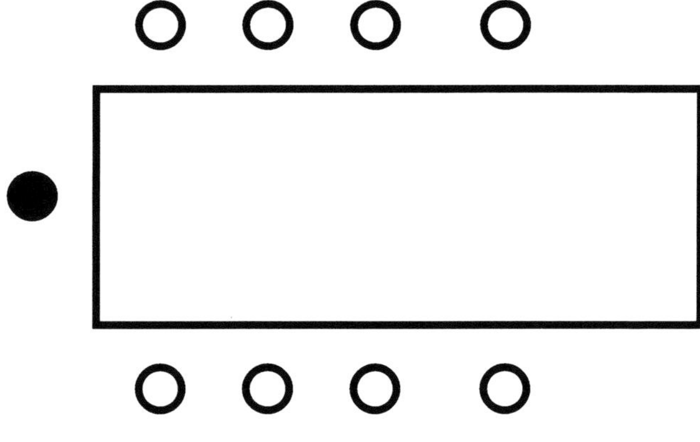

Figure 12.B

Now, apply this concept to the selection of a counselor's desk and arrangement of chairs. First, if counselors choose a round desk, they will establish an atmosphere that can lead to equality of participation and responsibility more easily than if they choose a rectangular desk. Let's assume, however, that they choose a rectangular desk. Where should they place chairs around their desk? To answer this question they should determine what they hope to accomplish in their financial counseling relationships and consider the following classifications of seating arrangements: If the counseling strategy is to teach and control client behaviors concerning their financial behavior, Figure 12.C would provide the greatest *power*.

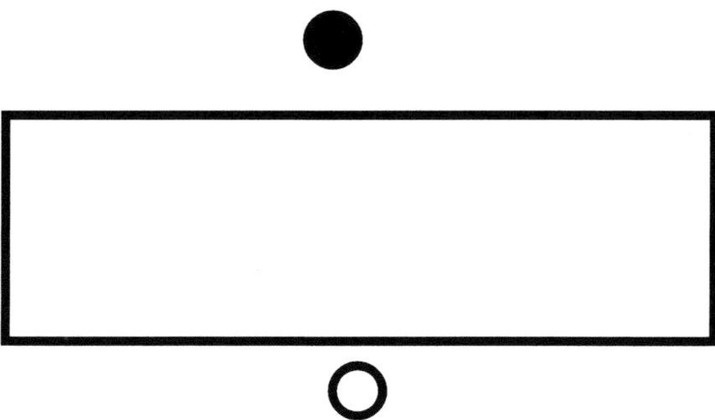

Figure 12.C

In a competitive arrangement, a counselor's seat commands the environment by using the desk as a source of *power.* It provides a physical barrier between counselor and client.

If the counselor's strategy is planning and/or productive counseling rather than teaching, the following arrangement (Figure 12.D) would be more appropriate.

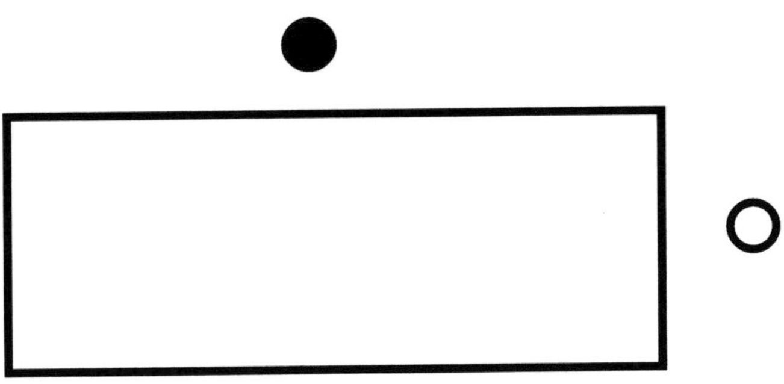

Figure 12.D

In the cooperative arrangement, the corner of the desk offers the client some security while establishing an atmosphere conducive to equality.

If the counselor's strategy is neither teaching nor planning, but rather counseling or mutual problem solving, then the arrangement presented in Figure 12.E should be considered. In this arrangement both the counselor and client are removed from the desk's influence.

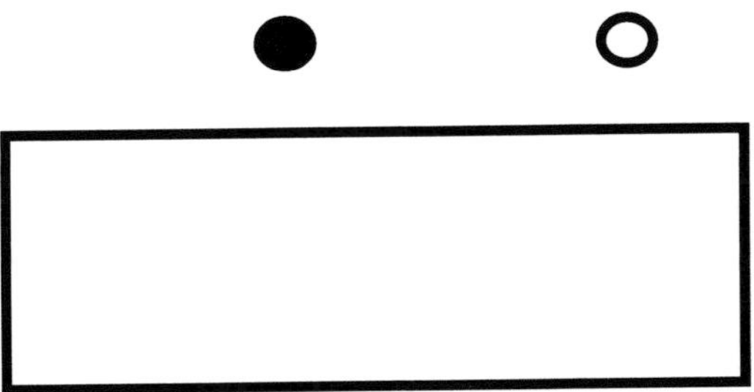

Figure 12.E

In the co-optive arrangement, both of the counselor and client have equal *power* and equal responsibility.

An additional seating arrangement is possible (Figure 12.F). However, it is seldom used in financial counseling.

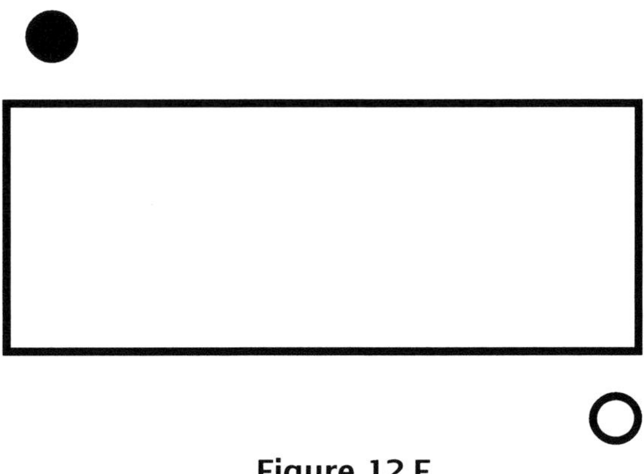

Figure 12.F

In most financial counseling environments, either the competitive or cooperative arrangements are preferred. Counselors are encouraged to examine their strategy and what type of atmosphere they wish to establish, and then arrange their furniture accordingly. It should be kept in mind that in doing so, counselors make arrangements that include client options. For example, counselors can place chairs in a variety of places and let their clients choose where they *want* to sit. The client's selection can provide counselors insight into their client's self-confidence, willingness to participate, or desire for control of the relationship.

Other Sources of Power

There are a variety of other sources of power in the physical environment.

- **Relative Height**: When one person is standing and another is sitting, the person standing will generally have more power. When applying this concept to seating, if one person's chair is higher than another's, the person in the higher chair will have greater influence.

- **Comparative Value Of Chairs:** Types of chairs can generate power or influence. If counselors sit in expensive leather chairs and their clients sit in inexpensive cloth chairs, counselors will have greater influence.

- **Positioning Of Chairs:** Location of chairs in the room can be a source of power. If the counselor's chair faces the door to the room, he/she will have greater influence than the client.

Obviously, to control the greatest power in financial counseling, counselors would try to employ as many of these concepts as possible. Conversely, to establish an equal relationship counselors would utilize these concepts to minimize the potential influence of furniture arrangement.

Office Décor

Another significant environmental consideration in effective communication is how counselors decorate their office and how they display items that attest to their professional competence. In this regard, counselors should keep in mind their personal preferences, their clients' needs, and their counseling goals. For example, a physical atmosphere that *is sterile* may interfere with the counselor's ability to develop a relationship with clients; whereas one that is too *homey* may give clients the idea that the counselor lacks professional competence. The development of an optimum atmosphere that will be most helpful will depend on the counselor's use of furniture, colors, decorations, textures, and professional acquisitions.

Furniture

Almost everything about furniture is important. In addition to furniture positioning, furniture texture, style, and location impact the situation. In general, most people will respond more positively to a room decorated with wood furniture and natural fibers such as wool or cotton than to a room decorated with metal or plastic furniture and artificial fibers or synthetics. If the counselor's office is large enough, addition of a sofa or easy chair can soften the atmosphere while additional tables or chairs can allow for alternative arrangements for professional discussions. The following arrangement of furniture (Figure 12.G) could be used to provide a psychologically pleasing, flexible environment.

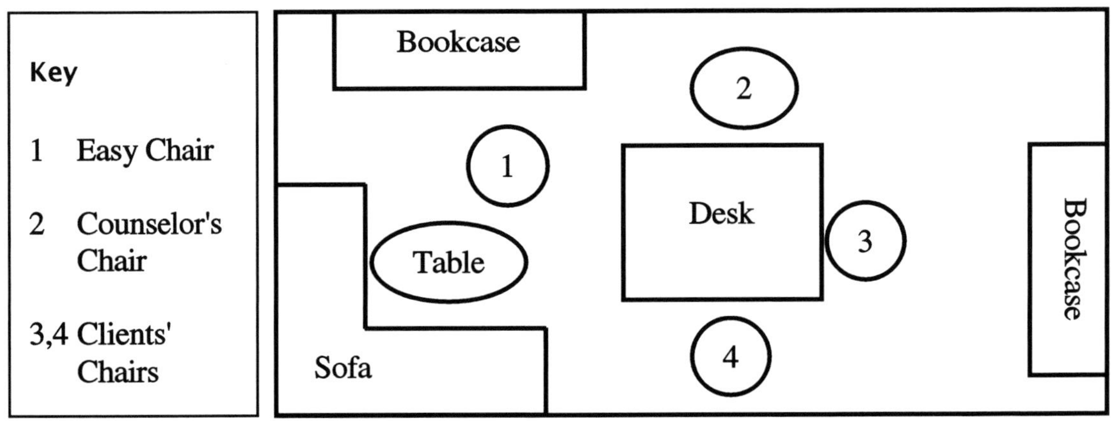

Figure 12.G

Color

In addition to furniture arrangement and texture, *color* is influential. Most people feel psychologically comfortable in rooms that use pastel or earth tone colors. Vibrant colors may be more energizing, but are less acceptable for professional relationships. In this regard, subtle artwork is viewed positively by a higher percentage of people than bold, highly creative designs.

Natural Elements

Plants,, flowers, and small trees add significantly to the psychological comfort of an office.

Awards and Certificates

It is important to include *evidence of the counselor's professional accomplishment and competency* in the decorating plan. Items such as licenses, diplomas, certificates of achievement, and professional awards should be openly displayed. Remember, in addition to the counselor's feeling of competence it is important how clients view a counselor's competence. A counselor's influence is increased when clients see evidence that counselors are skilled professionals. Professional credentials, openly displayed, set the stage for open professional communication.

Personal Characteristics

The way counselors are viewed by clients depends on their reputation, individual communicative style, level of expertise, and personal appearance. All of these variables are under a counselor's control. The first three result from professional preparation and personal style of delivery. One's appearance is somewhat different. This variable is based on the counselor's social consistency, carriage, hygiene, clothes, communicative ability, and responsiveness. Let's take each in order:

Social Consistency

Social consistency refers to how well counselors meet social expectations of others in specific social situations or how well they reflect social norms of their profession. If others expect counselors to behave in a certain manner and they don't, they may respond negatively. Consider an institution manager who attends a professional meeting on governmental regulations dressed in sweatshirt and cut-off jeans. Admittedly, this may be a farfetched example, but the point is that certain behavior is professionally unacceptable, some in a dramatic way, some in a subtle manner. In this example, the manager is dressed inappropriately for the professional situation. However, if a picnic were held to allow institution managers and government personnel to meet informally, then the manager *would be* dressed appropriately. By contrast, attending the picnic in a three-piece, navy blue pinstriped suit might be quite inappropriate!

Social Expectations

We have expectations that are based on our experiences and familiarity with specific social groups and specific situations. We learn to know when a behavior is appropriate and when it isn't. These expectations are the basis for what is socially acceptable in the above example and in the following personal variables.

Personal variables such as carriage, clothes, and hygiene all affect how others view counselors. Most of what follows is common sense. We mention it only as a reminder of how one's appearance can affect how people respond. People can use these three variables to form an opinion about counselors even without communicating with them.

Carriage

Some individuals walk with their heads held high, their shoulders back, and an alert look on their face, while others walk in a slouched manner and look at the ground as they walk. As we observe people, we classify some as proud, others as shy, pompous, or relaxed. We form our opinions from subtle clues people emit. We then classify people into categories. Our opinions of, and possibly our actions toward people are based upon our classifications.

Clothes

A second observation we make centers around how people are dressed. Appropriateness of professional dress follows subtle, informal rules. Through professional training and experience, counselors learn most of these rules. There may be situations, however, in which one does not know what is appropriate and, consequently, a feeling of being out of place, ill at ease, or embarrassed can result. When in doubt, a conservative clothing choice usually proves to be the safer course. Steering clear of bright colors, bold patterns, and unconventional styles ensures a more professional image.

In addition to the choice of appropriate clothes, how one wears clothes is important. Clothes that are too large, too tight, or wrinkled create a negative image, as do shoes that need polish or a shirt that is not tucked in. Clothes need to be appropriate for the situation, be properly tailored and cleaned, and be worn in an acceptable fashion.

Hygiene

Personal hygiene is closely tied to what one wears. A professional who neglects this important area communicates a negative or unsavory image to clients. The areas to be attended to most diligently are hair, fingernails, teeth, breath, and body odor. Hair style and maintenance is an obvious reflection of personal self-image and professional awareness. It is true that the subtle rules for professional hairstyle differ. Whereas managers, lawyers, doctors, and executives have one acceptable style, college professors have another, and artists still another.

Despite moderate differences in informal rules set by the counseling profession, almost all professions expect cleanliness. To be slightly outside the informal rules for the profession can be tolerated. To have unclean hair usually is not tolerated and probably will result in a negative image. Dirty fingernails, unsightly teeth, bad breath, and body odor can lead others to have a negative image of the offender. The message frequently transferred through these personal variables is "If they don't care enough about themselves to comb their hair, clean their fingernails, take care of their teeth, cleanse their breath, or to wash away body odor, how could they care enough about me to attend to my needs in a competent manner?" Personal sloppiness communicates an uncaring attitude that clients can generalize to perceived professional competence.

Communicative Ability

Communicative ability has a number of dimensions. First, *when* counselors choose to talk is important. For instance, do they talk when they should be listening? Do they interrupt other people as they talk? Do they finish others' sentences for them? Are they impatient while others present their ideas? A typical individual would probably answer yes to some of these questions in some circumstances. What do good communicators do? One answer to this question would be that good financial counselors attempt to listen attentively to their clients and to talk when their clients have finished what they have to say.

In addition to when counselors talk, *what* they have to say is important. The statement, "I thought he was a fool, and when he opened his mouth it removed all doubt," is a negative judgement about someone. Clients who hear financial counselors make such judgements might wonder what kinds of negative judgements the financial counselors are making about them. Verbal communication should be purposeful and appropriate to the counselor's strategy.

Third, *how* counselors talk is important. How rapidly they speak, how loudly they talk, how much emphasis they put on words, how well they enunciate, their diction, and whether they have an accent all influence how much clients get from what is said. In general, moderation in most of these aspects is best. That is, most people prefer to listen to someone who does not speak too fast or too slow, too loud or too soft, too high pitched or too low pitched, and with too much of an accent. Take notice of how national news and television personnel talk. Most have identical accent and speaking styles. They are chosen because their styles reflect what most people like. They have *general* believability. In most financial counseling, a low-keyed, straightforward manner of presentation is most believable and productive.

Interpersonal Responsiveness

A counselor's personal method of responding to clients is important. How counselors use eye contact, how and when they smile, how and when they nod their head all can communicate attentiveness and interest. It is important for counselors to know how and when to respond so that they can respond in a manner that is consistent with their strategies and financial counseling goals.

Finally, a counselor's interaction with clients probably begins and ends with a subtle form of communication that can create a positive or negative attitude. This form of communication is the handshake. The manner in which counselors shake hands can have an influence on what a client thinks about the counselor, and conversely, what counselors think about their clients. In discussing communicative ability, we suggest that most clients prefer a moderate approach. We make the same observation with regard to handshakes. It is important to be firm but not overly assertive. A feeble grip will suggest weakness on the counselor's part, whereas too powerful a grip can lead clients to question the counselor's intent. We suggest that counselors adopt a moderate grip that will communicate concern without being overbearing.

Final Considerations

It is obvious that many things can and do influence communication. Earlier in this chapter, we addressed those that where related to physical and personal variables. Now we discuss a number of elements relating to the environment in which communication takes place. This includes the use of time, sounds, auxiliary personnel, and clients' records.

Time

Time is a finite element, and consequently extremely important in communication. Probably most counselors and clients are busy people. If counselors do not respect this probability and do not use their client's time in an efficient manner, they will run the chance of alienating their clients. Time can be inappropriately used. There are several ways this happens. Time is used inappropriately when counselors keep clients waiting; fail to answer their telephone calls in a timely manner; appear to be inflexible in their schedule; fail to provide an able backup when they cannot attend to clients' needs; or answer the phone call of one client while serving another.

When financial counselors use time inappropriately, they communicate a lack of respect for their clients. In essence, they communicate, "My time is important; yours is not!" Obviously, we suggest that counselors guard against this possibility and use time to convey respect for their clients by attending to their needs in an efficient, expedient manner.

Sound

Sound, like time, can be used in a productive or negative way. Low-volume classical or semi-classical background music facilitates communication. Consequently, this type of music provides an excellent backdrop for professional conversations. From a negative perspective, loud music, unusually noisy voices, or disquieting background sounds can interfere with communications and should be avoided.

Personnel

A third element to consider is the communicative benefits of appropriately trained *auxiliary personnel.* In most professional situations clients seek information when they feel a need for it. Counselors may be able to provide their clients a consistently timely response. If they cannot, however, auxiliary personnel such as a knowledgeable secretary or assistant can be used to provide clients pertinent information when they need it. They can extend a counselor's professional usefulness by allowing them to communicate with more than one client at a time; the one they communicate with directly and the one they communicate with indirectly through auxiliary personnel. Trained auxiliary personnel can help counselors communicate that their professional service is convenient, efficient, and responsive to clients' needs.

Records

Properly maintained, readily accessible *records* foster communications. Clients expect counselors to be knowledgeable about their professional field and able to use information in their behalf. Further, clients probably expect counselors to understand their personal situation, to be able to apply their knowledge and to make appropriate recommendations. This can occur only if counselors maintain accurate records and have a system for obtaining information in an efficient manner. When clients see that counselors' records are professionally developed, accurately updated, confidentially maintained, and readily accessible, they *get the message* that counselors are efficient, competent, and professional. This, we assume, is exactly what counselors would like to communicate!

SECTION II

DEVELOPING A FINANCIAL COUNSELING PROGRAM

Determining Industry Attitudes

Each financial institution and its membership are different, and each has a unique set of needs and services. Attitudes toward providing professional financial counseling within any institution can be determined in a variety of ways. First, counselors should be aware of the written philosophy put forth by their institution. Most institutions will have a charter and/or bylaws that specify basic philosophy and goals. Individuals interested in establishing a counseling program should become well versed in formal and informal institution goals and objectives, and determine how a financial counseling program can add to the overall mission of their institution.

Second, counselors must assess how people within the institution interpret rules or bylaws and/or view the need for financial counseling. Significant individuals within the institution should be involved in the decision-making process of developing a financial counseling program. For example, the board of directors could be asked if they view financial counseling as being a service consistent with institutional bylaws. The directors could share their perspectives on financial counseling as a service to clients. Managers and staff could provide their opinion on whether financial counseling was consistent with the institution mission and provide insight on the need for financial counseling. Randomly sampled clients could share their viewpoint on the need for a financial counseling program.
The need for financial counseling programs can be determined by searching materials that discuss and interpret industry standards, by investigating governing body recommendations, and by exploring government regulations that promote financial counseling programs.

If results of the individual institution and industry investigations are positive, then development of a financial counseling program would be warranted. Assuming this to be the case, the following sections highlight elements that would be needed in the development of a financial counseling program.

Identifying Personnel To Become Counselors

How can potential counselors be identified? All who show an interest and who demonstrate an ability to effectively communicate should be considered. Among those who volunteer and those who are asked to participate, certain personal characteristics are essential. People's values, beliefs, and attitudes influence their ability to counsel, while other elements also influence their ability to establish and maintain effective counseling relationships. Persons who demonstrate positive, interpersonal communicative styles are more likely to become effective counselors than those who don't. Characteristics of a positive style are numerous.

The following list is representative of many important characteristics of effective financial counselors. The list is not inclusive, nor is it ordered in any particular sequence. Each characteristic is important. Although some financial counselors could be effective without manifesting each characteristic, most effective financial counselors are able to demonstrate all characteristics to some degree.

Commitment

Effective financial counselors must have a commitment to both *people* and *things*. In an institution the *things* that are important include financial items such as programs, budgets, savings accounts, and passbooks. Commitment to *people* would be reflected in one's willingness to spend time and energy to help clients to grow/develop.

Intelligence

Effective financial counselors must be able to establish a philosophy of life that facilitates the counseling relationship, one that is able to incorporate a sound rationale for counseling interactions. The financial counselor's rationale for operation must result in systematic strategies for helping clients reach their financial counseling goals and objectives. Financial counselors also must be able to remember significant details of the client's story, know how and when to use specific counseling strategies or tactics, and be knowledgeable about the world of finances.

Sensitivity

Through their verbal and nonverbal communication effective financial counselors demonstrate awareness of other people's feelings, attitudes, and beliefs. Financial counselors must be able to accurately assess what is important for the client and to use this assessment in a thoughtful manner.

Openness

Openness to new ideas, knowledge, and information is essential if financial counselors are to be effective. They must be open to new information and flexible enough to incorporate new information into their counseling approach.

Communicative Ability

Financial counselors must be able to communicate thoughts and feelings. Sensitivity by itself is insufficient. Financial counselors must be able to communicate their sensitivity in a way that will foster growth and development of the clients with whom they work.

Privacy

Financial counseling is built on the foundation of confidentiality. Financial counselors who are unable to maintain confidentiality will not be effective. In fact, they may be destructive. Without confidentiality trust cannot be established, client expectations for financial counseling will be diminished, counseling will cease to be viewed as a positive service, and counseling will not be a meaningful offering of the institution.

Facilitative Ability

Financial counselors must be able to help others help themselves. The tactics essential in this are congruence, empathy, acceptance, respect, and trust. These tactics have been discussed in detail within the text.

Professional

Financial counselors must always maintain a professional stance in the counseling relationship. This relationship must ascribe to clearly defined rules and regulations. These rules and regulations must reflect both the financial and psychological foundations on which counseling is based.

Being Real

One cannot *play* the role of being a financial counselor. Rather, financial counselors are *real*. To be real within the counseling relationship means to share oneself in an open, honest way. To do otherwise will destroy any chance for a meaningful relationship and impede the counseling process.

Financial counselors cannot play at being supportive, honest, encouraging, friendly, enthusiastic, or spontaneous. If these characteristics are not natural to the counselor, clients will know it and the financial counseling relationship will not develop, trust will not be established, and counseling will not occur. Honesty *is* the best policy. Individuals who have the ability to be honest with themselves and in the relationship are likely to become effective financial counselors.

Developing Training Programs For Counselors

The training of personnel to become financial counselors can be done in a number of ways. Financial counselors can be developed outside of the institution in which they will work. Individuals interested in financial counseling can take course offerings at universities and colleges or online over the Internet. Courses dealing with communication skills or interviewing procedures are directly applicable to becoming a financial counselor. Coupled with these courses are those designed to communicate specific, relevant educational material. Courses in business, accounting, and economics all would help individuals to become better financial counselors. While courses can be taken on an independent basis through correspondence courses or the Internet, interpersonal skills, tactics, and strategies are developed most effectively when practice and supervision is available.

Many institutions offer in-service opportunities for individuals to learn how to become financial counselors. Programs aimed specifically at developing counseling skills are held in a number of locations throughout the country. Potential financial counselors should consider one of the many possibilities offered through professional organizations such as those offered by the National Association, or various state institution leagues or chapters.

A second method of training is available through extensive resource materials. The reader is advised to consider materials and programs available through the following organizations.

- Institute for Personal Finance: Columbus, Ohio,
- Credit Union National Association: Madison, Wisconsin
- College for Financial Planning: Denver, Colorado
- National Institute for Consumer Education: Eastern Michigan University Ypsilanti, Michigan.

Courses, books, slides, tapes, and other resources are available to provide a basis for developing appropriate financial counseling skills.

A third way for developing financial counselors within a particular institution is to use individuals who have participated in college programs or financial counseling schools to provide training sessions within their respective institutions. The advantage of this approach is that individuals can receive direct feedback from fellow employees who have been trained to become financial counselors. More of this approach is needed. One of the best ways of learning to be a financial counselor is to work with individuals who are competent as counselors. As in the development of any skill, daily practice coupled with feedback will lead to skill development.

Finally, individuals interested in becoming financial counselors should take advantage of the wealth of printed information. Numerous books, articles, and other resources are available which deal with development of financial counseling skills. A number of materials are listed in the Reference and Additional Resources sections of this book.

Providing Adequate Counseling Facilities

There are several conditions that optimize the possibility of having an effective financial counseling program. Adequate facilities are one of these conditions. A description of the most relevant facility needs is included in Section I of this chapter. Please refer to that discussion for details.

Supporting Financial Counseling

Two areas of support for counseling must be considered: *financial* and *personal* support.

Financial Support

Financial support comes in three forms. First, financial counselors must be allowed time to work with clients. Financial counseling requires that counselors be available when clients wish to receive counseling and that sufficient time is allocated for counseling interviews. While counseling, financial counselors will not be able to do other tasks. They will be limited to direct work with clients. The time they spend in direct client involvement is beneficial for helping clients meet financial obligations and in providing meaningful institutional services.

Second, the institution must demonstrate financial support by providing counselors with training and allowing them to attend conferences and seminars to develop and update skills. Institutional expenditures for these provisions will benefit financial counselors and clients. Finally, counselors should have financial support for program materials - materials needed for development, implementation and evaluation. Financial support also could include resource texts and recordings, audio and visual taping equipment, materials for questionnaire development and usage, and auxiliary personnel.

Personal Support

As with any new service, getting started is most difficult because support from clients is not yet apparent. Therefore, in order to establish a counseling service, it will take a manager or a group of individuals with sufficient foresight to propose that the service be instituted. Materials found in various financial counseling magazines and publications can be used to attest to the fact that a counseling service does benefit the institution financially and clients personally.

Once financial counseling services have been started, a better educated membership should emerge, one that is able to handle financial cares more productively, with better awareness of preventive measures and, in time, with diminished need for remediation. Rewards for the institution include increased financial gains because of a reduced loan delinquency rate. Evidence of such a financial benefit will develop support for a number of services. Clients who have benefited from counseling will most readily lend their support to continuation of financial counseling. Once a financial counseling service has been established and has had time to affect the financial lives of people, the people usually become its staunchest supporters.

A second source of support will become evident. Administrative personnel, aware of counseling benefits to clients and financial benefits to the institution, should champion the service. Finally, the financial counseling service will be viewed as one more way the institution demonstrates concern for clients. This probably will be viewed positively and conceivably could increase institutional support and affiliation.

Initiating A Counseling Program

In initiating a counseling program one must keep in mind that a completely operational financial counseling program can be costly in terms of personnel, time, and resources. Issues related to these costs have been discussed above. In addition to these costs, a number of other considerations must be entertained. The four that we believe are the most salient are *timing*, *location*, *approach*, and *policies*. These four address the basic questions of when, where, how, and who.

Timing

When should one begin development of a financial counseling program? Although there is no definitive answer to this question, the best answer is "When there is a need." This need could have many faces. First, a good time to initiate a financial counseling program is when there are signs of a societal economic slowdown or recession, a time when clients have greater difficulty in meeting their financial obligations, or when they are more concerned about their financial situations for now and the future. Another time to initiate a financial counseling program is when your institution is experiencing an unusually high delinquency rate or when the rate of delinquency is increasing. These two conditions often occur together. Financial counseling should be considered as one way to decrease this concern. Third, providing financial counseling as a service can help your institution establish a competitive edge in the financial marketplace. Does this need exist? If it does, the timing may be right for initiating a program. Finally, societal demands may be *right* for starting or expanding a financial counseling program. For example, productive counseling has many of the characteristics of financial planning, a process that a number of financial institutions have incorporated into their mission. The question is, "Can financial counseling provide your membership a needed financial service?" An auxiliary question is, "Can your institution afford to *avoid providing* the service?" The external pressure may be sufficient to lead you to the conclusion that a financial counseling program is needed *now*.

Location

Where should the financial counseling service be provided? For some institutions the answer to this is easy, "At the office!" For others, however, it can be more difficult. For instance, consider the institution with a main office and four branch offices in the same city. Where do they house the financial counseling service? To arrive at a solution for this problem one must be aware of *specific* membership characteristics, personnel considerations, and space allocations.

Would clients in one branch have greater need for remedial counseling? For preventive counseling? For productive counseling? Is there a population of clients that should be targeted? If so, where do they live? Where are the personnel that will be employed as counselors presently employed? If they will be part time counselors, will they remain at their present locations? Which of the offices has the best physical space for a financial counseling service? Answers to these and similar questions, can shed light on *where* the service should be provided.

Approach

The question of *how* the counseling program will be initiated must be addressed. *How*, in this instance, refers to whether the financial counseling program is to be instituted all at once, or bit by bit. Most institutions take the latter approach, bit by bit. However, frequently they approach this from different perspectives. Some start the full program on a part-time basis. That is, they offer a full program, one including remedial, productive, and preventive financial counseling on a half-day, or possibly, on a one-day-a-week basis. As the demand for the service increases, they increase the number of hours per week that financial counseling is provided. A number of institutions have developed full-time programs in this way.

A second approach is to offer one aspect of the service initially, and then add elements as the program is accepted. In using this approach, remedial counseling could be offered initially. As the program develops and membership becomes aware of the program, preventive counseling could be added. Still later, productive counseling could be included to complete the program. Obviously, the two approaches outlined above could be integrated, e.g., start a program by providing remedial counseling on a part-time basis. Finally, a full-time, complete financial counseling program could be instituted. The advantage of this approach is that all services can be provided from the start and membership has the greatest access to the program. There are obvious disadvantages to this approach. The per client costs are higher at the beginning because of under-utilization of the service and the program is fully operational before membership response to the program can be determined.

Policies

It is important to determine, specifically, the target population(s) of the financial counseling program. Will delinquent clients be the primary focus of the program? Will clients who have loans turned down be recommended for counseling? Will *all* clients be informed about the availability of counseling for remedial, preventive, and productive purposes? Will families be targeted for consumer counseling concerns? In general, the type of formal and informal policies that will operate to assure that the financial counseling program reaches the widest membership with the greatest impact must be determined and specified.

CONCLUSION

This chapter examined importance of the physical environment in counseling. In Section I, physical and human considerations were discussed, including the physical environment, placement of furniture, and personalities of perspective counselors. Section II then addressed seven key areas in the development of a financial counseling program. They include: determining client needs; identifying institutional/industry attitudes toward providing help; identifying personnel who are capable of becoming counselors; training counselors; providing adequate counseling facilities; determining ways for supporting counseling; and issues relevant to initiating a counseling program. All of these considerations are important if institutions wish to establish financial counseling programs to meet clients' needs.

RESOURCES

Hall, E.T. (1981). *The Silent Language*. New York: Doubleday Publishing Company.

Hamilton, C., Parker, C. & Smith, D.D. (1982). *Communicating For Results.* Belmont: Wadsworth Publishing Company.

13 EVALUATION

Nasrudin went into a shop to buy a pair of trousers. Then he changed his mind and chose a cloak instead, at the same price.

"You have not paid" shouted the merchant.

"I left you the trousers, which were of the same value as the cloak." said Nasrudin.

"But you did not pay for the trousers either" said the merchant.

"Of course not, said Nasrudin, "Why should I pay for something I did not want to buy?"

Idries Shah (1971,24) *Nasrudin*

INTRODUCTION

Some consider evaluation to be the final event in the process of counseling. We consider it to be a step along the way. Systematic evaluation *can be* the final step or it can be a step that leads to continued efforts of counselors' and clients' to satisfy clients' needs. This chapter addresses ingredients central to evaluation. Elements of client self-renewal and follow-up also are highlighted.

TERMINATION

Termination should be mutually agreed upon and occur when outcomes meet needs. Counselors should not bring counseling relationships to a close before termination is warranted. Premature termination can leave clients unable to use skills or demonstrate behaviors that have been presented through the counseling process. Premature termination can provide clients and counselors with a false sense of accomplishment. Both parties may feel that termination is important and necessary, but if counselors push for termination before clients are ready, clients could feel abandoned.

Counselors must assure clients that counseling is an ongoing process, one that can stop or start at any moment in time. Clients should be assured that if the need arises, they can return for future counseling. If counseling has been adequate, objectives will have been achieved. Counselors can help clients to examine the total process from introduction of vague needs, through development of meaningful objectives, to enactment of behaviors consistent with objectives. By reviewing frames that were used in arriving at new behaviors, clients should be able to see how they might resolve problems in the future. Counselors should leave clients with the belief that the process that has been used is one that can be used independent of the counselor. Learning this process is one of the most productive outcomes of counseling. If clients learn how to use the process, termination is a logical consequence.

Example: The Case of Linda (Presented on the first page of Chapter Nine).

> Linda entered the counselor's office and said, "Mr. Brown, may I shut the door?" Mr. Brown said, "Sure, Linda, shut the door." Linda did and sat down. She started to cry. She cried for about five minutes and Mr. Brown said, "Linda, can I help you?" Linda said, "No, Mr. Brown" and continued to cry. She cried for twenty-five minutes longer, looked up and said, "Thank you Mr. Brown," got up and left the office.

In the case of Linda termination of counseling was initiated by Linda. The counselor may have felt that termination was premature, whereas Linda may have felt that it was at exactly the right time. Which opinion is correct? Linda came to the financial counselor to seek help. The help she sought, however, was not of the normal kind. Apparently she did not need the counselor's verbal input to resolve her problems or concerns. Rather, she appeared to want the counselor to be with her as another human being as she worked through her concerns. Mr. Brown, the counselor in this situation, had apparently established a relationship with Linda at a previous time. This relationship was developed in such a way that Linda was able to deal with her needs in Mr. Brown's presence, but without his verbal assistance. Mr. Brown did not generate alternatives, at least not as described in the vignette. However, the fact that Linda felt free to cry, cease her crying, say, "Thank you, Mr. Brown," get up and leave indicates that she had an opportunity to think through her concerns and possibly to generate alternatives for them. Linda felt satisfied. Mr. Brown, however, may have wondered exactly what transpired. Since counseling is for clients and not for counselors, Mr. Brown's need is less important than Linda's. Counselors should be willing to be used in whatever way is appropriate and ethical for the growth and development of clients. Although it would be nice for Mr. Brown to feel satisfied, it is not crucial that he does. It is important, however, that Linda achieved a measure of satisfaction from the client counselor interchange.

This case points to the fact that the counseling relationship is for clients, not to meet the needs of counselors. Termination should occur when clients reach a point where they are responsible for their own behavior. Linda demonstrated that she was able to work through her problems, arrive at solutions, and behave accordingly. Mr. Brown should feel satisfied that Linda accepted the responsibility that was hers. Mr. Brown's responsibility beyond the relationship would be to contact Linda later to assure that she was working through her concerns and that she no longer needed counseling.

ESTABLISHING A MEANS FOR CLIENT SELF-RENEWAL

Financial counseling can be seen as a continuous process that does not necessarily end when clients terminate counseling interviews. Success can be total or it can be partial. If it is total, termination can occur. If partial success has been determined, counselors may have to review what has been accomplished, modify counseling until total success has been achieved, and then initiate termination. Upon termination, financial counselors should help clients realize that both their personal and financial growth and development are ongoing, lifelong processes and that resources are available for continued growth. Several resources are discussed below.

The Financial Counselor

The financial counselor is the first of the continuous services that must be offered to clients. If at a future time a client feels a need for financial counseling, the counselor should be available or be able to advise the client of other counseling services.

Self-Help Groups

Financial counselors can help clients become aware of resources that are not necessarily formal referral agencies. Many communities have voluntary self-help group activities that focus on a variety of topics. As examples, assertiveness training groups provide an opportunity to learn how to live more effectively, anxiety reduction groups help individuals cope with debilitating anxiety, and self-help groups are available for cancer survivors. Groups such as these can help clients cope, learn new skills, or develop areas of perceived weaknesses. The advantage of the self-help approach for clients is that they can pursue development along chosen lines at their own pace and in their own way. Responsibility for involvement is the client's, and should be seen as a step in a logical developmental sequence which began with their choice to enter financial counseling.

Reading

Financial counselors can help clients become aware of self-help literature. There is material available that deals with how one can overcome difficulties. This literature appears in books and tape recordings that deal with self-help procedures, and is available through most bookstores. The topics covered deal with most concerns that clients might have. The advantage of using written or recorded materials is that clients can go at their own pace and at the depth they believe to be desirable.

In all of these methods of client self-renewal, financial counselors can serve as resource persons for clients. The responsibility for using financial counselors should be the client's. As clients develop independence, financial counselors will be used less frequently. Financial counselors should be aware of this natural progression. Finally, financial counselors are warned against delaying termination because of their own personal needs to be important in clients' lives. It is important that financial counselors have as an ultimate goal for every client that the client be personally independent and responsible.

USING FOLLOW-UP PROCEDURES

The final phase of termination is follow-up. Follow-up procedures are short or long-term. Short-term follow-up deals with immediate evaluation of the financial counseling process and outcomes. It is used to determine additional sources that might be employed or to investigate usefulness of the financial counselors' intervention with a particular client. Short-term follow-up can be classified as *formative evaluation*, - a continuous process that provides information that can be used to alter financial counseling as it progresses. Results of this type of evaluation or follow-up are immediate and will have an effect on strategies and tactics used with individual clients.

Long-term follow-up has a different purpose. This type of follow-up is designed to investigate whether the overall financial counseling program is effective. Evaluation done in this manner can have programmatic implications; can lead to long-term decisions about more appropriate ways to organize financial counseling services; can highlight strengths and weaknesses of facilities; and can provide cues for directions that the financial counseling service might develop.

Evaluation of this type is called *summative evaluation*. Summative evaluation tends to examine the overall picture. It provides an overview of the financial counseling enterprise whereas formative evaluation looks at the service from within individual interactions. Taken together, formative and summative evaluation provide a continuous, systematic way for assessing financial counseling services and provide the data needed for changing services in the direction that will be most helpful for meeting client needs.

To undertake either type of follow-up procedure, whether formative or summative, financial counselors must know how data will be gathered and used. It is important that before financial counselors collect data, they have a clear idea of ways that data will be used, who will have access to it, and how data eventually will be preserved. Once financial counselors have made decisions about these issues, they must determine methods for collecting data. Usually, there are a number of potential sources for data. Clients provide the primary source, while significant others in the client's lives such as financial counselors and financial institution personnel provide a secondary source. A variety of methods can be used to gather data from each of these sources. Before data collection occurs, however, a systematic plan for assessment incorporating four key variables should be developed. A discussion of these variables follows.

Administrative Variables

A number of decisions must be made regarding assessment. Most of these decisions deal with specific issues that must be addressed before assessment begins. The following list of issues is not intended to be inclusive, but to provide the reader with an idea of what must be considered.

Outcome or Process

In financial counseling, both outcome and process are important and closely related. Whereas the client and institutions may be concerned with outcomes, the financial counselor may measure the effectiveness of counseling by examining the counseling process or by examining outcomes.

Financial institutions might consider positive financial counseling outcomes to be decreased loan delinquency, more consistent savings, more timely loan payments, or better financial decisions. Many of these outcomes are observable and therefore lend themselves to assessment. Other financial counseling outcomes are less observable but equally as important. Clients may change beliefs and attitudes about themselves, determine ways to use their financial resources more productively, or learn decision-making skills that will have long-term benefits. These are outcomes, although not readily observable.

The financial counseling process also is open to assessment. Has the financial counselor used the most efficient, most productive strategies for helping clients achieve their goals? This question must continuously be asked and attempts made to answer it. Are outcomes most important? Is process most important? Can and should both be assessed? The way in which counselors address these issues is an administrative decision.

Longitudinal Or Short-Term Assessment

Financial counseling goals vary. In some cases, financial counselors are interested in knowing whether a particular strategy was effective with a specific client, and at other times, they are interested in knowing if financial counseling benefited clients *generally*. Longitudinal assessment tends to provide data about the long-term impact of financial counseling on an individual or particular group. Short term, as the name implies, looks at immediate results, e.g., did the client follow through on a decision that was made in counseling?

Both types of assessment have value. Longitudinal assessment is meaningful in making decisions referent to the total financial counseling program (summative consequences) whereas short-term assessment lends itself to immediate changes (formative consequences). Which type of assessment to use is an administrative decision.

Group Or Individual Assessment

Continual development of a financial counseling program is dependent on assessment of individual client progress and a collective assessment of groups of clients who have had similar financial counseling experiences, e.g., all those clients who received productive counseling. In both instances, assessment can measure outcome and process and be useful in a formative or summative manner. Whether emphasis is to be placed on individual or group assessment is an administrative decision.

What assessment procedures can be used? Assessment can occur in a variety of ways. Financial counselors can use interviews, questionnaires, census data, financial institution records, personal observations, behavioral records, or self-reports to gather data. The procedure used with individuals or groups is dependent on the goals of financial counseling and the objectives of the financial counseling program. The decision to employ any of the above methods is administrative.

What kind and how much data is needed? At times it is possible to obtain considerable data about a client or group of clients. At other times, it is not. Administrative decisions must be made as to the nature of data to be gathered and the amount to be solicited. Financial counseling goals and objectives provide a basis for determining what kind of data to collect, whereas the breadth and depth of data to be collected is dependent on financial counseling needs, data availability, potential data use, and cost of collection. At times, it may be desirable to gather information from all clients of a group. At other times a random sample of group members may be sufficient.

How much flexibility will exist in assessment procedures? The amount of change that will be tolerated during assessment procedures should be determined *before* initiating procedures. Decisions made in advance can affect the quality and quantity of data gathered. Changes in procedures made in *mid-stream* can render data collected early useless, whereas adherence to rigid early guidelines can prevent taking advantage of new information.

How will data be used? Who will use it? Before data is collected an administrative decision should be made concerning the use of data. Knowing how data will be used, and by whom, facilitates collection of useful data. If data is to be used by financial counselors to assess counseling strategies, a particular type of data is needed. If, however, data is to be used by administrators to determine the effect of financial counseling on loan delinquency rates, another class of data may be warranted.

Will there be a secondary analysis to assess assessment? Who will determine if the assessment procedure accomplished its purpose? If financial counselors perform assessment about the counseling service, they may be biased about results. If an independent assessment is used, individuals performing the assessment may be unfamiliar with significant aspects of financial counseling outcomes or strategies. An administrative decision is needed to determine the most appropriate individual or group to develop and implement all or any assessment procedures.

Technical Variables

Once administrative decisions have been made, efforts must center on developing assessment schema that are technically sound. The two major considerations that should be addressed are validity and reliability.

Validity

Validity refers to whether assessment procedures measure what they were designed to measure. A procedure that accurately measures the concept under scrutiny is valid. If elements of the procedure are technically appropriate and accurate, the procedure has internal validity. If results can be generalized appropriately to a wider population of participants, settings, or occasions, the assessment procedure has external or predictive validity.

Reliability

Reliability refers to the consistency of the assessment procedure. A procedure that provides inconsistent results obviously is not as useful as one that provides consistent results. Assessment of financial counseling should be based on valid and reliable procedures. If valid and reliable procedures are not used the usefulness of findings is negligible.

Control Variables

Assessment has inherent threats associated with it. Clients being assessed must know how assessment will be used and who will have access to data. At another level, the decision to assess can be threatening to financial counselors. Results of assessment can be used to develop or disband programs. Therefore, financial counselors should be involved in conceptualization of assessment procedures, discussions relevant to use of assessment results, and program changes that result from assessment.

Ethical Variables

Two ethical variables must be taken into account in assessment, - privacy and confidentiality. Clients have a right to maintain privacy and to refrain from sharing information. At the same time, financial counseling services can be improved if clients share their insights and relevant information with financial counselors. Usually, clients willingly share and assessment can occur. However, in situations where clients choose not to participate in assessment, their right to privacy *must* be maintained. Also, in all situations, efforts must be made to assure confidentiality of data.

The variables outlined above are important whenever assessment is used. They provide a basis for developing assessment. They also help prevent inappropriate use of assessment. Assessment should also be based on a model of interaction, one in which assessment is an integral part. Pulvino (1971) developed a counseling model using assessment as a primary means for measuring counselor accountability. This model, developed over thirty years ago, is still useful for conceptualizing assessment in financial counseling. In this model, assessment of process and outcome determines whether counseling goals have been reached (see Accountability Model diagram).

If measurable objectives have been reached, communication of evaluation results back to original publics (Step Five) can occur and financial counseling can cease. If, however, assessment (Step Four) reveals that objectives have not been reached, financial counselors must determine what remains to be accomplished, e.g., a renewed look at determining measurable objectives or additional counseling. This process continues until counseling goals have been reached.

ACCOUNTABILITY MODEL

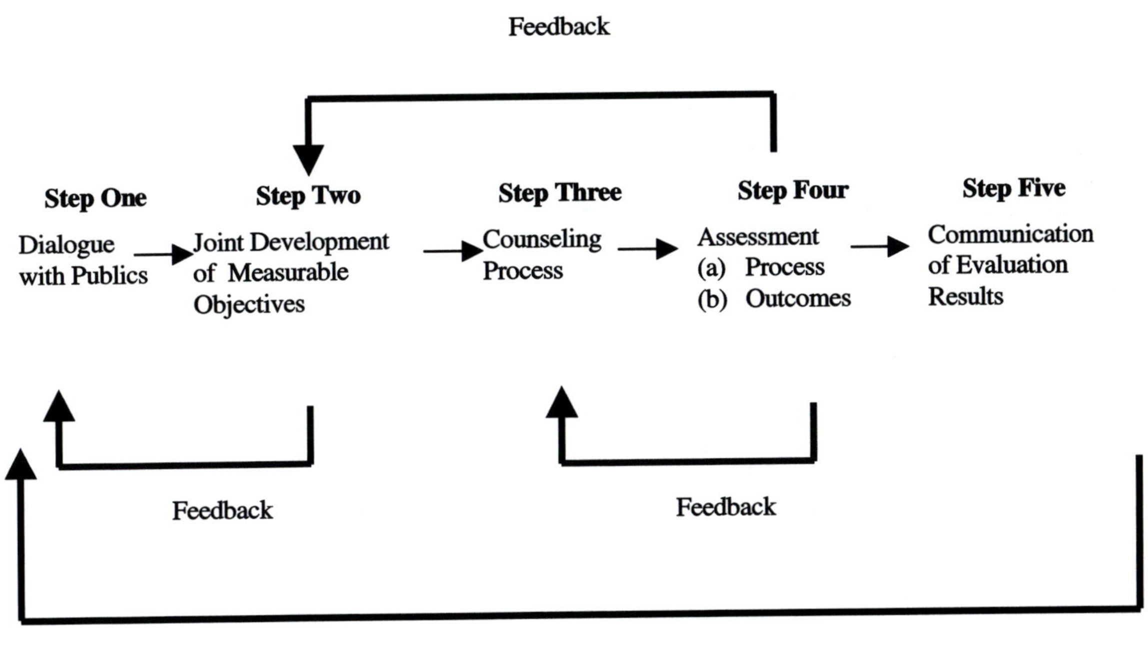

PROCESS/OUTCOME ASSESSMENT

PROCESS ASSESSMENT

Counselors, clients, or other capable professionals can assess financial counseling formally or informally. A number of scales are presented to show how formal assessment might be accomplished.

Client Rating Scale: Clients can be asked to rate financial counselors on variables that deal with counseling process/strategies and counseling goals. A form like the one that follows could be used for this purpose.

Client Rating Form 1

Directions: We are interested in knowing how you feel about the counseling you have received. Your observations will be valuable in helping us improve counseling services. Please circle the appropriate number for each item using the following scale.

1. Never or rarely2. Usually 3. Most of the time 4. All the time 5. Not relevant

1 2 3 4 5	(1)	The counselor acted as if he/she had all the answers.
1 2 3 4 5	(2)	The counselor helped me decide what I wanted to do.
1 2 3 4 5	(3)	The counselor helped me develop a plan to solve my problem.
1 2 3 4 5	(4)	The counselor offered me good suggestions
1 2 3 4 5	(5)	The counselor seemed to understand my problem.
1 2 3 4 5	(6)	The counselor seemed to understand my feelings.
1 2 3 4 5	(7)	The counselor could understand what I wanted and needed.
1 2 3 4 5	(8)	The counselor's remarks helped me to understand myself and my problem.
1 2 3 4 5	(9)	I felt accepted by the counselor.
1 2 3 4 5	(10)	The counselor was honest with me.

This is another form that could be used for client rating of a counselor.

Client Rating Form 2

Directions: We are interested in knowing what you think about the counseling you have received. For each group, check the statement that most clearly represents what you perceive.

_______	My counselor thoroughly understands my situation.
_______	My counselor generally understands my situation.
_______	My counselor somewhat understands my situation.
_______	My counselor does not understand my situation.
_______	I don't know if the counselor understands my situation.

_______	My counselor cares about me very much.
_______	My counselor cares about me some.
_______	My counselor cares about me a little.
_______	My counselor does not care about me.
_______	I don't know if the counselor cares about me.

Financial Counselor Self-Rating Scale: Counselors can serve as their own critics. One way to organize their efforts is exemplified below:

Self Evaluation Form

Directions: This form is used for self evaluation. It provides a basic outline for critical inquiry concerning your performance. You can use it to critically examine yourself. Please circle the appropriate number for each item using the following scale.

1. Inferior Quality   2. Some Indication of Ability   3. Acceptable Quality
4. Good Quality   5. Superior Quality

1 2 3 4 5	(1)	Ability to handle responsibility.
1 2 3 4 5	(2)	Flexibility of responses.
1 2 3 4 5	(3)	Ability to listen and identify themes and/or clues.
1 2 3 4 5	(4)	Sensitivity to feelings and ability to react to them.
1 2 3 4 5	(5)	Ability to analyze and react to the counselor-client relationship.
1 2 3 4 5	(6)	Facility of self-appraisal, relating your own behavior to your theory of philosophy of people.

In addition to formalized assessment procedures, financial counselors can benefit from discussions with clients about the counseling process and strategies used. Clients should be encouraged to share positive and negative observations of the process. Questions such as the following can be used. "What benefits did you gain from financial counseling?" "What other kinds of services do you wish the financial counselor would have offered?" "In what areas of financial counseling would you like to see improvement?" "What strategies did the financial counselor use which were particularly beneficial to you?" and "What might the financial counselor do that would be more helpful for you?" Questions can provide financial counselors more information about the service that they offer.

Outcome Assessment

Like process, financial counseling outcomes can be assessed formally and informally. If a formal approach is desired, an orderly sequence should be developed and followed.

It is important for financial counselors to know the *context* in which counseling outcomes will occur and what provisions exist for continued intervention if outcomes are not achieved. To do this, a systematic intervention strategy must exist in which client needs are identified and financial counselor strategies and tactics are used in an appropriate and beneficial way. A number of authors have addressed this issue. Most identify key ingredients in the process. These ingredients are synthesized in the following flow chart.

Model for Counselor Intervention

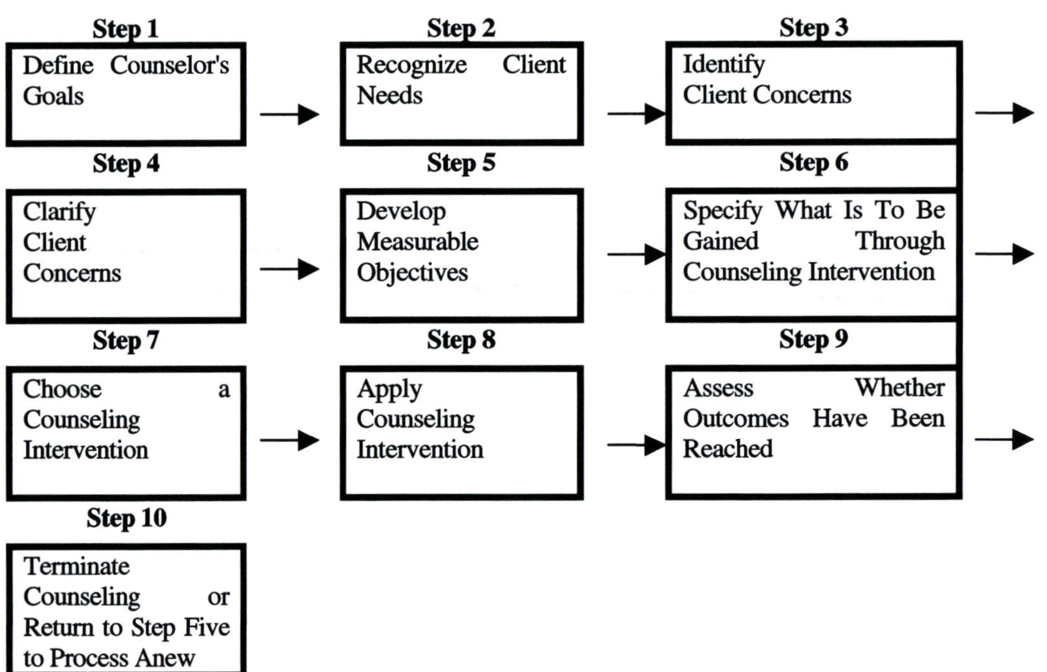

Financial counseling applications of this model can occur in numerous ways. One method is for the financial counselor to encourage the client to discuss concerns. These concerns should then be examined so that major ones might be isolated and ranked for importance. Specific outcomes for each concern also should be identified. From these concerns a chart can be developed in which the likelihood of specific outcomes can be arranged in a hierarchical manner (see example below). The chart should represent a continuum of observable measures from the *worst* to the *best* anticipated outcome. *Expected* outcomes appear in the center of the chart.

Outcome Achievement Chart

Outcome Value		**Outcomes**	
	Goal	**Goal**	**Goal**
	To be debt free	*To be able to make financial decisions*	*To develop a budget*
Worst Possible Outcome	*Owe more than the $500 I presently owe*	*Can't decide if I should save or not*	*Don't use a budget*
Expected Outcome	*Owe no money*	*Make and follow through on a decision to start savings plan*	*Use a budget most of the time*
Best Possible Outcome	*Have at least $100 in savings*	*Make numerous financial decisions*	*Follow a budget regularly*

Specifying the worst to best possible outcomes helps financial counselors and clients approach goal setting realistically. Financial counseling outcomes are seldom *all* or *nothing* situations. There are usually degrees of success or failure. Stating possible outcomes as a continuum from worst to best eliminates the all-or-nothing attitude and focuses evaluation on degrees of success rather than on absolute success *or* failure.

At termination of financial counseling (Step 10 in the Model for Counselor Intervention Flow chart), the client's outcomes should be examined. The client's outcome achievement is assessed and recorded on the chart.

Joint financial counselor-client examination of this chart can help both parties understand what has been achieved through counseling. If the client's goals have been reached, termination can occur. If they have not, the financial counselor and the client may wish to return to Step five of the flow-chart (develop measurable objectives) and begin the counseling process anew.

Finally, outcome assessment also can occur informally. The financial counselor, through discussion with the client, can determine if outcomes have been achieved or if additional counseling is needed. In addition, financial counselors can use their position in the financial institution to determine if the client is meeting financial obligations and, in general, achieving financial goals established in counseling. If goals have been achieved and outcomes are satisfactory, counseling can terminate. If not, this can be discussed and counseling can continue.

CONCLUSION

Financial counseling is a process with specific steps. It establishes goals and objectives and is comprised of both process and specific content. The specific steps should be taken to assess the effectiveness of the counseling interchange. This chapter has addressed a number of evaluation issues.

RESOURCES

DeJong, P. & Berg, I.K. (1998). *Interviewing For Solutions*. Pacific Grove: Brooks Cole.

Poindexter, C.C., Valentine, D. & Conway, P. (1999). *Essential Skills For Human Services.* Pacific Grove: Brooks Cole.

Pulvino, C.J. (1971). *Feedback: A needed component of counselor accountability*. Summer Symposium Report. University of Wisconsin, Madison, Vol.1, 52-60.

Shah, I. (1971), *Nasrudin*. New York: E. P. Dutton.

Young, M.E. (1998). *Learning The Art Of Helping*. Upper Saddle River: Prentice-hall.

14 MULTIPLE INTERVIEWING

... What is REAL? asked the rabbit one day... "Does it mean having things inside you and a stick- out handle?"

"Real isn't how you are made," said the Skin Horse. "It's a thing that happens to you. When a child loves you for a long, long time, not just to play with, but REALLY loves you, then you become Real."

"Does it hurt?" asked the Rabbit.

"Sometimes," said the Skin Horse, for he was always truthful..

"When you are Real you don't mind being hurt."

"Does it happen all at once, like being wound up," he asked, "or bit by bit?"

"It doesn't happen all at once," said the Skin Horse. "You become. It takes a long time. That's why it doesn't happen to people who break easily, or have sharp edges, or who have to be carefully kept. Generally, by the time you are Real, most of your hair has been loved off, and your eyes drop out and you get loose in the joints and very shabby. But these things don't matter at all, because once you are Real you can't be ugly, except to people who don't understand."

Margery Williams (1975, 16-17) *The Velveteen Rabbit*

INTRODUCTION

We have discussed counseling strategies and tactics as they apply to two-person sessions, the financial counselor and a client. Many times, however, financial counselors will counsel with more than one person at a time. Probably the most common occurrence will be when counselors work with couples. In this chapter we will discuss special concerns when dealing with two or more clients. A significant question that must be addressed is, "How do you simultaneously pace, motivate, explore, and deal with two or more distinct client personalities?"

MULTIPLE COMMUNICATIVE PATTERNS

When two people interact, a pattern of communication exists which relates to the flow of information between the two. As discussed previously, the output from one person becomes the input for the second and *vice versa.* There is mutual influence because one person's outputs place expectations on the form and kind of output of the second person.

In *multiple* communicative interactions, the patterns of communication and potential for influence expand rapidly. When a third person is added to an existing two-person interaction, a three-way pattern of communication results. If we assume that the financial counselor is at the tip of the following triangle in position C, there is an interaction among both clients and the financial counselor. In addition, there is potential for a fourth pattern, when any of the three persons, in one message, directs communication to both of the other two persons.

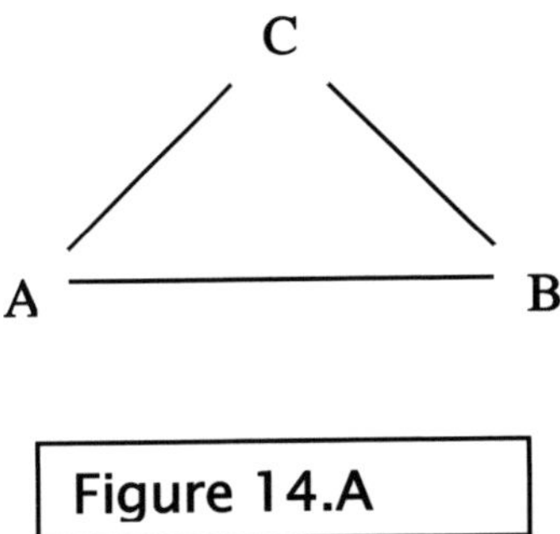

Figure 14.A

Adding more people to the interaction increases the number of communicative patterns. For example, when a fourth person is added to the group there is the potential for at least seven distinct patterns to develop, i.e., six different pair configurations and one that represents an address to the entire group from any of the four participants.

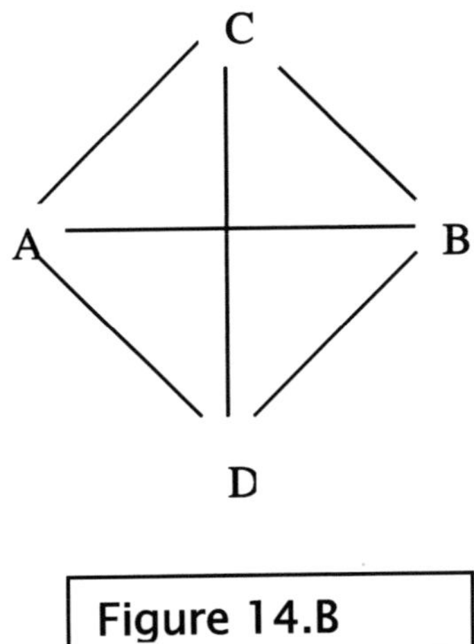

Figure 14.B

While potential patterns of communication and influence increase with each additional person, counseling strategies and tactics necessary to deal with such complexities remain constant. You can use verbal and nonverbal pacing skills and exploring skills with groups, just as with individuals. These same tactics can be used to reduce the complexity of interaction and to control patterns of communication. Each of the above diagrams shows the number of *potential* patterns. However, an effective financial counselor can control the number of *active* patterns by controlling the centrality of communication. That is, effective financial counselors can establish themselves as the center of communication flow. Geometrically, this would look a little like a wheel, with all communication being directed through the hub.

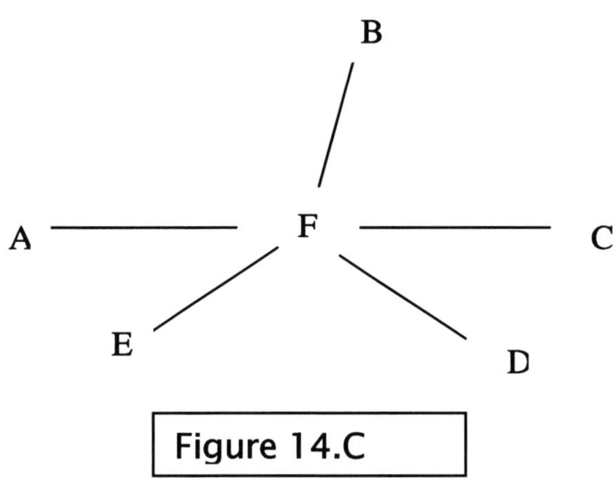

Figure 14.C

Notice in this figure that the person in the middle has the potential to act as gatekeeper. Most communication, indicated by the solid lines, is directed by, and funneled through, the person in the center. There is little communication, indicated by the lack of lines, among the other participants. The difference between Figure 14.B and Figure 14.C is roughly equivalent to the difference between a group discussion and a teaching situation. In a group discussion each participant can take an active part and talk or respond to every other person. In teacher-student situations, teachers usually control communication so that it is channeled through them.

We recommend that in financial counseling you establish patterns of communication similar to the teaching model. We are not implying that you should become a "teacher," but that it is easier to control communicative patterns if you become the hub of the process. This allows you to control the focus of communication while allowing group clients to openly communicate with each other. In this approach, you have more control over both the content and the process of communication.

Skills are applied in a slightly different manner in multiple communicative interactions. In the standard two-person counseling session, tactics are used to focus on information and the manner in which the client processes information. Although you must still focus on information in the multiple interview, you probably will need to concentrate more on *how* your clients communicate about the information under discussion. This shift in focus occurs for a number of reasons.

- First, in the multiple interview you must focus on the needs of more than one person. This automatically limits your ability to attend to any *one* person. You may miss information being transmitted through subtle clues of voice inflection, body gestures, or space usage. The data you have about any one person will be much less than what you would gather in an individual interview, while the information you have about the group will increase.

- Second, the group format prevents you from responding to every client need. You must "spread" yourself around by responding to the needs of *all* clients of the group. To do this, the level or intensity of your response to any one person will be less than it would be in an individual interaction.

The multiple interview forces you to be aware of the group at the expense of any one individual.

MULTIPLE COUNSELING PROCESSES AND ISSUES

Pacing

Verbal pacing skills of restating, paraphrasing, and summarizing are used in the multiple counseling interactions just as in individual counseling sessions. You can restate, paraphrase, or summarize individual statements made by any client. You also can summarize, from time to time, the discussion that has taken place among all participants.

By contrast, the use of nonverbal pacing in multiple interactions demands further discussion.

When you non-verbally pace, you attempt to match another person's important nonverbal behavior to communicate acceptance, warmth, and understanding. This helps build trust, which is necessary for effective relationships. But whom do you non-verbally pace when talking to more than one person at a time?

Realistically you can't non-verbally pace everyone. Yet, the process of nonverbal pacing in multiple counseling is rather simple. You non-verbally pace the person who is talking. You will find that when you non-verbally pace a person, the person will tend to direct more communication toward you than to others in the multiple situations. As you pace each speaker, you *will* become the hub of the communicative pattern. This allows you to use your own nonverbal behavior to lead and direct the flow of communication. For example, one of the authors was counseling a couple who were having minor difficulties in their relationship. The meeting took place in late afternoon during the summer. The wife was a teacher who was on summer vacation. She came to the interview dressed in casual slacks and a blouse. The husband came to the interview directly from work, dressed in a three-piece suit. The wife sat in a relaxed manner in her chair. She eventually slid down, stretched her feet out in front of her, and rested her head on the back of the chair. Her husband, by contrast, sat erect with both feet on the floor, and clasped the arms of the chair.

As frequently happens in counseling couples, each spouse began by sharing with the author his/her perception of the relationship. Both the husband and wife directed most of their dialogue to the author, who was sitting in front and between them. The author selectively non-verbally paced each speaker. When the wife spoke, the author leaned back in his chair and matched her general body orientation. When the husband spoke, the author sat erect in his chair and focused his attention on him. The author said little during this initial part of the interview, responding most frequently by using the verbal pacing skills of paraphrasing and summarization. By doing so, he established trust between him and each client.

At one point in the interview, the author felt that it was important for the couple to talk directly to each other rather than through him. The author accomplished this by leaning forward in his chair and alternately looking at the wife and the husband. The author repeated the process by looking at the husband and then at the wife, paused, and then looked at a point between them. After a few seconds had elapsed, the wife sat straighter in her chair, leaned forward toward her husband, and began to address him directly. The husband, without hesitation, responded directly to her.

In this example, the author used verbal and nonverbal pacing to establish an effective relationship. By verbally and non-verbally pacing each speaker, the author became the hub of the communication. After trust was established, the author, through non-verbal behavior was able to help the couple communicate with each other.

Exploring

Exploring strategies can be used in multiple counseling much as they are used in individual counseling sessions. However, in multiple counseling, exploration tactics also can be used to focus on the clients' communication process. This requires counselors to pay attention to *how* group clients respond to what is being said, as well as to the information that is being shared.

For example, in working with a couple, a counselor might notice that when one person is talking, the other person non-verbally expresses an emotional reaction to what is being said. Whether the person signals confusion, anger, frustration, happiness, disagreement, agreement, or another emotion, you can facilitate communication. Be alert to these responses, examine the interaction to determine what specifically is triggering these responses, observe the interaction process in its entirety, and lead clients to focus on issues that foster particular responses. Consider the following example.

> **Financial Counselor:** I noticed that while your spouse was talking you didn't seem to agree. Tell me what you disagree with.

In this example, the financial counselor has first shared an observation and then used an imperative lead to explore how the person feels about what is being said. In the example that follows, the financial counselor notices that one of the clients looks confused as the other talks.

> **Financial Counselor:** I think I understand what you are trying to say. It would help me and maybe your spouse, if you would tell us a little more about what you mean by a secure investment.

In this example, the financial counselor has asked for concept clarification and has brought the spouse into the exploration. This broader form of exploration occurs because the financial counselor notices that the spouse has non-verbally expressed confusion.

Sources of Conflict

In general, there are four major sources of conflict in multiple counseling.

- Differences in male-female communication styles
- Differences in learning styles
- Differences in basic needs
- Differences in values

Gender differences

Males and females frequently express their thoughts in different ways. For example, females are *generally* more likely to respond to the specifics of a statement, while males are more likely to respond to the overall meaning of the message. In a multiple counseling session with both male and female participants, *differences in communication styles* can lead to misunderstanding. As a facilitative financial counselor, you can help individuals communicate more effectively by helping them recognize and bridge their individual differences. Consider the following interchange as an example of this point.

> **Financial Counselor:** If we choose the direction that we've been discussing, you may feel that your resources are being stretched too thin. In my opinion, this would last for a short time and then you would start to feel that you could handle it okay.
>
> Martha might ask, "How long would we feel this heavy burden?" whereas Dan might say, "In the long run it looks like we could benefit from this."

To be most helpful, the financial counselor should respond to both, possibly in the following manner.

Financial Counselor: We do have two situations, the short term and the long term. Martha, in response to your question, I believe that you'd feel the financial burden for less than six months. Dan, I would agree with you. I think that if you are willing to put up with the financial difficulty for the six months you will reap substantial long-term gains.

In this interchange, the financial counselor indicates an understanding of how both Martha and Dan view the problem, acknowledges both clients, and attends to differences in their individual communicative styles.

Learning styles Differences

A difference in clients' learning styles is a second potential source for communicative difficulty. Consider the following.

Financial Counselor: Tell me what type of savings plan you would consider at this point.

Mary: I would like a savings plan that makes sense given all of our present debts and the goals that we've established.

John: Umm hmm, but I feel that it is very important that whatever we do we don't get bound up or tied in knots!

In this interchange Mary's learning style seems to be auditory, whereas John's appears to be kinesthetic. Mary's statements reflect *thinking* about what needs to be done, while John's words are *action-oriented.* The financial counselor, in working with these clients, should determine if these early statements represent how Mary and John communicate *generally.*

Once this is known, the financial counselor can communicate more effectively with both persons by using their preferred style. Also, the counselor can help Mary and John communicate more effectively with each other.

Basic Needs Differences

A third area of potential conflict results from *differences in individual needs.* Abraham Maslow (1954) suggests that individuals operate on a need hierarchy that incorporates seven basic needs.

Maslow's Hierarchy of Needs

A basic need for food, drink, and sexual contact

A need for security from the environment

A need for social contact and acceptance

A need for self-esteem

A need for self-actualization

A need for truth

A need for beauty

Not all individuals have the same need, or combination of needs, at the same time. Consequently, conflict can occur when two or more clients have different needs. For example, consider the following.

Financial Counselor: What type of savings plan is most appealing to you?

Wife: I'd like to put our money into something that has a good chance for secure growth. I'm interested in having our money make money so that we can do the things we've always wanted to do, but I don't want to take a lot of chances.

Husband: I think that we have to invest for our retirement. I want to make sure that when I retire we have enough to live on!

It is obvious in this interchange that the spouses have slightly different needs. One is more concerned with social or possibly self-esteem needs, while the other is concerned with security. The financial counselor must be aware of these differences and help both clients understand their needs and, possibly, resolve their differences.

Value Differences

Finally, *differences in basic values* can lead to conflict in interpersonal interactions. The five basic values that are important in financial counseling revolve around issues of *power, status, love, security,* and *autonomy.* Consider the following statements that reflect financial values:

Money should be used to control others! (*Power*)

Wealth allows me to belong to the "right" country club. (*Status*)

I want to use my financial resources to help the needy. (*Love*)

The greatest value of money is that I don't have to worry about the future. (*Security*)

Money allows me to do the things I want! (*Autonomy*)

Individuals display all values. Yet, people behave in a manner that suggests that at least one or more are most important. Be on the alert for dramatic differences in your clients' value orientations and be ready to use communication skills to help resolve apparent differences.

In all of the potential conflict-producing circumstances described above, your role as a financial counselor is constant. You must be alert to client differences and be able to facilitate communication between or among clients, effectively pace clients verbally and non-verbally within multiple counseling, and control the flow and direction of communication.

CONFLICT SITUATIONS

Dobson and Miller (1974) in *Giving In To Get Your Own Way* discuss four potentially hazardous situations that can arise in multiple relationships. The first revolves around being a *Participant Observer.* In this situation, conflict erupts between or among clients, while the financial counselor is left to observe the ensuing argument. The second, *The Vise,* results in the financial counselor being pressured from two sides at once. Usually it begins as a disagreement between two clients and frequently progresses to a second stage, a joint attack on the well-intentioned financial counselor. The third type of conflict situation is *Getting Caught in the Middle,* where disagreements arise and the financial counselor is asked to take sides. Finally, the fourth type is the *Multiple Attack,* a group attack on the counselor, which may occur when the financial counseling session includes three or more clients. A discussion of these follows with suggestion of ways to deal with them.

Participant Observer

In this situation the financial counselor can be found "in" communication with participants while maintaining a psychological position for observing interaction of participants. As clients discuss their situations, the counselor can observe their differing values, needs, learning styles, communicative styles, and goals. In some cases, differences can lead to verbally expressed conflict. By being a participant observer in the clients' conflict situation, the financial counselor can observe the process, intervene, and focus discussion on problem resolution. Resolution will occur when financial counselors move clients to a common ground for examining decisions or problems under discussion. Below is an example of a financial counselor who is left to observe a couple's interaction. The focus of the counseling has been on a productive use of the couple's money. The financial counselor has not made any recommendations, but has helped the couple look at various forms of investment.

Financial counselor: Well, we have discussed a number of options, and I'm wondering what you two would like to do.

Bob: Yes. Well, I think we ought to really look into some of those various kinds of stocks you talked about. They sound like we would have a real potential for fast growth! I mean we could double our money real quick that way.

Pat: But Bob, those are so risky! I think it would be like giving our money away. I don't want to invest in something where we might lose all our money overnight!

Bob: Well, it's extra cash we have for investing. It's not like we will be in the poorhouse if we lose it. I want to invest in something where we have a chance of making it big.

Pat: We worked hard for that money, and I don't want to just throw it away! I think we should be a lot more conservative, investing in something where we will have a guarantee like some of those certificates of deposit.

Bob: You sound as though the only thing you want to do with the money is put it in the financial institution.

Pat: You seem to want to make all the decisions!

Notice that in this interchange the financial counselor has been on the sidelines as an observer. Besides the obvious feelings of embarrassment a financial counselor might have watching clients argue, there would be a natural desire to want to help. If the counselor did try to help, there is a danger of being *Getting Caught in the Middle,* or of being caught in *The Vise* and of having both people use the counselor to vent their emotions. The task for the financial counselor is to discover clients' basic differences and help them to focus on resolving them.

In this interchange there are some obvious value and attitudinal differences between the two on how to invest their money. However, the couple's goals are unclear. It might be assumed that their differences in values and attitudes stem from differences in goals. The financial counselor can test this possibility by focusing the discussion.

Financial Counselor: It sounds as though both of you have strong feelings about how to invest your money. I'm wondering if you have discussed what you want to accomplish through investments. It would help me if we could spend a few minutes talking about your goals. Pat, what do you want to accomplish by investing?

Pat: What is most important to me is getting ready for the kids' college education and then having a nice nest egg so that we don't have to worry about money when we retire.

Financial Counselor: I can understand that. Bob, what are your thoughts on this?

Bob: Well, I figure that with both of us working we will be able to handle the college expenses out of our normal income, and we both have pretty good retirement plans at work. So I think we ought to invest our money so that we can buy and do things when we retire.

Financial Counselor: That helps. On the surface it sounds like you want to go in different directions, and that may be where the disagreement is coming from. I'm wondering if they are really that different, though.

Pat: What do you mean?

Financial Counselor:*:* Well, one way of approaching things is investing your money to provide for both college and the nest egg you talked about. This would release more of your current income to buy the things Bob talked about. On the other hand, if you use ordinary income to cover the college expenses, you could use your investments to build a nest egg and to buy the things Bob wants. I'm wondering if you might do both.

The key to helping in this form of conflict is to identify underlying themes that the clients do not seem to be dealing with directly. In the example, the financial counselor's hypothesis appeared to be accurate, the couple *does* have different underlying goals.

The Vise

In the *Vise,* financial counselors are attacked by both clients. Let's return to the example above and see how that might happen.

Financial Counselor: It sounds as though both of you have strong feelings about how to invest your money. I'm wondering if you have discussed what you want to accomplish through investments. It would help me if we could spend a few minutes talking about your goals. Pat, what do you want to accomplish by investing?

Pat: Of course we've discussed our goals. We want to invest so that we can make our money grow securely. Isn't that right, Bob?

Bob: Yeah! We know what we want to accomplish and we have the same goals. We want to get ahead of inflation!

A financial counselor's best efforts may turn a situation into a pattern in which the couple vents their emotions. The emotions usually subconsciously are intended for each other, but the financial counselor becomes an easy and safe target, safe in the sense that the couple won't have to deal with their emotions with each other. When caught in *a vise*, the financial counselor's immediate goal should be to move back to the participant observer position so that any continued attacks will be between clients. Continuing with the dialogue:

Financial Counselor: There seems to be a lot of emotion tied up in this issue of how to invest your money. Bob, tell me, how do you think you should invest your money?

Bob (*still attacking*): Well, I don't think it is a matter of goals. I want to invest in something where we have a chance of making it big. I don't mind taking a few chances.

Pat: Wait a minute, Bob! I don't want to take any big chances with our money. We need to save that for the kids' college education and retirement.

Bob: I'm worried about the kids' education just as much as you are, but I want to make some money so that we can do things we can't do now.

Notice in this short interchange the financial counselor did not respond directly to attacks that put the counselor in a vise. Rather, the counselor directed attention to the strong emotions being expressed and then focused back on what the couple wanted to accomplish. As Bob expressed his desires, Pat then responded to what she didn't like in Bob's approach. The attack was redirected back to the *clients*, and then the financial counselor moved again to the participant observer position.

At this point, the immediate goal should be to reduce conflict so that effective problem solving can take place. The financial counselor's first attempt was not successful. Remember the general principle that *if what you are doing isn't producing what you want, try something different*. It is fairly certain that if the financial counselor repeats the original response, a repeat of the initial reaction will occur, an attack on the counselor! As an example of trying something different, the financial counselor might say something like the following:

> **Financial Counselor:** (*looking for resolution*): I guess there is a lot more emotion in this issue of how to invest than I thought. Let's see if we can find some common ground, and then go from there. One thing I heard both of you say is that you are concerned with the kids' college education.
>
> **Pat:** Well, yes. That is the most important thing to me right now.
>
> **Bob:** Yeah, we need to know that we can provide them with whatever assistance we can. My folks helped me a lot through college, and I know it meant a lot to me.
>
> **Pat:** My parents provided all the money for me to go to college, and I think it was one of the best things they ever did for me.
>
> **Financial Counselor:** This seems to be something you both feel very strongly about. But the difference seems to be how you want to accomplish it.

The financial counselor initially used a good summarizing response focused on how the couple was feeling. Then the communication was focused on reaching a common understanding where the discussion could begin anew. Again, in a multiple counseling situation, the tactics used are the same as those used in one-to-one counseling, but the focus is often on communicative process rather than on content itself. When there is strong emotion being expressed in the communicative pattern, it is often most helpful to focus on the theme and the process rather than on defending oneself.

Getting Caught In The Middle

This form of conflict occurs when financial counselors are asked to take sides on an issue. Intuitively, counselors know that if they take sides, they will be used by one client to convince another client how to think or act. Obviously, when counselor succumb to this ploy they may alienate one or both of the clients. This situation begins with each client trying to pull the financial counselor into his or her way of thinking. The financial counselor probably will get the feeling that he/she is being pulled in two different directions at once. For example:

> **Bob:** I think that we should invest in something that gives us the quickest potential for doubling our money. That way we can be sure of having money for the kids' education.
>
> **Pat:** But, if we put the money in a CD for three or more years we can get at least 6% and it will be insured, and we wouldn't have to worry about losing it.

In this interchange, spouses express their opinions, each in a different direction. At this point there probably will not be a direct overture for agreement from the financial counselor. However, if the financial counselor watches nonverbal behavior closely, usually there will be some indirect bid for agreement: looking at the financial counselor while making a point, nodding as a form of asking for a "yes" from the financial counselor, or gesturing toward the financial counselor when speaking. Financial counselors should not respond verbally or non-verbally to these indirect bids. Any kind of response, such as a nod that is intended to communicate, "I understand you," can be taken as agreement. If financial counselors do not respond non-verbally to the bids for agreement, they might hear something like the following:

> **Bob:** Well, Robbie (financial counselor's name) knows that I'm right, because by putting our money in a guaranteed CD we will just keep up with inflation.

At this point the financial counselor has a direct bid for agreement. The counselor is being *caught in the middle,* by being asked to take sides. The counselor's first move should be to move toward the participant observer position.

> **Financial Counselor:** You both seem to have strong opinions on how to accomplish saving money for your kids' education. It sounds to me as though you, Pat, need a greater sense of security about investing and you, Bob, would like to take more risks.

> **Bob:** Well, if we don't take risks we won't ever get ahead of the game.
>
> **Pat:** But, if we take risks that are too big we might lose everything we have worked so hard for and jeopardize the money for college.

> **Financial Counselor:** I'm wondering what you think about investments that have some risk but not the same high risk as the stock market.

In the first response the financial counselor focused again on the process and feelings being expressed. Notice, the response slowed the conflict and moved the financial counselor back to the participant observer position. In that position the financial counselor could focus on the underlying theme of "risk taking" as a basis for resolving client conflict.

A second form of *Getting Caught in the Middle* can occur when two people give a third person contradictory advice. This can happen when a client consults two different financial counselors. One counselor may suggest one course of action, while the other suggests something entirely different. At this point the client might not know which way to turn.

Financial counselors may experience this form of *Getting Caught in the Middle* when a client seeks a third opinion. Frequently clients will attempt to use financial counselors to decide for them. In these situations, financial counselors may offer advice that agrees with one of the two previously consulted financial counselors or advice that is completely different. In either case, we recommend that financial counselors move to the participant observer role and help clients resolve their own conflict. For example:

> **Client:** I have talked with several financial counselors and I keep getting different stories. One told me that purchasing universal life insurance is the way to go, while another told me that it is better to purchase term insurance. Which do you think is better?
>
> **Financial Counselor:** It can be very confusing trying to figure out which way to invest, and those two options are certainly viable. Have you figured out the relative costs and benefits of each?

The financial counselor effectively sidesteps getting caught in the middle by focusing on client feelings and then redirects communication to the client's responsibility to logically examine the situation. In this example, the counselor is being asked to evaluate options as a basis for future decision making. The financial counselor moved to the participant observer role and attempted to facilitate the client's problem solving. The financial counselor avoided making the decision for the client or adding a third alternative; both actions could make the situation more confusing for the client. Again, the best approach usually is to become a participant observer. From here financial counselors can facilitate client decision making and problem solving. There will be times however, that a client may ask for the financial counselor's opinion, and the counselor may get caught in the middle without knowing it.

Client: Which do you think is better, whole life or term insurance?

In this situation the client does not explain that he or she has been out shopping for opinions. However, in this case a similar response to the one above would work equally well and avoid potential conflict.

The Multiple Attack

This conflict situation occurs when three or more people attack the financial counselor. The situation can occur when financial counselors are making presentations to groups of clients, presenting ideas in a seminar setting, or even when making presentations to a group of colleagues. As with other forms of conflict, the financial counselor's first response should be directed towards moving to a participant observer position. In this position, if the conflict continues, it will occur among participants rather than be directed at the financial counselor. From this participant observer position, counselors can redirect attacks to underlying themes and move discussion toward a common ground of understanding as a basis for resolution.

As an example of this process, consider the following situation in which a financial counselor has been asked to discuss various forms of investments as part of a financial planning seminar at the financial institution.

Financial Counselor: The most secure investments would be in insured certificates of deposit.

John: Do you mean those are safe? There sure are a lot of people who have lost their money when some of the savings and loans closed. Probably the best thing to do is just keep your money under your mattress like my grandfather did. He got through the depression just fine.

Betty: Yeah! From what I read there usually isn't enough money in those insurance reserves to pay everybody back. I think you should spread your investments around in small pots to protect yourself.

Susan: Yeah, she's right! Then we all have to pay for it through our taxes because the government will always bail people out. Why not invest in something else where the old government will bail us out anyway?

Three people are attacking the harried financial counselor. If the counselor agrees with any of the three, the other two will attack him immediately. To avoid this and to place himself in a position where he can be most helpful to the *entire* group, he should move to the participant observer position and redirect participant energies to underlying emotions and issues.

Financial counselor: I can see that you all have definite opinions about what might be best. That's good, but it would be helpful to me to understand your points of view better. John, you seem to believe that the only safe way to save is keeping your money near you. Why don't you share with Betty and Susan why you think that is so important.

The counselor has set the stage for getting the three participants to talk directly to one another and has provided himself an opportunity to step back into a *participant observer* role. From there he can respond to "group" needs and direct the flow of communication.

CONCLUSION

This chapter shares the belief that financial counselors must be aware of potential sources of conflict, able to help clients to see ways of resolving conflicts, and prepared to focus on the process of communication. Financial counselors will be most helpful to all clients in a multiple interaction if they adopt the role of *participant observer* and control the process of communication.

RESOURCES

Dobson, T. & Miller, V.J. (1974). *Giving In To Get Your Way.* New York: Delacourt Press.

Heitler, S.M. (1990). *From Conflict To Resolution.* New York: W.W. Norton.

Lee, J.L., Pulvino, C.J. & Perrone, P.A. (1998). *Restoring Harmony*. Columbus: Prentice Hall Publishing Company.

Markova, D. (1991). *The Art Of The Possible.* New York: Conari Press.

Maslow, A. H. (1954). *Towards a Psychology of Being.* New York: Van Nostrand Reinhold

Thompson, G.J. (1993). *Verbal Judo.* New York: William Morrow.

Weeks, D. (1992). *The Eight Essential Steps To Conflict Resolution.* New York: G.P. Putnam's Sons.

Williams, M. (1975). *The Velveteen Rabbit.* New York: AVON Books

Index

A

B

C

D

E

F

G

H

I

J

K

L